Data Visualization with JavaScript

STEPHEN A. THOMAS

Printed in USA

First printing

19 18 17 16 15   1 2 3 4 5 6 7 8 9

ISBN-10: 1-59327-605-2

ISBN-13: 978-1-59327-605-8

Text stock is SFI Certified

Publisher: William Pollock

Production Editor: Laurel Chun

Cover Illustration: Beth Middleworth

Developmental Editor: Seph Kramer

Technical Reviewer: Christopher Keen

Copyeditor: Rachel Monaghan

Compositor: Lynn L'Heureux

Proofreader: Emelie Burnette

Indexer: BIM Indexing & Proofreading Services

The visualization on the cover is inspired by the work of Mike Bostock.
It is described in "Creating a Unique Visualization" on page 252.

For information on distribution, translations, or bulk sales, please contact No Starch Press, Inc. directly:

No Starch Press, Inc.

245 8th Street, San Francisco, CA 94103

phone: 415.863.9900; info@nostarch.com

www.nostarch.com

The Library of Congress Cataloging-in-Publication Data

Thomas, Stephen A., 1962-
  Data visualization with JavaScript / by Stephen A. Thomas.
      pages cm
  ISBN 978-1-59327-605-8 -- ISBN 1-59327-605-2
  1. Information visualization--Data processing. 2. JavaScript (Computer program language) I. Title.
  QA76.9.I52T46 2015
  005.2'762--dc23
                                2014039759

About the Author

Stephen A. Thomas specializes in frontend development at Georgia Tech's Department of Education Technology and has developed complex JavaScript visualizations for the health-care and security industries. He writes and speaks about data visualization in publications and at conferences around the world.

About the Technical Reviewer

Chris Keen resides in Atlanta, Georgia, and has been writing JavaScript since 2004. Chris has had the honor of working on visualizations ranging from an SVG tweet map at Weather.com to full-blown interactive maps with Leaflet.js at Endgame Systems. Chris is currently infatuated with making data dashboards using Backbone, Epoxy, and D3. Chris recently founded Keen Concepts (*http://keenconcepts.io/*), and he consults on JavaScript-rich web applications.

Brief Contents

Contents in Detail

Acknowledgments

Even though it's been said many times, there's no getting around the fact that a book is the work of many people other than the author. This book certainly wouldn't have been possible without the patience of Seph and the other fine folks at No Starch Press. There simply is no better publisher for technical books. Kudos also to Chris for the technical review, though, of course, the remaining mistakes are mine alone. I owe a special thanks to NickC for his generosity; it's such a pleasure to meet folks that appreciate the true community spirit of the Web and web development. Finally, shout-outs to the team developing the Open Academic Environment and my colleagues at the Georgia Institute of Technology; working with them is a true pleasure.

Introduction

It's getting hard to ignore the importance of data in our lives. Data is critical to the largest social organizations in human history (giants like Facebook and Google), and its collection has widespread geopolitical implications, as we all saw with the NSA surveillance scandal. But it's also getting easier to ignore the data itself. One estimate suggests that 99.5% of the data our systems collect goes to waste.

Data visualization is a tool that addresses this gap. Effective visualizations clarify; they transform abstract collections of numbers into shapes and forms that viewers quickly grasp and understand. The best visualizations impart this understanding intuitively. Viewers comprehend the data immediately—without thinking. This frees viewers to more fully consider the implications of the data: the stories it tells, the insights it reveals, or even the warnings it offers.

If you're developing websites or web applications today, there's a good chance you have data to communicate—data best presented in a good visualization. But how do you know what kind of visualization is appropriate? And even more importantly, how do you actually create one? In the chapters that follow, we explore dozens of different visualizations, techniques, and toolkits. Each example discusses the appropriateness of the visualization (and suggests possible alternatives) and provides step-by-step instructions for adding the visualization to your web pages.

The Book's Philosophy

In creating this book, I've tried to follow four main principles to make sure it provides meaningful and practical guidance.

Implementation vs. Design

This book won't teach you how to design data visualizations. Quite honestly, there are other authors far better qualified than me for that (Edward Tufte, for example). Instead, this book will focus on implementing visualizations. When appropriate, I'll take a slightly bigger picture view to discuss the strengths and weaknesses of particular visualization strategies, but the main goal is to show you how to create a wide range of visualizations. (I recognize that sometimes the boss absolutely insists on a pie chart.)

Code vs. Styling

As you might guess from the title, this book focuses on how to use Java-Script code to create visualizations. The examples don't assume you're a JavaScript expert—and I'll be sure to explain any code more complicated than a basic jQuery selector—but I won't spend much time discussing styles for the visualizations. Fortunately, styling visualizations is pretty much the same as styling other web content. Basic experience with HTML and CSS will serve you well when you add visualizations to your pages.

Simple vs. Complex

Most of the book's examples are simple, straightforward visualizations. Complex visualizations can be engaging and compelling, but studying a lot of advanced code usually isn't the best way to learn the craft. In these examples, I'll try to stay as simple as possible so you can clearly see how to use the various tools and techniques. Simple doesn't mean boring, however, and even the simplest visualizations can be enlightening and inspiring.

Reality vs. an Ideal World

When you begin building your own visualizations, you'll discover that the real world is rarely as kind as you'd wish. Open source libraries have bugs, third-party servers have security issues, and not every user has updated to the latest and greatest web browser. I've addressed these realities in the examples in this book. I'll show you how to accommodate older browsers when it's practical, how to comply with security constraints such as Cross-Origin Resource Sharing (CORS), and how to work around bugs in other folks' code.

The Book's Contents

The chapters that follow cover a variety of visualization techniques and the JavaScript libraries that we can use to implement them.

▶ **Chapter 1** begins with the most basic visualizations—static charts and plots—using the Flotr2 library.

▶ **Chapter 2** adds interactivity to the visualizations, giving users the chance to select content, zoom in, and track values. The chapter also shows how to retrieve data for visualizations directly from the Web. For variety, its examples use the Flot library, which is based on jQuery.

▶ **Chapter 3** looks at integrating multiple visualizations and with other content on a web page; it uses the jQuery sparklines library.

▶ In **Chapter 4**, we consider visualizations other than standard charts and plots, including tree maps, heat maps, network graphs, and word clouds. Each example focuses on a particular JavaScript library designed specifically for the visualization type.

▶ **Chapter 5** covers time-based visualizations. It looks at several ways to visualize timelines, including traditional libraries; pure HTML, CSS, and JavaScript; and full-featured web components.

▶ In **Chapter 6**, we consider geographic data as we look at different ways to incorporate maps into our visualizations.

▶ **Chapter 7** introduces the powerful D3.js library, a flexible and full-featured toolkit for building custom visualizations of almost any type.

▶ Beginning in **Chapter 8,** we consider other aspects of web-based visualizations. This chapter shows off the Underscore.js library, which makes it easy to prepare the data that drives our visualizations.

▶ Finally, **Chapters 9 and 10** walk through the development of a complete, single-page web application that relies on data visualization. Here we'll see how to use modern development tools such as Yeoman and the Backbone.js library.

Source Code for Examples

To make the text as clear and readable as possible, examples usually contain isolated snippets of JavaScript, plus occasional fragments of HTML or CSS. Complete source code for all examples is available on GitHub at *http://jsDataV.is/source/*.

1

Graphing Data

Many people think of data visualization as intricate interactive graphics of dazzling complexity. Creating effective visualizations, however, doesn't require Picasso's artistic skill or Turing's programming expertise. In fact, when you consider the ultimate purpose of data visualization—helping users *understand* data—simplicity is one of the most important features of an effective visualization. Simple, straightforward charts are often the easiest to understand.

After all, users have seen hundreds or thousands of bar charts, line charts, X/Y plots, and the like. They know the conventions that underlie these charts, so they can interpret a well-designed example effortlessly. If a simple, static chart presents the data best, use it. You'll spend less effort creating your visualization, and your users will spend less effort trying to understand it.

There are many high-quality tools and libraries to help you get started with simple visualizations. With these tools, you can avoid reinventing the wheel, and you can be assured of a reasonably attractive presentation by sticking with the library defaults. We'll look at several of these tools throughout the book, but for this chapter we'll use the Flotr2 library (*http://www.humblesoftware.com/flotr2/*). Flotr2 makes it easy to add standard bar charts, line charts, and pie charts to any web page, and it also supports some less common chart types. We'll take a look at all of these techniques in the examples that follow. Here's what you'll learn:

▶ How to create a basic bar chart

▶ How to plot continuous data with a line chart

▶ How to emphasize fractions with a pie chart

▶ How to plot X/Y data with a scatter chart

▶ How to show magnitudes of X/Y data with a bubble chart

▶ How to display multidimensional data with a radar chart

Creating a Basic Bar Chart

If you're ever in doubt about what type of chart best explains your data, your first consideration should probably be the basic bar chart. We see bar charts so often that it's easy to overlook how effective they can be. Bar charts can show the evolution of a value over time, or they can provide a straightforward comparison of multiple values. Let's walk through the steps to build one.

Step 1: Include the Required JavaScript

Since we're using the Flotr2 library to create the chart, we need to include that library in our web pages. The Flotr2 package isn't currently popular enough for public content distribution networks, so you'll need to download a copy and host it on your own web server. We'll use the minimized version (flotr2.min.js) since it provides the best performance.

Flotr2 doesn't require any other JavaScript libraries (such as jQuery), but it does rely on the HTML canvas feature. Major modern browsers (Safari, Chrome, Firefox) support canvas, but until version 9, Internet Explorer (IE) did not. Unfortunately, there are still millions of users with IE8 (or even earlier). To support those users, we can include an additional library (excanvas.min.js) in our pages. That library is available from Google (*https://code.google.com/p/explorercanvas/*). Start with the following skeleton for your HTML document:

```
<!DOCTYPE html>
<html lang="en">
```

```
<head>
  <meta charset="utf-8">
  <title></title>
</head>
<body>
  <!-- Page Content Here -->
  <!--[if lt IE 9]><script src="js/excanvas.min.js"></script><![endif]-->
  <script src="js/flotr2.min.js"></script>
</body>
</html>
```
❶

Since other browsers don't need excanvas.min.js, we use some special markup at ❶ to make sure that only IE8 and earlier will load it. Also, notice that we're including the JavaScript libraries at the end of the document. This approach lets the browser load the document's entire HTML markup and begin laying out the page while it waits for the server to provide the JavaScript libraries.

Step 2: Set Aside a <div> Element to Hold the Chart

Within our document, we need to create a <div> element to contain the chart. This element must have an explicit height and width, or Flotr2 won't be able to construct the chart. We can indicate the element's size in a CSS style sheet, or we can place it directly on the element itself. Here's how the document might look with the latter approach.

```
<!DOCTYPE html>
<html lang="en">
  <head>
    <meta charset="utf-8">
    <title></title>
  </head>
  <body>
    <div id="chart" style="width:600px;height:300px;"></div>
    <!--[if lt IE 9]><script src="js/excanvas.min.js"></script><![endif]-->
    <script src="js/flotr2.min.js"></script>
  </body>
</html>
```

Note that we've given the <div> an explicit id ("chart") so we can reference it later. You'll need to use a basic template like this (importing the Flotr2 library and setting up the <div>) for all the charts in this chapter.

Step 3: Define the Data

Now we can tackle the data that we want to display. For this example, I'll use the number of Manchester City wins in the English Premier League for the past seven years. Of course you'll want to substitute your actual data values, either with inline JavaScript (like the following example) or by another means (such as an AJAX call to the server).

```
<script>
var wins = [[[2006,13],[2007,11],[2008,15],[2009,15],[2010,18],[2011,21],
          [2012,28]]];
</script>
```

As you can see, we have three layers of arrays. Let's start from the inside and work our way out. For Flotr2 charts, each data point is entered in a two-item array with an x-value and y-value. In our case we're using the year as the x-value and the number of wins as the y-value. We collect all these values in another array called a *series*. We place this series inside one more outer array. We could enter multiple series into this outer array, but for now we're showing only one series. Here's a quick summary of each layer:

▶ Each data point consists of an x-value and a y-value packaged in an array.

▶ Each series consists of a set of data points packaged in an array.

▶ The data to chart consists of one or more series packaged in an array.

Step 4: Draw the Chart

That's all the setup we need. A simple call to the Flotr2 library, as shown here, creates our first attempt at a chart.

```
window.onload = function () {
    Flotr.draw(
        document.getElementById("chart"),
        wins,
        {
            bars: {
                show: true
            }
        }
    );
};
```

First we make sure the browser has loaded our document; otherwise, the chart `<div>` might not be present. That's the point of `window.onload`. Once that event occurs, we call `Flotr.draw` with three parameters: the HTML element to contain the chart, the data for the chart, and any chart options (in this case, we specify options only to tell Flotr2 to create a bar chart from the data).

Since Flotr2 doesn't require jQuery, we haven't taken advantage of any of jQuery's shortcuts in this example. If your page already includes jQuery, you can use the standard jQuery conventions for the Flotr2 charts in this chapter to execute the script after the window has loaded, and to find the `<div>` container for the chart.

Figure 1-1 shows what you'll see on the web page.

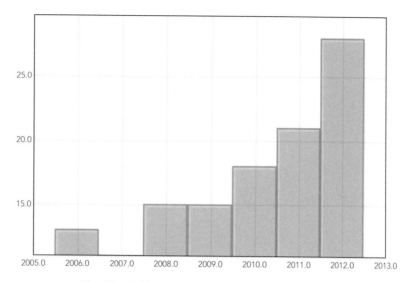

FIGURE 1-1: *The Flotr2 library turns data into a basic (if unpolished) bar chart.*

Now you have a bar chart, but it's not showing the information very effectively. Let's add some options incrementally until we get what we want.

Step 5: Fix the Vertical Axis

The most glaring problem with the vertical axis is its scale. By default, Flotr2 automatically calculates the range of the axis from the minimum and maximum values in the data. In our case the minimum value is 11 wins (from 2007), so Flotr2 dutifully uses that as its y-axis minimum. In bar charts, however, it's almost always best to make 0 the y-axis minimum. If you don't use 0, you risk overemphasizing the differences between values and confusing your users. Anyone who glances at the chart in Figure 1-1, for example, might think that Manchester City did not win any matches in 2007. That certainly wouldn't do the team any justice.

Another problem with the vertical axis is the formatting. Flotr2 defaults to a precision of one decimal place, so it adds the superfluous ".0" to all the labels. We can fix both of these problems by specifying some y-axis options.

```
Flotr.draw(document.getElementById("chart"), [wins], {
    bars: {
        show: true
    },
    yaxis: {
        min: 0,
        tickDecimals: 0
    }
});
```

The **min** property sets the minimum value for the y-axis, and the **tickDecimals** property tells Flotr2 how many decimal places to show for the labels. In our case we don't want any decimal places.

As you can see in Figure 1-2, adding these options definitely improves the vertical axis since the values now start at zero and are formatted appropriately for integers.

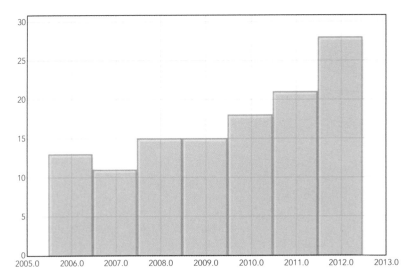

FIGURE 1-2: *Simple options help Flotr2 construct a better vertical axis.*

Step 6: Fix the Horizontal Axis

The horizontal axis needs some work as well. Just as with the y-axis, Flotr2 assumes that the x-axis values are real numbers and shows one decimal place in the labels. Since we're charting years, we could simply set the precision to 0, as we did for the y-axis. But that's not a very general solution, since it won't work when the x-values are non-numeric categories (like team names). For the more general case, let's first change our data to use simple numbers rather than years for the x-values. Then we'll create an array that maps those simple numbers to arbitrary strings, which we can use as labels.

```
var wins = [[[0,13],[1,11],[2,15],[3,15],[4,18],[5,21],[6,28]]];
var years = [
    [0, "2006"],
    [1, "2007"],
    [2, "2008"],
    [3, "2009"],
    [4, "2010"],
    [5, "2011"],
    [6, "2012"]
];
```

As you can see, instead of using the actual years for the x-values, we're simply using 0, 1, 2, and so on. We then define a second array that maps those integer values to strings. Although here our strings are years (and thus numbers), they could be anything.

Another problem is a lack of spacing between the bars. By default, each bar takes up its full horizontal space, but that makes the chart look very cramped. We can adjust that with the `barWidth` property. Let's set it to `0.5` so that each bar takes up only half the available space.

Here's how we pass those options to Flotr2.

```
Flotr.draw(document.getElementById("chart"), wins, {
    bars: {
        show: true,
        barWidth: 0.5
    },
    yaxis: {
        min: 0,
        tickDecimals: 0
    },
    xaxis: {
❶       ticks: years
    }
});
```

Note at ❶ that we use the `ticks` property of the x-axis to tell Flotr2 which labels match which x-values. Now we're starting to get somewhere with our chart, as shown in Figure 1-3. The x-axis labels are appropriate for years, and there is space between the bars to improve the chart's legibility.

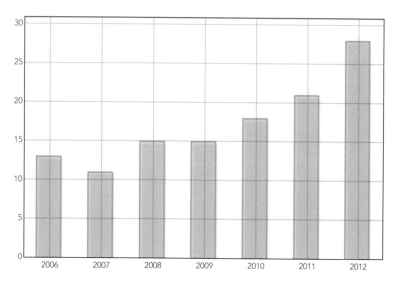

FIGURE 1-3: *We can define our own labels for the horizontal axis.*

Step 7: Adjust the Styling

Now that the chart is functional and readable, we can pay some attention to the aesthetics. Let's add a title, get rid of the unnecessary grid lines, and adjust the coloring of the bars.

```
Flotr.draw(document.getElementById("chart"), wins, {
    title: "Manchester City Wins",
    colors: ["#89AFD2"],
    bars: {
        show: true,
        barWidth: 0.5,
        shadowSize: 0,
        fillOpacity: 1,
        lineWidth: 0
    },
    yaxis: {
        min: 0,
        tickDecimals: 0
    },
    xaxis: {
        ticks: years
    },
    grid: {
        horizontalLines: false,
        verticalLines: false
    }
});
```

As you can see in Figure 1-4, we now have a bar chart that Manchester City fans can be proud of.

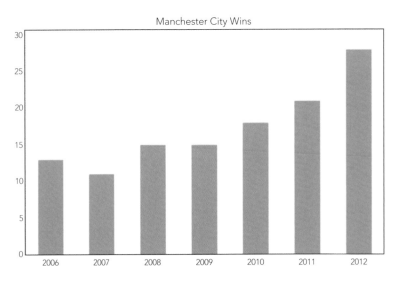

FIGURE 1-4: *Additional options let us adjust the visual styles of the chart.*

For any data set of moderate size, the standard bar chart is often the most effective visualization. Users are already familiar with its conventions, so they don't have to put any extra effort into understanding the format. The bars themselves offer a clear visual contrast with the background, and they use a single linear dimension (height) to show differences between values, so users easily grasp the salient data.

Step 8: Vary the Bar Color

So far our chart has been monochromatic. That makes sense because we're showing the same value (Manchester City wins) across time. But bar charts are also good for comparing different values. Suppose, for example, we wanted to show the total wins for multiple teams in one year. In that case, it makes sense to use a different color for each team's bar. Let's go over how we can do that.

First we need to restructure the data somewhat. Previously we've shown only a single series. Now we want a different series for each team. Creating multiple series lets Flotr2 color each independently. The following example shows how the new data series compares with the old. We've left the `wins` array in the code for comparison, but it's the `wins2` array that we're going to show now. Notice how the nesting of the arrays changes. Also, we're going to label each bar with the team abbreviation instead of the year.

```
var wins = [[[0,13],[1,11],[2,15],[3,15],[4,18],[5,21],[6,28]]];
var wins2 = [[[0,28]],[[1,28]],[[2,21]],[[3,20]],[[4,19]]];
var teams = [
    [0, "MCI"],
    [1, "MUN"],
    [2, "ARS"],
    [3, "TOT"],
    [4, "NEW"]
];
```

With those changes, our data is structured appropriately, and we can ask Flotr2 to draw the chart. When we do that, let's use different colors for each team. Everything else is the same as before.

```
Flotr.draw(document.getElementById("chart"), wins2, {
    title: "Premier League Wins (2011-2012)",
    colors: ["#89AFD2", "#1D1D1D", "#DF021D", "#0E204B", "#E67840"],
    bars: {
        show: true,
        barWidth: 0.5,
        shadowSize: 0,
        fillOpacity: 1,
        lineWidth: 0
    },
    yaxis: {
        min: 0,
        tickDecimals: 0
    },
```

```
    xaxis: {
        ticks: teams
    },
    grid: {
        horizontalLines: false,
        verticalLines: false
    }
});
```

As you can see in Figure 1-5, with a few minor adjustments we've completely changed the focus of our bar chart. Instead of showing a single team at different points in time, we're now comparing different teams at the same point in time. That's the versatility of a simple bar chart.

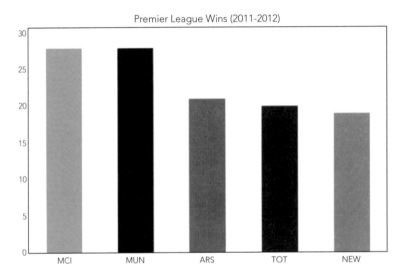

FIGURE 1-5: *Bar charts can compare different quantities at one point in time as well as the same quantity at different points in time.*

We've used a lot of different code fragments to put together these examples. If you want to see a complete example in a single file, check out this book's source code at *http://jsDataV.is/source/*.

Step 9: Work Around Flotr2 "Bugs"

If you're building large web pages with a lot of content, you may run into a Flotr2 "bug" that can be quite annoying. I've put "bug" in quotation marks because the Flotr2 behavior is deliberate, but I believe it's not correct. In the process of constructing its charts, Flotr2 creates dummy HTML elements so it can calculate their sizes. Flotr2 doesn't intend these dummy elements to be visible on the page, so it "hides" them by positioning them off the screen. Unfortunately, what Flotr2 thinks is off the screen isn't always. Specifically, line 2,281 of flotr2.js is:

```
D.setStyles(div, { "position" : "absolute", "top" : "-10000px" });
```

Flotr2 intends to place these dummy elements 10,000 pixels above the top of the browser window. However, CSS absolute positioning can be relative to the containing element, which is not always the browser window. So if your document is more than 10,000 pixels high, you may find Flotr2 scattering text in random-looking locations throughout the page. There are a couple of ways to work around this bug, at least until the Flotr2 code is revised.

One option is to modify the code yourself. Flotr2 is open source, so you can freely download the full source code and modify it appropriately. One simple modification would position the dummy elements far to the right or left rather than above. Instead of `"top"` you could change the code to `"right"`. If you're not comfortable making changes to the library's source code, another option is to find and hide those dummy elements yourself. You should do this *after* you've called `Flotr.draw()` for the last time. The latest version of jQuery can banish these extraneous elements with the following statement:

```
$(".flotr-dummy-div").parent().hide();
```

Plotting Continuous Data with a Line Chart

Bar charts work great for visualizing a modest amount of data, but for more significant amounts of data, a line chart can present the information much more effectively. Line charts are especially good at revealing overall trends in data without bogging the user down in individual data points.

For our example, we'll look at two measures that may be related: carbon dioxide (CO_2) concentration in the atmosphere and global temperatures. We want to show how both measures have changed over time, and we'd like to see how strongly related the values are. A line chart is a perfect visualization tool for looking at these trends.

Just like for the bar chart, you'll need to include the Flotr2 library in your web page and create a `<div>` element to contain the chart. Let's start prepping the data.

Step 1: Define the Data

We'll begin with CO_2 concentration measurements. The US National Oceanographic and Atmospheric Administration (NOAA) publishes measurements (*http://www.esrl .noaa.gov/gmd/ccgg/trends/co2_data_mlo.html*) taken at Mauna Loa, Hawaii, from 1959 to the present day. The first few values are shown in the following excerpt.

```
var co2 = [
    [ 1959, 315.97 ],
    [ 1960, 316.91 ],
    [ 1961, 317.64 ],
    [ 1962, 318.45 ],
    // Data set continues...
```

NOAA also publishes measurements of mean global surface temperature (*http://www.ncdc.noaa.gov/cmb-faq/anomalies.php*). These values measure the difference from the baseline, which is currently taken to be the average temperature over the entire 20th century. Since the CO_2 measurements begin in 1959, we'll use that as our starting point for temperature as well.

```
var temp = [
    [ 1959,  0.0776 ],
    [ 1960,  0.0280 ],
    [ 1961,  0.1028 ],
    [ 1962,  0.1289 ],
    // Data set continues...
```

Step 2: Graph the CO_2 Data

Graphing one data set is quite easy with Flotr2. We simply call the `draw()` method of the `Flotr` object. The only parameters the method requires are a reference to the HTML element in which to place the graph, and the data itself. The `lines` property of the data object indicates that we want a line chart.

```
Flotr.draw(
    document.getElementById("chart"),
    [{ data: co2, lines: {show:true} }]
);
```

Since Flotr2 does not require jQuery, we're not using any jQuery convenience functions in our example. If you do have jQuery on your pages, you can simplify the preceding code a little. In either case, Figure 1-6 shows the result.

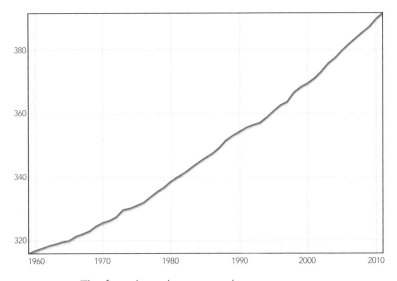

FIGURE 1-6: *The first chart shows one data set.*

The chart clearly shows the trend in CO_2 concentration for the past 50-plus years.

Step 3: Add the Temperature Data

With a simple addition to our code, we can include temperature measurements in our chart.

```
Flotr.draw(
    document.getElementById("chart"),
    [
        { data: co2, lines: {show:true} },
        { data: temp, lines: {show:true}, yaxis: 2 }
    ]
);
```

Note that we include the **yaxis** option for the temperature data and give it a value of **2**. That tells Flotr2 to use a different y-scale for the temperature data.

The chart in Figure 1-7 now shows both measurements for the years in question, but it's gotten a little cramped and confusing. The values butt up against the edges of the chart, and the grid lines are hard for users to interpret when there are multiple vertical axes.

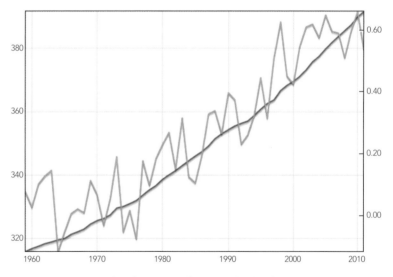

FIGURE 1-7: *A single chart can show multiple data sets.*

Step 4: Improve the Chart's Readability

By using more Flotr2 options, we can make several improvements in our line chart's readability. First we can eliminate the grid lines, since they aren't relevant for the temperature measurements.

We can also extend the range of both vertical axes to provide a bit of breathing room for the chart. Both of these changes are additional options to the draw() method.

```
Flotr.draw(
    document.getElementById("chart"),
    [
        { data: co2, lines: {show:true} },
        { data: temp, lines: {show:true}, yaxis: 2 }
    ],{
❶      grid: {horizontalLines: false, verticalLines: false},
❷      yaxis: {min: 300, max: 400},
❸      y2axis: {min: -0.15, max: 0.69}
    }
);
```

The grid options at ❶ turn off the grid lines by setting both the horizontalLines and verticalLines properties to false. The yaxis options at ❷ specify the minimum and maximum value for the first vertical axis (CO_2 concentration), while the y2axis options at ❸ specify those values for the second vertical axis (temperature difference).

The resulting graph in Figure 1-8 is cleaner and easier to read.

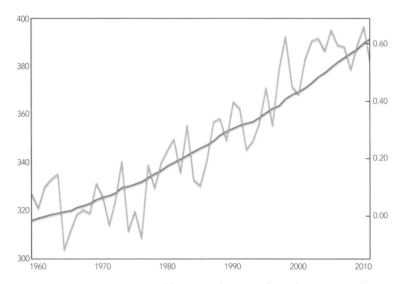

FIGURE 1-8: *Removing grid lines and expanding the axes makes the chart easier to read.*

Step 5: Clarify the Temperature Measurements

The temperature measurements might still be confusing to users, since they're not really temperatures; they're actually deviations from the 20th-century average. Let's convey that distinction by adding a line for that 20th-century average and explicitly labeling it. The simplest way to do that is to create a "dummy" data set and add that to the chart. The extra data set has nothing but zeros.

```
var zero = [];
for (var yr=1959; yr<2012; yr++) { zero.push([yr, 0]); };
```

When we add that data set to the chart, we need to indicate that it corresponds to the second y-axis. And since we want this line to appear as part of the chart framework rather than as another data set, let's deemphasize it somewhat by setting its width to one pixel, coloring it dark gray, and disabling shadows.

```
Flotr.draw(
    document.getElementById("chart"),
    [
        { data: zero, lines: {show:true, lineWidth: 1}, yaxis: 2,
          shadowSize: 0, color: "#545454" },
        { data: co2, lines: {show:true} },
        { data: temp, lines: {show:true}, yaxis: 2 }
    ],{
        grid: {horizontalLines: false, verticalLines: false},
        yaxis: {min: 300, max: 400},
        y2axis: {min: -0.15, max: 0.69}
    }
);
```

As you can see, we've placed the zero line first among the data sets. With that order, Flotr2 will draw the actual data on top of the zero line, as shown in Figure 1-9, reinforcing its role as chart framework instead of data.

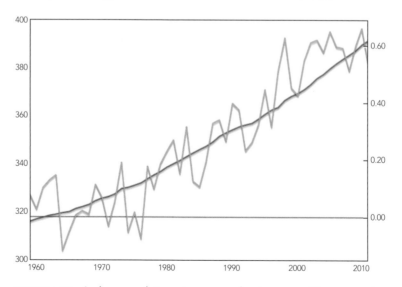

FIGURE 1-9: *A dummy data set can emphasize a position on a chart axis.*

Step 6: Label the Chart

For the last step in this example, we'll add appropriate labels to the chart. That includes an overall title, as well as labels for individual data sets. And to make it clear which axis refers to temperature, we'll add a "°C" suffix to the temperature scale. We identify the label for each data series in the `label` option for that series. The overall chart title merits its own option, and we add the "°C" suffix using a `tickFormatter()` function.

```
Flotr.draw(
    document.getElementById("chart"),
    [ {
        data: zero,
        label: "20<sup>th</sup>-Century Baseline Temperature",
        lines: {show:true, lineWidth: 1},
        shadowSize: 0,
        color: "#545454"
    },
    {
        data: temp,
        label: "Yearly Temperature Difference (°C)",
        lines: {show:true}
    },
    {
        data: co2,
        yaxis: 2,
        label: "CO<sub>2</sub> Concentration (ppm)",
        lines: {show:true}
    }
    ],
    {
        title: "Global Temperature and CO<sub>2</sub> Concentration (NOAA Data)",
        grid: {horizontalLines: false, verticalLines: false},
        y2axis: {min: -0.15, max: 0.69,
❶            tickFormatter: function(val) {return val+" °C";}}
        yaxis: {min: 300, max: 400},
    }
);
```

For each value on the axis, the formatter function is called with the value, and Flotr2 expects it to return a string to use for the label. As you can see at ❶, we simply append the " °C" string to the value.

Notice that we've also swapped the position of the CO_2 and temperature graphs. We're now passing the temperature data series ahead of the CO_2 series. We did that so that the two temperature quantities (baseline and difference) appear next to each other in the legend, making their connection a little clearer to the user.

And because the temperature now appears first in the legend, we've also swapped the axes, so the temperature axis is on the left. Finally, we've adjusted the title of the chart for the same reason. Figure 1-10 shows the result.

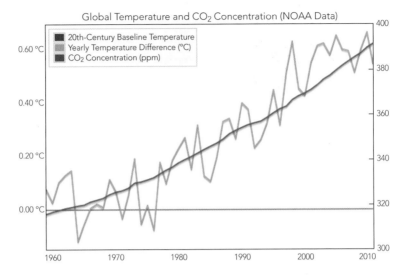

FIGURE 1-10: *Labeling the axes and adding a legend completes the chart.*

A line chart like Figure 1-10 excels in visualizing this kind of data. Each data set contains over 50 points, making it impractical to present each individual point. And in fact, individual data points are not the focus of the visualization. Rather, we want to show *trends*—the trends of each data set as well as that data set's correlation to the others. Connecting the points with lines leads the user right to those trends and to the heart of our visualization.

Step 7: Work Around Flotr2 "Bugs"

Be sure to refer to Step 9 of "Creating a Basic Bar Chart" on page 14 to see how to work around some "bugs" in the Flotr2 library.

Emphasizing Fractions Using a Pie Chart

Pie charts don't get a lot of love in the visualization community, and for a pretty good reason: they're rarely the most effective way to communicate data. We will walk through the steps to create pie charts in this section, but first let's take some time to understand the problems they introduce. Figure 1-11, for example, shows a simple pie chart. Can you tell from the chart which color is the largest? The smallest?

FIGURE 1-11: *Pie charts can make it hard to compare values.*

It's very hard to tell. That's because humans are not particularly good at judging the relative size of areas, especially if those areas aren't rectangles. If we really wanted to compare these five values, a bar chart works much better. Figure 1-12 shows the same values in a bar chart.

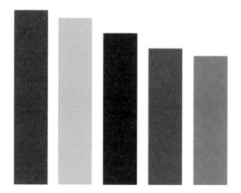

FIGURE 1-12: *Bar charts usually make comparisons easier.*

Now, of course, it's easy to rank each color. With a bar chart we only have to compare one dimension—height. This yields a simple rule of thumb: if you're comparing different values against one another, consider a bar chart first. It will almost always provide the best visualization.

One case, however, where pie charts can be quite effective is when we want to compare a single partial value against a whole. Say, for example, we want to visualize the percentage of the world's population that lives in poverty. In that case, a pie chart may work quite well. Here's how we can construct such a chart using Flotr2.

Just as in Step 1 of "Creating a Basic Bar Chart" on page 6, we need to include the Flotr2 library in our web page and set aside a `<div>` element to contain the chart we'll construct.

Step 1: Define the Data

The data here is quite straightforward. According to the World Bank (*http://www.newgeography.com/content/003325-alleviating-world-poverty-a-progress-report*), at the end of 2008, 22.4 percent of the world's population lived on less than $1.25/day. That's the fraction that we want to emphasize with our chart.

```
var data = [[[0,22.4]],[[1,77.6]]];
```

Here we have an array with two data series: one for the percentage of the population in poverty (22.4) and a second series for the rest (77.6). Each series itself consists of an array of points. In this example, and for pie charts in general, there is only one point in each series, with an x-value and a y-value (which are each stored together in yet another, inner array). For pie charts, the x-values are irrelevant, so we simply include the placeholder values 0 and 1.

Step 2: Draw the Chart

To draw the chart, we call the `draw()` method of the `Flotr` object. That method takes three parameters: the element in our HTML document in which to place the chart, the data for our chart, and any options. We'll start with the minimum set of options required for a pie chart.

```
window.onload = function () {
    Flotr.draw(document.getElementById("chart"), data, {
        pie: {
            show: true
        },
        yaxis: {
❶          showLabels: false
        },
        xaxis: {
❷          showLabels: false
        },
        grid: {
❸          horizontalLines: false,
❹          verticalLines: false
        }
    });
}
```

As you can see, Flotr2 requires a few more options for a minimum pie chart than it does for other common chart types. For both the x- and y-axes we need to disable labels, which we do by setting the `showLabels` property to `false` at ❶ and ❷. We also have to turn off the grid lines, as a grid doesn't make a lot of sense for a pie chart. We accomplish that by setting the `verticalLines` and `horizontalLines` properties of the `grid` option to `false` at ❸ and ❹.

Since Flotr2 doesn't require jQuery, we're not using any of the jQuery convenience functions in this example. If you do have jQuery for your pages, you can simplify this code a bit.

Figure 1-13 is a start, but it's hard to tell exactly what the graph intends to show.

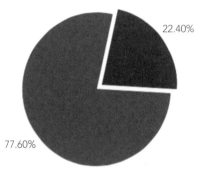

22.40%

77.60%

FIGURE 1-13: *Without effective labeling, pie charts can be difficult to interpret.*

Step 3: Label the Values

The next step is to add some text labels and a legend to indicate what the chart is displaying. To label each quantity separately, we have to change the structure of our data. Instead of using an array of series, we'll create an object to store each series. Each object's **data** property will contain the corresponding series, and we'll add a **label** property for the text labels.

```
var data = [
    {data: [[0,22.4]], label: "Extreme Poverty"},
    {data: [[1,77.6]]}
];
```

With our data structured this way, Flotr2 will automatically identify labels associated with each series. Now when we call the **draw()** method, we just need to add a **title** option. Flotr2 will add the title above the graph and create a simple legend identifying the pie portions with our labels. To make the chart a little more engaging, we'll pose a question in our title. That's why we're labeling only one of the areas in the chart: the labeled area answers the question in the title.

```
Flotr.draw(document.getElementById("chart"),data, {
    title: "How Much of the World Lives on $1.25/Day?",
    pie: {
        show: true
    },
    yaxis: {
        showLabels: false
    },
    xaxis: {
        showLabels: false
    },
```

```
    grid: {
        horizontalLines: false,
        verticalLines: false
    }
});
```

The chart in Figure 1-14 reveals the data quite clearly.

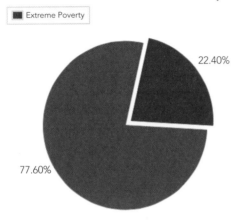

How Much of the World Lives on $1.25/Day?

■ Extreme Poverty

22.40%

77.60%

FIGURE 1-14: *Labels and titles can help make a chart engaging.*

Although pie charts have a bad reputation in the data visualization community, there are some applications for which they are quite effective. They're not very good at letting users compare multiple values, but as shown in this example, they do provide a nice and easily understandable picture showing the proportion of a single value within a whole.

Step 4: Work Around Flotr2 "Bugs"

Be sure to refer to Step 9 of "Creating a Basic Bar Chart" on page 14 to see how to work around some "bugs" in the Flotr2 library.

Plotting X/Y Data with a Scatter Chart

A bar chart is often most effective for visualizing data that consists primarily of a single quantity (such as the number of wins in the bar charts we created earlier). But if we want to explore the relationship between two different quantities, a scatter chart can be more effective. Suppose, for example, we wish to visualize the relationship between a country's health-care spending (one quantity) and its life expectancy (the second quantity). Let's step through an example to see how to create a scatter chart for that data.

Just as in Step 1 of "Creating a Basic Bar Chart" on page 6, we need to include the Flotr2 library in our web page and set aside a `<div>` element to contain the chart we'll construct.

Step 1: Define the Data

For this example, we'll use the 2012 report from the Organisation for Economic Co-operation and Development (OECD; *http://www.oecd-ilibrary.org/social-issues-migration-health/data/oecd-health-statistics_health-data-en*). This report includes figures for health-care spending as a percent of gross domestic product, and average life expectancy at birth. (Although the report was released in late 2012, it contains data for 2010.) Here you can see a short excerpt of that data stored in a JavaScript array:

```
var health_data = [
    { country: "Australia",    spending:  9.1,   life: 81.8  },
    { country: "Austria",      spending: 11.0,   life: 80.7  },
    { country: "Belgium",      spending: 10.5,   life: 80.3  },
    // Data set continues...
```

Step 2: Format the Data

As is often the case, we'll need to restructure the original data a bit so that it matches the format Flotr2 requires. The JavaScript code for that is shown next. We start with an empty **data** array and step through the source data. For each element in the source **health_data**, we extract the data point for our chart and push that data point into the **data** array.

```
var data = [];
for (var i = 0; i < health_data.length; i++) {
    data.push([
        health_data[i].spending,
        health_data[i].life
    ]);
};
```

Since Flotr2 doesn't require jQuery, we're not using any of the jQuery convenience functions in this example. But if you're using jQuery for other reasons in your page, you could, for example, use the `.map()` function to simplify the code for this restructuring. (In Step 7 of "Selecting Chart Content" on page 55, there's a detailed example of the jQuery `.map()` function.)

Step 3: Plot the Data

Now all we need to do is call the `draw()` method of the `Flotr` object to create our chart. For a first attempt, we'll stick with the default options.

```
Flotr.draw(
    document.getElementById("chart"),
    [{ data: data, points: {show:true} }]
);
```

As you can see, Flotr2 expects at least two parameters. The first is the element in our HTML document in which we want the chart placed, and the second is the data for the chart. The data takes the form of an array. In general, Flotr2 can draw multiple series on the same chart, so that array might have multiple objects. In our case, however, we're charting only one series, so the array has a single object. That object identifies the data itself, and it tells Flotr2 not to show points instead of lines.

Figure 1-15 shows our result. Notice how the points are pressed right up against the edges of the chart.

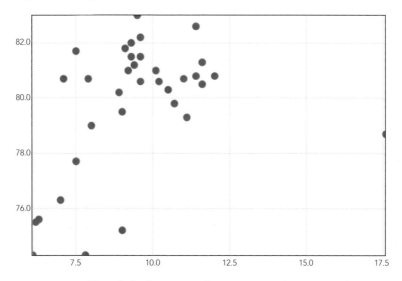

FIGURE 1-15: *The default scatter chart options don't provide any margins.*

Step 4: Adjust the Chart's Axes

The first attempt isn't too bad, but Flotr2 automatically calculates the ranges for each axis, and its default algorithm usually results in a chart that's too cramped. Flotr2 does have an **autoscale** option; if you set it, the library attempts to find sensible ranges for the associated axes automatically. Unfortunately, in my experience the ranges Flotr2 suggests rarely improve the default option significantly, so in most cases we're better off explicitly setting them. Here's how we do that for our chart:

```
Flotr.draw(
    document.getElementById("chart"),
    [{
        data: data,
```

```
        points: {show:true}
    }],
    {
        xaxis: {min: 5, max: 20},
        yaxis: {min: 70, max: 85}
    }
);
```

We've added a third parameter to the `draw()` method that contains our options, which in this case are properties for the x- and y-axes. In each case, we're explicitly setting a minimum and maximum value. By specifying ranges that give the data a little breathing room, we've made the chart in Figure 1-16 much easier to read.

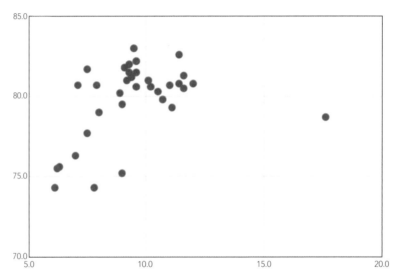

FIGURE 1-16: *Specifying our own axes makes the chart easier to read.*

Step 5: Label the Data

Our chart so far looks reasonably nice, but it doesn't tell users what they're seeing. We need to add some labels to identify the data. A few more options can clarify the chart:

```
Flotr.draw(
    document.getElementById("chart"),
    [{
        data: data, points: {show:true}
    }],
    {
        title: "Life Expectancy vs. Health-Care Spending",
        subtitle: "(by country, 2010 OECD data)",
        xaxis: {min: 5, max: 20, ❶tickDecimals: 0,
                title: "Spending as Percentage of GDP"},
```

```
          yaxis: {min: 70, max: 85, ❷tickDecimals: 0, title: "Years"}
    }
);
```

The **title** and **subtitle** options give the chart its overall title and subtitle, while the **title** properties within the **xaxis** and **yaxis** options name the labels for those axes. In addition to adding labels, we've told Flotr2 to drop the unnecessary decimal point from the x- and y-axis values by changing the **tickDecimals** property at ❶ and ❷. The chart in Figure 1-17 looks much better.

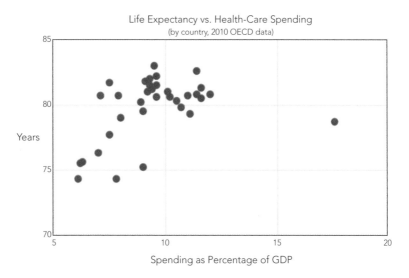

FIGURE 1-17: *Labels and titles clarify the chart's content.*

Step 6: Clarify the X-Axis

Although our chart has definitely improved since our first attempt, there is still one nagging problem with the data presentation. The x-axis represents a percentage, but the labels for that axis show whole numbers. That discrepancy might cause our users some initial confusion, so let's get rid of it. Flotr2 allows us to format the axis labels however we want. In this example, we simply wish to add a percentage symbol to the value. That's easy enough:

```
Flotr.draw(
    document.getElementById("chart"),
    [{
        data: data, points: {show:true}
    }],
    {
        title: "Life Expectancy vs. Health-Care Spending",
        subtitle: "(by country, 2010 OECD data)",
```

```
      xaxis: {min: 5, max: 20, tickDecimals: 0,
              title: "Spending as Percentage of GDP",
❶             tickFormatter: function(val) {return val+"%"}},
      yaxis: {min: 70, max: 85, tickDecimals: 0, title: "Years"}
   }
);
```

The trick is the `tickFormatter` property of the `xaxis` options at ❶ in the preceding code. That property specifies a function. When `tickFormatter` is present, Flotr2 doesn't draw the labels automatically. Instead, at each point where it would draw a label, it calls our function. The parameter passed to the function is the numeric value for the label. Flotr2 expects the function to return a string that it will use as the label. In our case we're simply adding a percent sign after the value.

In Figure 1-18, with the addition of the percentage values labeling the horizontal axis, we have a chart that presents the data clearly.

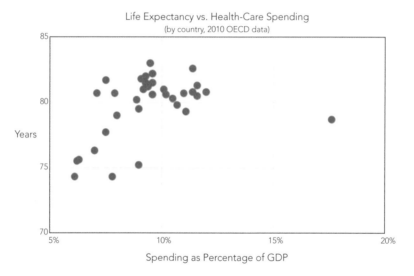

FIGURE 1-18: *Formatting the axis labels clarifies the content.*

The scatter chart excels at revealing relationships between two different variables. In this example, we can see how life expectancy relates to health-care spending. In aggregate, more spending yields longer life.

Step 7: Answer Users' Questions

Now that our chart successfully presents the data, we can start to look more carefully at the visualization from our users' perspective. We especially want to anticipate any questions that users might have and try to answer them directly on the chart. There are at least three questions that emerge in the chart as it now stands:

1. What countries are shown?
2. Are there any regional differences?
3. What's that data point way over on the right?

One way to answer those questions would be to add mouseovers (or tool tips) to each data point. But we're not going to use that approach in this example for a couple of reasons. First (and most obviously), interactive visualizations are the subject of Chapter 2; this chapter considers only static charts and graphs. Secondly, mouseovers and tool tips are ineffective for users accessing our site on a touch device, such as a smartphone or tablet. If we required users to have a mouse to fully understand our visualization, we might be neglecting a significant (and rapidly growing) number of them.

Our approach to this problem will be to divide our data into multiple series so that we can color and label each independently. Here's the first step in breaking the data into regions:

```
var pacific_data = [
    { country: "Australia",      spending:  9.1,  life: 81.8  },
    { country: "New Zealand",    spending: 10.1,  life: 81.0  },
];
var europe_data = [
    { country: "Austria",        spending: 11.0,  life: 80.7  },
    { country: "Belgium",        spending: 10.5,  life: 80.3  },
    { country: "Czech Republic", spending:  7.5,  life: 77.7  },

// Data set continues...

var us_data = [
    { country: "United States",  spending: 17.6,  life: 78.7  }
];
```

Here, we're giving the United States its own series, separate from the Americas series. That's because the United States is the outlier data point on the far right of the chart. Our users probably want to know the specific country for that point, not just its region. For the other countries, a region alone is probably enough identification. As before, we need to restructure these arrays into Flotr2's format. The code is the same as in Step 4; we're just repeating it for each data set.

```
var pacific=[], europe=[], americas=[], mideast=[], asia=[], us=[];
for (i = 0; i < pacific_data.length; i++) {
    pacific.push([ pacific_data[i].spending, pacific_data[i].life ]);
}
for (i = 0; i < europe_data.length; i++) {
    europe.push([ europe_data[i].spending, europe_data[i].life ]);
}
// Code continues...
```

Once we've separated the countries, we can pass their data to Flotr2 as distinct series. Here we see why Flotr2 expects arrays as its data parameter. Each series is a separate object in the array.

```
Flotr.draw(
    document.getElementById("chart"),
    [
        { data: pacific,  points: {show:true} },
        { data: europe,   points: {show:true} },
        { data: americas, points: {show:true} },
        { data: mideast,  points: {show:true} },
        { data: asia,     points: {show:true} },
        { data: us,       points: {show:true} }
    ],{
        title: "Life Expectancy vs. Health-Care Spending",
        subtitle: "(by country, 2010 OECD data)",
        xaxis: {min: 5, max: 20, tickDecimals: 0,
                title: "Spending as Percentage of GDP",
                tickFormatter: function(val) {return val+"%"}},
        yaxis: {min: 70, max: 85, tickDecimals: 0, title: "Years"}
    }
);
```

With the countries in different data series based on regions, Flotr2 now colors the regions distinctly, as shown in Figure 1-19.

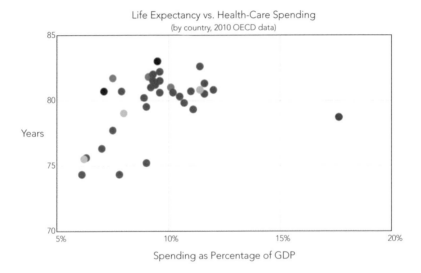

FIGURE 1-19: *Splitting the data into multiple data sets lets us assign different colors to each.*

For the final enhancement, we add a legend to the chart identifying the regions.

```
Flotr.draw(
    document.getElementById("chart"),
    [
        { data: pacific,  label: "Pacific", points: {show:true} },
        { data: europe,   label: "Europe", points: {show:true} },
        { data: americas, label: "Americas", points: {show:true} },
        { data: mideast,  label: "Middle East", points: {show:true} },
        { data: asia,     label: "Asia", points: {show:true} },
        { data: us,       label: "United States", points: {show:true} }
    ],{
        title: "Life Expectancy vs. Health-Care Spending (2010 OECD data)",
❶       xaxis: {min: 5, max: 25, tickDecimals: 0,
                title: "Spending as Percentage of GDP",
                tickFormatter: function(val) {return val+"%"}},
        yaxis: {min: 70, max: 85, tickDecimals: 0, title: "Years"},
❷       legend: {position: "ne"}
    }
);
```

In order to make room for the legend, we increase the range of the x-axis at ❶ and position the legend in the northeast quadrant at ❷.

This addition gives us the final chart shown in Figure 1-20.

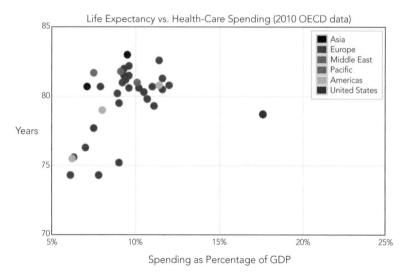

FIGURE 1-20: *Adding a legend completes the chart.*

Step 8: Work Around Flotr2 "Bugs"

Be sure to refer to Step 9 of "Creating a Basic Bar Chart" on page 14 to see how to work around some "bugs" in the Flotr2 library.

Adding Magnitudes to X/Y Data with a Bubble Chart

Traditional scatter charts, like those described in the previous example, show the relationship between two values: the x-axis and the y-axis. Sometimes, however, two values are not adequate for the data we want to visualize. If we need to visualize three variables, we could use a scatter plot framework for two of the variables and then vary the size of the points according to the third variable. The resulting chart is a bubble chart.

Using bubble charts effectively requires some caution, though. As we saw earlier with pie charts, humans are not very good at accurately judging the relative areas of nonrectangular shapes, so bubble charts don't lend themselves to precise comparisons of the bubble size. But if your third variable conveys only the general sense of a quantity rather than an accurate measurement, a bubble chart may be appropriate.

For this example we'll use a bubble chart to visualize the path of Hurricane Katrina in 2005. Our x- and y-values will represent position (latitude and longitude), and we'll ensure our users can interpret those values very accurately. For the third value—the bubble area—we'll use the storm's sustained wind speed. Since wind speed is only a general value anyway (as the wind gusts and subsides), a general impression is sufficient.

Just as in Step 1 of "Creating a Basic Bar Chart" on page 6, we need to include the Flotr2 library in our web page and set aside a `<div>` element to contain the chart we'll construct.

Step 1: Define the Data

We'll start our example with data taken from Hurricane Katrina observations by United States National Oceanic and Atmospheric Administration (NOAA). The data includes the latitude and longitude of the observation and the sustained wind speed in miles per hour.

```
var katrina = [
    { north: 23.2, west: 75.5, wind:  35 },
    { north: 24.0, west: 76.4, wind:  35 },
    { north: 25.2, west: 77.0, wind:  45 },
    // Data set continues...
```

For the bubble chart, Flotr2 needs each data point to be an array rather than an object, so let's build a simple function to convert the source data into that format. To make the function more general, we can use an optional parameter to specify a filter function. And while we're extracting data points, we can reverse the sign of the longitude so that west to east displays left to right.

```
function get_points(source_array, filter_function) {
❶    var result = [];
    for (var i=0; i<source_array.length; i++) {
        if ( (typeof filter_function === "undefined")
            || (typeof filter_function !== "function")
            || filter_function(source_array[i]) ) {
            result.push([
                source_array[i].west * -1,
                source_array[i].north,
                source_array[i].wind
            ]);
        }
    }
    return result;
}
```

The code for our function starts by setting the return value (result) to an empty array at ❶. Then it iterates through the input source_array one element at a time. If the filter_function parameter is available, and if it is a valid function, our code calls that function with the source array element as a parameter. If the function returns true, or if no function was passed in the parameter, then our code extracts the data point from the source element and pushes it onto the result array.

As you can see, the filter_function parameter is optional. If the caller omits it (or if it is not a valid function), then every point in the source ends up in the result. We won't use the filter function right away, but it will come in handy for the later steps in this example.

Step 2: Create a Background for the Chart

Because the x- and y-values of our chart will represent position, a map makes the perfect chart background. To avoid any copyright concerns, we'll use map images from Stamen Design (*http://stamen.com/*) that use data from OpenStreetMap (*http://openstreetmap.org/*). Both are available under Creative Commons licenses, CC BY 3.0 (*http://creativecommons.org/licenses/by/3.0*) and CC BY SA (*http://creativecommons.org/licenses/by-sa/3.0*), respectively.

Projections can be a tricky issue when you're working with maps, but the smaller the mapped area, the less of an effect projections have, and they're less critical in the center of the mapped region. For this example, with its relatively small area and action focused in the center, we'll assume the map image uses a Mercator projection. That assumption lets us avoid any advanced mathematical transformations when converting from latitude and longitude to x- and y-values.

Figure 1-21 shows the map image on which we'll overlay the hurricane's path.

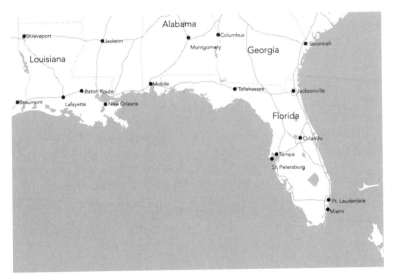

FIGURE 1-21: A map image can be used as the background for a chart.

Step 3: Plot the Data

It will take us several iterations to get the chart looking the way we want, but let's start with the minimum number of options. One parameter we will need to specify is the bubble radius. For static charts such as this example, it's easiest to experiment with a few values to find the best size. A value of **0.3** seems effective for our chart. In addition to the options, the **draw()** method expects an HTML element that will contain the chart, as well as the data itself.

```
Flotr.draw(
    document.getElementById("chart"),
    [{
      data: get_points(katrina),
      bubbles: {show:true, baseRadius: 0.3}
    }]
);
```

As you can see, we're using our transformation function to extract the data from our source. The return value from that function serves directly as the second parameter to **draw()**.

For now, we haven't bothered with the background image. We'll add that to the chart once we've adjusted the data a bit. The result in Figure 1-22 still needs improvement, but it's a working start.

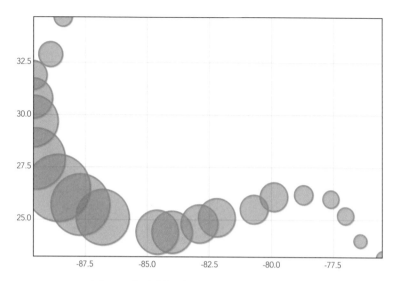

FIGURE 1-22: *A basic bubble chart varies the size of the data points.*

Step 4: Add the Background

Now that we've seen how Flotr2 will plot our data, we can add in the background image. We'll want to make a few other additions at the same time. First, as long as we're adding the background, we can remove the grid lines. Second, let's disable the axis labels; latitude and longitude values don't have much meaning for the average user, and they're certainly not necessary with the map. Finally, and most importantly, we need to adjust the scale of the chart to match the map image.

```
Flotr.draw(
    document.getElementById("chart"),
    [{
      data: get_points(katrina),
      bubbles: {show:true, baseRadius: 0.3}
    }],
    {
❶     grid: {
            backgroundImage: "img/gulf.png",
            horizontalLines: false,
            verticalLines: false
        },
❷       yaxis: {showLabels: false, min: 23.607, max: 33.657},
❸       xaxis: {showLabels: false, min: -94.298, max: -77.586}
    }
);
```

We've added **grid** options starting at ❶ to tell Flotr2 to omit both horizontal and vertical grid lines, and they designate the background image. Our image shows latitude values from 23.607°N to 33.657°N and longitude from 77.586°W to 94.298°W. At ❷ and ❸ we provide those values as ranges for the xaxis and yaxis options, and disable labels for both axes. Note that because we're dealing with longitudes west of 0, we're using negative values.

At this point the chart in Figure 1-23 is looking pretty good. We can clearly see the path of the hurricane and get a sense of how the storm strengthened and weakened.

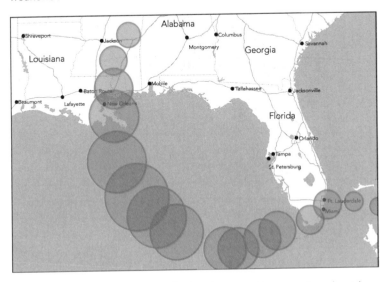

FIGURE 1-23: *With a map as the background image, the chart has a meaningful context.*

Step 5: Color the Bubbles

This example gives us a chance to provide even more information to our users without overly distracting them: we have the option to modify the bubble colors. Let's use that freedom to indicate the Saffir-Simpson classification for storm intensity at each measurement point.

Here's where we can take advantage of the filter option we included in the data formatting function. The Saffir-Simpson classification is based on wind speed, so we'll filter based on the **wind** property. For example, here's how to extract only those values that represent a Category 1 hurricane, with wind speeds from 74 to 95 miles per hour. The function we pass to get_points returns **true** only for appropriate wind speeds.

```
cat1 = get_points(katrina, function(obs) {
    return (obs.wind >= 74) && (obs.wind < 95);
});
```

To have Flotr2 assign different colors to different strengths, we divide the data into multiple series with the following code. Each series gets its own color. In addition to the five hurricane categories, we've also parsed out the points for tropical storm and tropical depression strength.

```
Flotr.draw(
    document.getElementById("chart"),
    [
        {
            data: get_points(katrina, function(obs) {
                    return (obs.wind < 39);
                }),
            color: "#74add1",
            bubbles: {show:true, baseRadius: 0.3, lineWidth: 1}
        },{
        // Options continue...
        },{
            data: get_points(katrina, function(obs) {
                    return (obs.wind >= 157);
                }),
            color: "#d73027",
            label: "Category 5",
            bubbles: {show:true, baseRadius: 0.3, lineWidth: 1}
        }
    ],{
        grid: {
            backgroundImage: "img/gulf.png",
            horizontalLines: false,
            verticalLines: false
        },
        yaxis: {showLabels: false, min: 23.607, max: 33.657},
        xaxis: {showLabels: false, min: -94.298, max: -77.586},
        legend: {position: "sw"}
    }
);
```

We've also added labels for the hurricane categories and placed a legend in the lower left of the chart, as you can see in Figure 1-24.

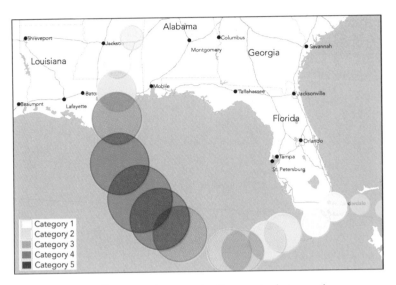

FIGURE 1-24: *Different colors can indicate wind strength.*

Step 6: Adjust the Legend Styles

By default, Flotr2 seems to prefer all elements as large as possible. The legend in Figure 1-24 is a good example: it looks cramped and unattractive. Fortunately, the fix is rather simple: we simply add some CSS styles to give the legend padding. We can also set the legend's background color explicitly rather than relying on Flotr2's manipulation of opacity.

```
.flotr-legend {
    padding: 5px;
    background-color: #ececec;
}
```

To prevent Flotr2 from creating its own background for the legend, set the opacity to 0.

```
Flotr.draw(
    document.getElementById("chart")
        // Additional options...
        legend: {position: "sw", backgroundOpacity: 0,},
        // Additional options...
```

With that final tweak, we have the finished product of Figure 1-25. We don't want to use the Flotr2 options to specify a title, because Flotr2 will shrink the chart area by an unpredictable amount (since we cannot predict the font sizing in the users' browsers). That would distort our latitude transformation. Of course, it's easy enough to use HTML to provide the title.

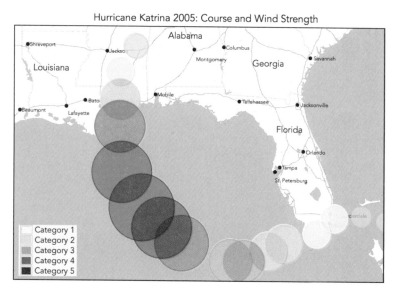

Hurricane Katrina 2005: Course and Wind Strength

FIGURE 1-25: *A bubble chart shows a third dimension (wind speed), as well as position.*

The bubble chart adds another dimension to the two-dimensional scatter chart. In fact, as in our example, it can add two further dimensions. The example uses bubble size to represent wind speed and color to indicate the hurricane's classification. Both of these additional values require care, however. Humans are not good at comparing two-dimensional areas, nor can they easily compare relative shades or colors. We should never use the extra bubble chart dimensions to convey critical data or precise quantities. Rather, they work best in examples such as this—neither the exact wind speed nor the specific classification need be as precise as the location. Few people can tell the difference between 100- and 110-mile-per-hour winds, but they certainly know the difference between New Orleans and Dallas.

Step 7: Work Around Flotr2 "Bugs"

Be sure to refer to Step 9 of "Creating a Basic Bar Chart" on page 14 to see how to work around some "bugs" in the Flotr2 library.

Displaying Multidimensional Data with a Radar Chart

If you have data with many dimensions, a radar chart may be the most effective way to visualize it. Radar charts are not as common as other charts, though, and their unfamiliarity makes them a little harder for users to interpret. If you design a radar chart, be careful not to increase that burden.

Radar charts are most effective when your data has several characteristics:

▸ You don't have too many data points to show. Half a dozen data points is about the maximum that a radar chart can accommodate.

▸ The data points have multiple dimensions. With two or even three dimensions to your data, you would probably be better off with a more traditional chart type. Radar charts come into play with data of four or more dimensions.

▸ Each data dimension is a scale that can at least be ranked (from good to bad, say), if not assigned a number outright. Radar charts don't work well with data dimensions that are merely arbitrary categories (such as political party or nationality).

A classic use for radar charts is analyzing the performance of players on a sports team. Consider, for example, the 2012 starting lineup of Miami Heat, a team in the National Basketball Association (NBA). There are only five data points (the five players). There are multiple dimensions—points, assists, rebounds, blocks, steals, and so on—and each of those dimensions has a natural numeric value.

Table 1-1 shows the players' 2011–2012 season averages per game, as well as the team totals (which include the contributions of nonstarters).

Table 1-1: Miami Heat 2011–2012 Season

Player	Points	Rebounds	Assists	Steals	Blocks
Chris Bosh	17.2	7.9	1.6	0.8	0.8
Shane Battier	5.4	2.6	1.2	1.0	0.5
LeBron James	28.0	8.4	6.1	1.9	0.8
Dwyane Wade	22.3	5.0	4.5	1.7	1.3
Mario Chalmers	10.2	2.9	3.6	1.4	0.2
Team total	98.2	41.3	19.3	8.5	5.3

Just as in Step 1 of "Creating a Basic Bar Chart" on page 6, we need to include the Flotr2 library in our web page and set aside a `<div>` element to contain the chart we'll construct.

Step 1: Define the Data

We'll start with a typical JavaScript expression of the team's statistics. For our example we'll start with an array of objects corresponding to each starter, and a separate object for the entire team.

```
var players = [
    { player: "Chris Bosh",    points: 17.2, rebounds: 7.9, assists: 1.6,
      steals: 0.8, blocks: 0.8 },
    { player: "Shane Battier", points:  5.4, rebounds: 2.6, assists: 1.2,
      steals: 1.0, blocks: 0.5 },
```

```
        { player: "LeBron James",    points: 28.0, rebounds: 8.4, assists: 6.1,
          steals: 1.9, blocks: 0.8 },
        { player: "Dwyane Wade",     points: 22.3, rebounds: 5.0, assists: 4.5,
          steals: 1.7, blocks: 1.3 },
        { player: "Mario Chalmers", points: 10.2, rebounds: 2.9, assists: 3.6,
          steals: 1.4, blocks: 0.2 }
];
var team = {
    points:  98.2,
    rebounds: 41.3,
    assists:  19.3,
    steals:    8.5,
    blocks:    5.3
};
```

For an effective radar plot, we need to normalize all the values to a common scale. In this example, let's translate raw statistics into team percentage. For example, instead of visualizing LeBron James's scoring as 28.0, we'll show it as 29 percent (28.0/98.2).

There are a couple of functions we can use to convert the raw statistics into an object to chart. The first function returns the **statistics** object for a single player. It simply searches through the **players** array looking for that player's name. The second function steps through each statistic in the **team** object, gets the corresponding statistic for the named player, and normalizes the value. The returned object will have a **label** property equal to the player's name, and an array of normalized statistics for that player.

```
var get_player = function(name) {
    for (var i=0; i<players.length; i++) {
        if (players[i].player === name) return players[i];
    }
}
var player_data = function(name) {
    var obj = {}, i = 0;
    obj.label = name;
    obj.data = [];
    for (var key in team) {
        obj.data.push([i, 100*get_player(name)[key]/team[key]]);
        i++;
    };
    return obj;
};
```

For example, the function call **player_data("LeBron James")** returns the following object:

```
{
    label: "LeBron James",
    data:  [
              [0,28.513238289205702],
```

```
    [1,20.33898305084746],
    [2,31.60621761658031],
    [3,22.352941176470587],
    [4,15.09433962264151]
  ]
}
```

For the specific statistics, we're using a counter from 0 to 4. We'll see how to map those numbers into meaningful values shortly.

Since Flotr2 doesn't require jQuery, we aren't taking advantage of any jQuery convenience function in the preceding code. We're also not taking full advantage of the JavaScript standard (including methods such as `.each()`), because Internet Explorer releases prior to version 9 do not support those methods. If you have jQuery on your pages for other reasons, or if you don't need to support older IE versions, you can simplify this code quite a bit.

The last bit of code we'll use is a simple array of labels for the statistics in our chart. The order must match the order returned in `player_data()`.

```
var labels = [
    [0, "Points"],
    [1, "Rebounds"],
    [2, "Assists"],
    [3, "Steals"],
    [4, "Blocks"]
];
```

Step 2: Create the Chart

A single call to Flotr2's `draw()` method is all it takes to create our chart. We need to specify the HTML element in which to place the chart, as well as the chart data. For the data, we'll use the `get_player()` function shown previously.

```
Flotr.draw(document.getElementById("chart"),
    [
        player_data("Chris Bosh"),
        player_data("Shane Battier"),
        player_data("LeBron James"),
        player_data("Dwyane Wade"),
        player_data("Mario Chalmers")
    ],{
❶      title:
            "2011/12 Miami Heat Starting Lineup – Contribution to Team Total",
❷      radar:  { show: true },
❸      grid:   { circular: true, },
        xaxis:  { ticks: labels, },
        yaxis:  { showLabels: false, min:0, max: 33, }
    }
);
```

This code also includes a few options. The **title** option at ❶ provides an overall title for the chart, and the **radar** option at ❷ tells Flotr2 the type of chart we want. With a radar chart, we also have to explicitly specify a circular (as opposed to rectangular) grid, so we do that with the **grid** option at ❸. The final two options detail the x- and y-axes. For the x-axis, we use our **labels** array to give each statistic a name, and for the y-axis, we forgo labels altogether and explicitly specify the minimum and maximum values.

The only real trick is making the HTML container wide enough to hold both the chart proper and the legend, since Flotr2 doesn't do a great job of calculating the size appropriately. For a static chart such as this one, trial and error is the simplest approach and gives us the chart shown in Figure 1-26.

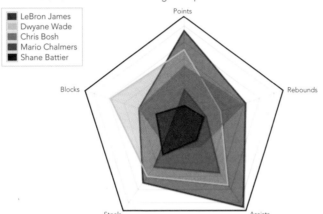

FIGURE 1-26: *Radar charts let users compare multiple data variables at once.*

Although it's certainly not a surprise to NBA fans, the chart clearly demonstrates the value of LeBron James to the team. He led the team in four of the five major statistical categories.

The radar chart lends itself only to a few specialized applications, but it can be effective when there is a modest number of variables, each of which is easily quantified. In Figure 1-26, each player's area on the chart roughly corresponds to his total contribution across all of the variables. The relative size of the red area makes James's total contribution strikingly clear.

Step 3: Work Around Flotr2 "Bugs"

Be sure to refer to Step 9 of "Creating a Basic Bar Chart" on page 14 to see how to work around some "bugs" in the Flotr2 library.

Summing Up

The examples in this chapter provide a quick tour of the many types of standard data charts, the simplest and most straightforward tool for visualizing data. Each of these charts is especially effective for certain types of visualizations.

Bar charts   The workhorse of charts. Effective at showing the change of a quantity over a small number of regular time intervals, or at comparing several different quantities against one another.

Line charts   More effective than bar charts when there is a large number of data values to show, or for showing quantities that vary on an irregular schedule.

Pie charts   Often overused but can be effective to highlight the proportion of a single value within a whole.

Scatter charts   Effective for showing possible relationships between two values.

Bubble charts   Adds a third value to scatter charts but should be used carefully, as it's difficult to accurately assess the relative areas of circular regions.

Radar charts   Designed to show several aspects of the subject on one chart. Not as familiar to many users but can be effective for certain specialized cases.

2
Making Charts Interactive

In Chapter 1 we saw how to create a wide variety of simple, static charts. In many cases such charts are the ideal visualization, but they don't take advantage of an important characteristic of the Web—interactivity. Sometimes you want to do more than just present data to your users; you want to give them a chance to explore the data, to focus on the elements they find particularly interesting, or to consider alternative scenarios. In those cases we can take advantage of the Web as a medium by adding interactivity to our visualizations.

Because they're designed for the Web, virtually all of the libraries and toolkits we examine in this book include support for interactivity. That's certainly true of the Flotr2 library used in Chapter 1. But let's take the opportunity to explore an alternative. In this chapter, we'll use the *Flot library* (*http://www.flotcharts.org/*), which is based on jQuery and features exceptionally strong support for interactive and real-time charts.

For this chapter, we're also going to stick with a single data source: the gross domestic product (GDP) for countries worldwide. This data is publicly available from the *World Bank* (*http://data.worldbank.org/*). It may not seem like the most exciting data to work with, but effective visualizations can bring even the most mundane data alive. Here's what you'll learn:

▶   How to let users select the content for a chart

▶   How to let users zoom into a chart to see more details

▶   How to make a chart respond to user mouse movements

▶   How to dynamically get data for a chart using an AJAX service

Selecting Chart Content

If you're presenting data to a large audience on the Web, you may find that different users are especially interested in different aspects of your data. With global GDP data, for example, we might expect that individual users would be most interested in the data for their own region of the world. If we can anticipate inquiries like this from the user, we can construct our visualization to answer them.

In this example, we're targeting a worldwide audience, and we want to show data for all regions. To accommodate individual users, however, we can make the regions selectable; that is, users will be able to show or hide the data from each region. If some users don't care about data for particular regions, they can simply choose not to show it.

Interactive visualizations usually require more thought than simple, static charts. Not only must the original presentation of data be effective, but the way the user controls the presentation *and* the way the presentation responds must be effective as well. It usually helps to consider each of those requirements explicitly.

1.   Make sure the initial, static presentation shows the data effectively.
2.   Add any user controls to the page and ensure they make sense for the visualization.
3.   Add the code that makes the controls work.

We'll tackle each of these phases in the following example.

Step 1: Include the Required JavaScript Libraries

Since we're using the Flot library to create the chart, we need to include that library in our web pages. And since Flot requires jQuery, we'll include that in our pages as well. Fortunately, both jQuery and Flot are popular libraries, and they are available on public *content distribution networks (CDNs)*. That gives you the option of loading both from a CDN instead of hosting them on your own site. There are several advantages to relying on a CDN:

Better performance If the user has previously visited other websites that retrieved the libraries from the same CDN, then the libraries may already exist in the browser's local cache. In that case the browser simply retrieves them from the cache, avoiding the delay of additional network requests. (See the second disadvantage in the next list for a different view on performance.)

Lower cost One way or another, the cost of your site is likely based on how much bandwidth you use. If your users are able to retrieve libraries from a CDN, then the bandwidth required to service their requests won't count against your site.

Of course there are also disadvantages to CDNs as well.

Loss of control If the CDN goes down, then the libraries your page needs won't be available. That puts your site's functionality at the mercy of the CDN. There are approaches to mitigate such failures. You can try to retrieve from the CDN and fall back to your own hosted copy if the CDN request fails. Implementing such a fallback is tricky, though, and it could introduce errors in your code.

Lack of flexibility With CDN-hosted libraries, you're generally stuck with a limited set of options. For example, in this case we need both the jQuery and Flot libraries. CDNs provide those libraries only as distinct files, so to get both we'll need two network requests. If we host the libraries ourselves, on the other hand, we can combine them into a single file and cut the required number of requests in half. For high-latency networks (such as mobile networks), the number of requests may be the biggest factor in determining the performance of your web page.

There isn't a clear-cut answer for all cases, so you'll have to weigh the options against your own requirements. For this example (and the others in this chapter), we'll use the CloudFlare CDN.

In addition to the jQuery library, Flot relies on the HTML canvas feature. To support IE8 and earlier, we'll include the excanvas.min.js library in our pages and make sure that only IE8 and earlier will load it, just like we did for our bar chart in Chapter 1. Also, since excanvas isn't available on a public CDN, we'll have to host it on our own server. Here's the skeleton to start with:

```
<!DOCTYPE html>
<html lang="en">
  <head>
    <meta charset="utf-8">
```

```
    <title></title>
  </head>
  <body>
    <!-- Content goes here -->
    <!--[if lt IE 9]><script src="js/excanvas.min.js"></script><![endif]-->
    <script src="//cdnjs.cloudflare.com/ajax/libs/jquery/1.8.3/jquery.min.js">
    </script>
    <script src="//cdnjs.cloudflare.com/ajax/libs/flot/0.7/jquery.flot.min.js">
    </script>
  </body>
</html>
```

As you can see, we're including the JavaScript libraries at the end of the document. This approach lets the browser load the document's entire HTML markup and begin laying out the page while it waits for the server to provide the JavaScript libraries.

Step 2: Set Aside a <div> Element to Hold the Chart

Within our document, we need to create a <div> element to contain the chart we'll construct. This element must have an explicit height and width, or Flot won't be able to construct the chart. We can indicate the element's size in a CSS style sheet, or we can place it directly on the element itself. Here's how the document might look with the latter approach.

```
<!DOCTYPE html>
<html lang="en">
  <head>
    <meta charset="utf-8">
    <title></title>
  </head>
  <body>
❶   <div id="chart" style="width:600px;height:400px;"></div>
    <!--[if lt IE 9]><script src="js/excanvas.min.js"></script><![endif]-->
    <script src="//cdnjs.cloudflare.com/ajax/libs/jquery/1.8.3/jquery.min.js">
    </script>
    <script src="//cdnjs.cloudflare.com/ajax/libs/flot/0.7/jquery.flot.min.js">
    </script>
  </body>
</html>
```

Note at ❶ that we've given the <div> an explicit id so we can reference it later.

Step 3: Prepare the Data

In later examples we'll see how to get the data directly from the World Bank's web service, but for this example, let's keep things simple and assume we have the data already downloaded and formatted for JavaScript. (For brevity, only excerpts are shown here. The book's source code includes the full data set.)

```
var eas = [[1960,0.1558],[1961,0.1547],[1962,0.1574], // Data continues...
var ecs = [[1960,0.4421],[1961,0.4706],[1962,0.5145], // Data continues...
var lcn = [[1960,0.0811],[1961,0.0860],[1962,0.0990], // Data continues...
var mea = [[1968,0.0383],[1969,0.0426],[1970,0.0471], // Data continues...
var sas = [[1960,0.0478],[1961,0.0383],[1962,0.0389], // Data continues...
var ssf = [[1960,0.0297],[1961,0.0308],[1962,0.0334], // Data continues...
```

This data includes the historical GDP (in current US dollars) for major regions of the world, from 1960 to 2011. The names of the variables are the World Bank region codes.

✴ **NOTE: At the time of this writing, World Bank data for North America was temporarily unavailable.**

Step 4: Draw the Chart

Before we add any interactivity, let's check out the chart itself. The Flot library provides a simple function call to create a static graph. We call the jQuery extension `plot` and pass it two parameters. The first parameter identifies the HTML element that should contain the chart, and the second parameter provides the data as an array of data sets. In this case, we pass in an array with the series we defined earlier for each region.

```
$(function () {
    $.plot($("#chart"), [ eas, ecs, lcn, mea, sas, ssf ]);
});
```

Figure 2-1 shows the resulting chart.

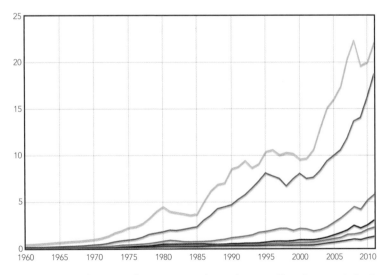

FIGURE 2-1: *Flot can show a static line chart well with just default options.*

It looks like we've done a good job of capturing and presenting the data statically, so we can move on to the next phase.

Step 5: Add the Controls

Now that we have a chart we're happy with, we can add the HTML controls to interact with it. For this example, our goal is fairly simple: our users should be able to pick which regions appear on the graph. We'll give them that option with a set of checkboxes, one for each region. Here's the markup to include the checkboxes.

```
<label><input type="checkbox"> East Asia & Pacific</label>
<label><input type="checkbox"> Europe & Central Asia</label>
<label><input type="checkbox"> Latin America & Caribbean</label>
<label><input type="checkbox"> Middle East & North Africa</label>
<label><input type="checkbox"> South Asia</label>
<label><input type="checkbox"> Sub-Saharan Africa</label>
```

You may be surprised to see that we've placed the `<input>` controls inside the `<label>` elements. Although it looks a little unusual, that's almost always the best approach. When we do that, the browser interprets clicks on the label as clicks on the control, whereas if we separate the labels from the controls, it forces the user to click on the tiny checkbox itself to have any effect.

On our web page, we'd like to place the controls on the right side of the chart. We can do that by creating a containing `<div>` and making the chart and the controls float (left) within it. While we're experimenting with the layout, it's easiest to simply add the styling directly in the HTML markup. In a production implementation, you might want to define the styles in an external style sheet.

```
<div id="visualization">
    <div id="chart" style="width:500px;height:333px;float:left"></div>
    <div id="controls" style="float:left;">
        <label><input type="checkbox"> East Asia & Pacific</label>
        <label><input type="checkbox"> Europe & Central Asia</label>
        <label><input type="checkbox"> Latin America & Caribbean</label>
        <label><input type="checkbox"> Middle East & North Africa</label>
        <label><input type="checkbox"> South Asia</label>
        <label><input type="checkbox"> Sub-Saharan Africa</label>
    </div>
</div>
```

We should also add a title and instructions and make all the `<input>` checkboxes default to **checked**. Let's see the chart now, to make sure the formatting looks okay (Figure 2-2).

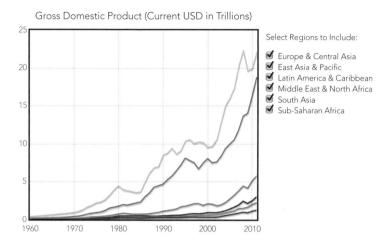

Gross Domestic Product (Current USD in Trillions)

Select Regions to Include:

☑ Europe & Central Asia
☑ East Asia & Pacific
☑ Latin America & Caribbean
☑ Middle East & North Africa
☑ South Asia
☑ Sub-Saharan Africa

FIGURE 2-2: *Standard HTML can create controls for chart interaction.*

Now we see how the controls look in relation to the chart in Figure 2-2, and we can verify that they make sense both for the data and for the interaction model. Our visualization lacks a critical piece of information, though: it doesn't identify which line corresponds to which region. For a static visualization, we could simply use the Flot library to add a legend to the chart, but that approach isn't ideal here. You can see the problem in Figure 2-3, as the legend looks confusingly like the interaction controls.

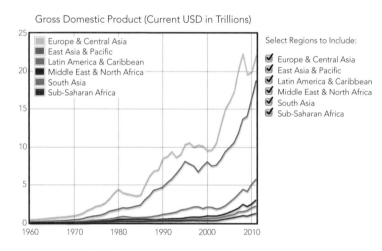

Gross Domestic Product (Current USD in Trillions)

Europe & Central Asia
East Asia & Pacific
Latin America & Caribbean
Middle East & North Africa
South Asia
Sub-Saharan Africa

Select Regions to Include:

☑ Europe & Central Asia
☑ East Asia & Pacific
☑ Latin America & Caribbean
☑ Middle East & North Africa
☑ South Asia
☑ Sub-Saharan Africa

FIGURE 2-3: *The Flot library's standard legend doesn't match the chart styles well.*

We can eliminate the visual confusion by combining the legend and the interaction controls. The checkbox controls will serve as a legend if we add color boxes that identify the chart lines.

We can add the colored boxes using an HTML <span> tag and a bit of styling. Here is the markup for one such checkbox with the styles inline. (Full web page implementations might be better organized by having most of the styles defined in an external style sheet.)

```
<label class="checkbox">
    <input type="checkbox" checked>
    <span style="background-color:rgb(237,194,64);height:0.9em;
                 width:0.9em;margin-right:0.25em;display:inline-block;"/>
    East Asia & Pacific
</label>
```

In addition to the background color, the <span> needs an explicit size, and we use an inline-block value for the display property to force the browser to show the span even though it has no content. As you can also see, we're using ems instead of pixels to define the size of the block. Since ems scale automatically with the text size, the color blocks will match the text label size even if users zoom in or out on the page.

A quick check in the browser can verify that the various elements combine effectively (Figure 2-4).

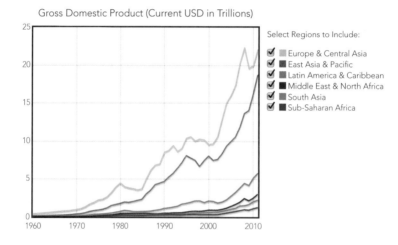

FIGURE 2-4: *Interaction controls can also serve as chart elements such as legends.*

That looks pretty good, so now we can move on to the interaction itself.

Step 6: Define the Data Structure for the Interaction

Now that the general layout looks good, we can turn back to JavaScript. First we need to expand our data to track the interaction state. Instead of storing the data as simple arrays of values, we'll use an array of objects. Each object will include the corresponding data values along with other properties.

```
var source = [
    { data: eas, show: true, color: "#FE4C4C", name: "East Asia & Pacific" },
    { data: ecs, show: true, color: "#B6ED47", name: "Europe & Central Asia" },
    { data: lcn, show: true, color: "#2D9999",
      name: "Latin America & Caribbean" },
    { data: mea, show: true, color: "#A50000",
      name: "Middle East & North Africa" },
    { data: sas, show: true, color: "#679A00", name: "South Asia" },
    { data: ssf, show: true, color: "#006363", name: "Sub-Saharan Africa" }
];
```

Each object includes the data points for a region, and it also gives us a place to define additional properties, including the label for the series and other status information. One property that we want to track is whether the series should be included on the chart (using the key show). We also need to specify the color for each line; otherwise, the Flot library will pick the color dynamically based on how many regions are visible at the same time, and we won't be able to match the color with the control legend.

Step 7: Determine Chart Data Based on the Interaction State

When we call plot() to draw the chart, we need to pass in an object containing the data series and the color for each region. The source array has the information we need, but it contains other information as well, which could potentially make Flot behave unexpectedly. We want to pass in a simpler object to the plot function. For example, the East Asia & Pacific series would be defined this way:

```
{
    data:  eas,
    color: "#E41A1C"
}
```

We also want to be sure to show the data only for regions the user has selected. That may be only a subset of the complete data set. Those two operations—transforming array elements (in this case, to simpler objects) and filtering an array to a subset—are very common requirements for visualizations. Fortunately, jQuery has two utility functions that make both operations easy: $.map() and $.grep().

Both .grep() and .map() accept two parameters. The first parameter is an array or, more precisely, an "array-like" object. That's either a JavaScript array or another JavaScript object that looks and acts like an array. (There is a technical distinction, but it's not something we have to worry about here.) The second parameter is a function that operates on elements of the array one at a time. For .grep(), that function returns true or false to filter out elements accordingly. In the case of .map(), the function returns a transformed object that replaces the original element in the array. Figure 2-5 shows how these functions convert the initial data into the final data array.

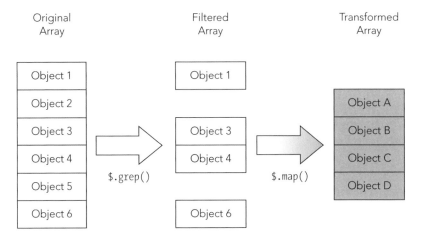

FIGURE 2-5: *The jQuery library has utility functions to help transform and filter data.*

Taking these one at a time, here's how to filter out irrelevant data from the response. We use `.grep()` to check the **show** property in our source data so that it returns an array with only the objects where **show** is set to **true**.

```
$.grep(
    source,
    function (obj) { return obj.show; }
)
```

And here's how to transform the elements to retain only relevant properties:

```
$.map(
    source,
    function (obj) { return { data: obj.data, color: obj.color }; }
)
```

There's no need to make these separate steps. We can combine them in a nice, concise expression as follows:

```
$.map(
    $.grep(
        source,
        function (obj) { return obj.show; }
    ),
    function (obj) { return { data: obj.data, color: obj.color }; }
)
```

That expression in turn provides the input data to Flot's **plot()** function.

Step 8: Add the Controls Using JavaScript

Now that our new data structure can provide the chart input, let's use it to add the checkbox controls to the page as well. The jQuery `.each()` function is a convenient way to iterate through the array of regions. Its parameters include an array of objects and a function to execute on each object in the array. That function takes two parameters, the array index and the array object.

```
$.each(source, function(idx, region) {
    var input = $("<input>").attr("type","checkbox").attr("id","chk-"+idx);
    if (region.show) {
        $(input).prop("checked",true);
    }
    var span = $("<span>").css({
        "background-color": region.color,
        "display":          "inline-block",
        "height":           "0.9em",
        "width":            "0.9em",
        "margin-right":     "0.25em",
    });
    var label = $("<label>").append(input).append(span).append(region.name);
    $("#controls").append(label);
});
```

Within the iteration function we do four things. First, we create the checkbox `<input>` control. As you can see, we're giving each control a unique `id` attribute that combines the `chk-` prefix with the source array index. If the chart is showing that region, the control's `checked` property is set to `true`. Next we create the `<span>` for the color block. We're setting all the styles, including the region's color, using the `css()` function. The third element we create in the function is the `<label>`. To that element we append the checkbox `<input>` control, the color box `<span>`, and the region's name. Finally, we add the `<label>` to the document.

Notice that we don't add the intermediate elements (such as the `<input>` or the `<span>`) directly to the document. Instead, we construct those elements using local variables. We then assemble the local variables into the final, complete `<label>` and add that to the document. This approach significantly improves the performance of web pages. Every time JavaScript code adds elements to the document, the web browser has to recalculate the appearance of the page. For complex pages, that can take time. By assembling the elements before adding them to the document, we've only forced the browser to perform that calculation once for each region. (You could further optimize performance by combining all of the regions in a local variable and adding only that single local variable to the document.)

If we combine the JavaScript to draw the chart with the JavaScript to create the controls, we need only a skeletal HTML structure.

```
<div id="visualization">
    <div id="chart" style="width:500px;height:333px;float:left"></div>
    <div id="controls" style="float:left;">
        <p>Select Regions to Include:</p>
```

```
    </div>
</div>
```

Our reward is the visualization in Figure 2-6—the same one as shown in Figure 2-4—but this time we've created it dynamically using JavaScript.

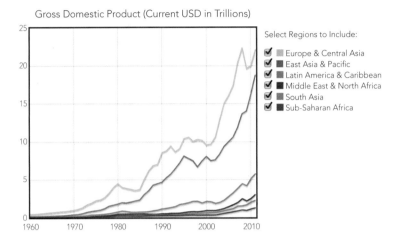

Gross Domestic Product (Current USD in Trillions)

FIGURE 2-6: *Setting the chart options ensures that the data matches the legend.*

Step 9: Respond to the Interaction Controls

We still haven't added any interactivity, of course, but we're almost there. Our code just needs to watch for clicks on the controls and redraw the chart appropriately. Since we've conveniently given each checkbox an **id** attribute that begins with **chk-**, it's easy to watch for the right events.

```
$("input[id^='chk-']").click(function(ev) {
    // Handle the click
})
```

When the code sees a click, it should determine which checkbox was clicked, toggle the **show** property of the data source, and redraw the chart. We can find the specific region by skipping past the four-character **chk-** prefix of the event target's **id** attribute.

```
idx = ev.target.id.substr(4);
source[idx].show = !source[idx].show
```

Redrawing the chart requires a couple of calls to the chart object that **plot()** returns. We reset the data and then tell the library to redraw the chart.

```
plotObj.setData(
    $.map(
        $.grep(source, function (obj) { return obj.show; }),
        function (obj) { return { data: obj.data, color: obj.color }; }
    )
);
plotObj.draw();
```

And that's it. We finally have a fully interactive visualization of regional gross domestic product, as shown in Figure 2-7.

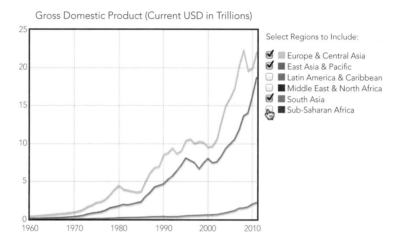

FIGURE 2-7: *An interactive chart gives users control over the visualization.*

The visualization we've created engages users more effectively than a static chart. They can still see the overall picture, but the interaction controls let them focus on aspects of the data that are especially important or interesting to them.

There is still a potential problem with this implementation. Two data sets (Europe and East Asia & Pacific) dominate the chart. When users deselect those regions, the remaining data is confined to the very bottom of the chart, and much of the chart's area is wasted. You could address this by rescaling the chart every time you draw it. To do this, you would call `plotObj.setupGrid()` before calling `plotObj.draw()`. On the other hand, users may find this constant rescaling disconcerting, because it changes the whole chart, not just the region they selected. In the next example, we'll address this type of problem by giving users total control over the scale of both axes.

Zooming In on Charts

So far, we've given users some interaction with the visualization by letting them choose which data sets appear. In many cases, however, you'll want to give them even more control, especially if you're showing a lot of data and details are hard to discern. If users can't see the details they need, our visualization has failed. Fortunately, we can avoid this problem by giving users a chance to inspect fine details within the data. One way to do that is to let users zoom in on the chart.

Although the Flot library in its most basic form does not support zooming, there are at least two library extensions that add this feature: the *selection* plug-in and the *navigation* plug-in. The navigation plug-in acts a bit like Google Maps. It adds a control that looks like a compass to one corner of the plot and gives users arrows and buttons to pan or zoom the display. This interface is not especially effective for charts, however. Users cannot control exactly how much the chart pans or zooms, which makes it difficult for them to anticipate the effect of an action.

The selection plug-in provides a much better interface. Users simply drag their mouse across the area of the chart they want to zoom in on. The effect of this gesture is more intuitive, and users can be as precise as they like in those actions. The plug-in does have one significant downside, however: it doesn't support touch interfaces.

For this example, we'll walk through the steps required to support zooming with the selection plug-in. Of course, the best approach for your own website and visualizations will vary from case to case.

Step 1: Prepare the Page

Because we're sticking with the same data, most of the preparation is identical to the last example.

```
<!DOCTYPE html>
<html lang="en">
  <head>
    <meta charset="utf-8">
    <title></title>
  </head>
  <body>
    <!-- Content goes here -->
    <!--[if lt IE 9]><script src="js/excanvas.min.js"></script><![endif]-->
    <script src="//cdnjs.cloudflare.com/ajax/libs/jquery/1.8.3/jquery.min.js">
    </script>
    <script src="//cdnjs.cloudflare.com/ajax/libs/flot/0.7/jquery.flot.min.js">
    </script>
❶   <script src="js/jquery.flot.selection.js"></script>
  </body>
</html>
```

As you can see, we do, however, have to add the selection plug-in to the page. It is not available on common CDNs, so we host it on our own server, as shown at ❶.

Step 2: Draw the Chart

Before we add any interactivity, let's go back to a basic chart. This time, we'll add a legend inside the chart since we won't be including checkboxes next to the chart.

```
$(function () {
    $.plot($("#chart") [
        { data: eas, label: "East Asia & Pacific" },
        { data: ecs, label: "Europe & Central Asia" },
        { data: lcn, label: "Latin America & Caribbean" },
        { data: mea, label: "Middle East & North Africa" },
        { data: sas, label: "South Asia" },
        { data: ssf, label: "Sub-Saharan Africa" }
    ], {legend: {position: "nw"}});
});
```

Here, we call the jQuery extension **plot** (from the Flot library) and pass it three parameters. The first parameter identifies the HTML element that should contain the chart, and the second parameter provides the data as an array of data series. These series contain regions we defined earlier, plus a label to identify each series. The final parameter specifies options for the plot. We'll keep it simple for this example— the only option we're including tells Flot to position the legend in the top-left (northwest) corner of the chart.

Figure 2-8 shows the resulting chart.

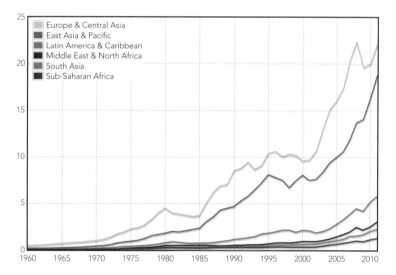

FIGURE 2-8: *The starting point for most interactive charts is a good static chart.*

It looks like we've done a good job of capturing and presenting the data statically, so we can move on to the next phase.

Step 3: Prepare the Data to Support Interaction

Now that we have a working static chart, we can plan how to support interaction. As part of that support, and for the sake of convenience, we'll store all the parameters we're passing to **plot()** in local variables.

```
❶  var $el = $("#chart"),
❷      data = [
            { data: eas, label: "East Asia & Pacific" },
            { data: ecs, label: "Europe & Central Asia" },
            { data: lcn, label: "Latin America & Caribbean" },
            { data: mea, label: "Middle East & North Africa" },
            { data: sas, label: "South Asia" },
            { data: ssf, label: "Sub-Saharan Africa" }
        ],
❸      options = {legend: {position: "nw"}};

❹  var plotObj = $.plot($el, data, options);
```

Before we call **plot()**, we create the variables **$el** ❶, **data** ❷, and **options** ❸. We'll also need to save the object returned from **plot()** at ❹.

Step 4: Prepare to Accept Interaction Events

Our code also has to prepare to handle the interaction events. The selection plug-in signals the user's actions by triggering custom **plotselected** events on the element containing the chart. To receive these events, we need a function that expects two parameters—the standard JavaScript event object and a custom object containing details about the selection. We'll worry about how to process the event shortly. For now let's focus on preparing for it.

```
$el.on("plotselected", function(ev, ranges) {
    // Handle selection events
});
```

The jQuery **.on()** function assigns a function to an arbitrary event. Events can be standard JavaScript events such as **click**, or they can be custom events like the one we're using. The event of interest is the first parameter to **.on()**. The second parameter is the function that will process the event. As noted previously, it also takes two parameters.

Now we can consider the action we want to take when our function receives an event. The **ranges** parameter contains both an **xaxis** and a **yaxis** object, which have information about the **plotselected** event. In both objects, the **from** and **to** properties specify the region that the user selected. To zoom to that selection, we can simply redraw the chart by using those ranges for the chart's axes.

Specifying the axes for the redrawn chart requires us to pass new options to the **plot()** function, but we want to preserve whatever options are already defined. The jQuery **.extend()** function gives us the perfect tool for that task. The function merges JavaScript objects so that the result contains all of the properties in each object. If the objects might contain other objects, then we have to tell jQuery to use "deep" mode when it performs the merge. Here's the complete call to **plot()**, which we place inside the **plotselected** event handler.

```
plotObj = $.plot($el, data,
    $.extend(true, {}, options, {
        xaxis: { min: ranges.xaxis.from, max: ranges.xaxis.to },
        yaxis: { min: ranges.yaxis.from, max: ranges.yaxis.to }
    })
);
```

When we use `.extend()`, the first parameter (`true`) requests deep mode, the second parameter specifies the starting object, and subsequent parameters specify additional objects to merge. We're starting with an empty object (`{}`), merging the regular options, and then further merging the axis options for the zoomed chart.

Step 5: Enable the Interaction

Since we've included the selections plug-in library on our page, activating the interaction is easy. We simply include an additional **selection** option in our call to `plot()`. Its `mode` property indicates the direction of selections the chart will support. Possible values include `"x"` (for x-axis only), `"y"` (for y-axis only), or `"xy"` (for both axes). Here's the complete `options` variable we want to use.

```
var options = {
    legend: {position: "nw"},
    selection: {mode: "xy"}
};
```

And with that addition, our chart is now interactive. Users can zoom in to see as much detail as they want. There is a small problem, though: our visualization doesn't give users a way to zoom back out. Obviously we can't use the selection plug-in to zoom out, since that would require users to select outside the current chart area. Instead, we can add a button to the page to reset the zoom level.

```
<!DOCTYPE html>
<html lang="en">
  <head>
    <meta charset="utf-8">
    <title></title>
  </head>
  <body>
    <div id="chart" style="width:600px;height:400px;"></div>
❶   <button id="unzoom">Reset Zoom</button>
    <!--[if lt IE 9]><script src="js/excanvas.min.js"></script><![endif]-->
    <script src="//cdnjs.cloudflare.com/ajax/libs/jquery/1.8.3/jquery.min.js">
    </script>
    <script src="//cdnjs.cloudflare.com/ajax/libs/flot/0.7/jquery.flot.min.js">
    </script>
    <script src="js/jquery.flot.selection.js"></script>
  </body>
</html>
```

You can see the button in the markup at ❶; it's right after the `<div>` that holds the chart.

Now we just need to add code to respond when a user clicks the button. Fortunately, this code is pretty simple.

```
$("#unzoom").click(function() {
    plotObj = $.plot($el, data, options);
});
```

Here we just set up a click handler with jQuery and redraw the chart using the original options. We don't need any event data, so our event handling function doesn't even need parameters.

That gives us a complete, interactive visualization. Users can zoom in to any level of detail and restore the original zoom with one click. You can see the interaction in Figure 2-9.

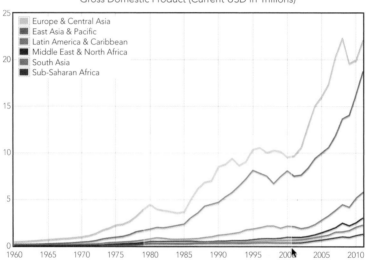

FIGURE 2-9: *Interactive charts let users focus on data relevant to their needs.*

Figure 2-10 shows what the user sees after zooming in.

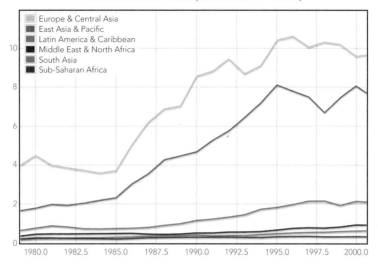

Gross Domestic Product (Current USD in Trillions)

FIGURE 2-10: *Users can zoom in on a section of particular interest.*

If you experiment with this example, you'll soon see that users cannot select an area of the chart that includes the legend. That may be okay for your visualization, but if it's not, the simplest solution is to create your own legend and position it off the chart's canvas, like we did for the first example in this chapter.

Tracking Data Values

A big reason we make visualizations interactive is to give users control over their view of the data. We can present a "big picture" view of the data, but we don't want to prevent users from digging into the details. Often, however, this can force an either/or choice on users: they can see the overall view, or they can see a detailed picture, but they can't see both at the same time. This example looks at an alternative approach that enables users to see overall trends and specific details at once. To do that, we take advantage of the mouse as an input device. When the user's mouse hovers over a section of the chart, our code overlays details relevant to that part of the chart.

This approach does have a significant limitation: it works only when the user has a mouse. If you're considering this technique, be aware that users on touch-screen devices won't be able to take advantage of the interactive aspect; they'll see only the static chart.

Since simple GDP data doesn't lend itself well to the approach in this example, we'll visualize a slightly different set of data from the World Bank. This time we'll look at exports as a percentage of GDP. Let's start by considering a simple line chart, shown in Figure 2-11, with data for each world region.

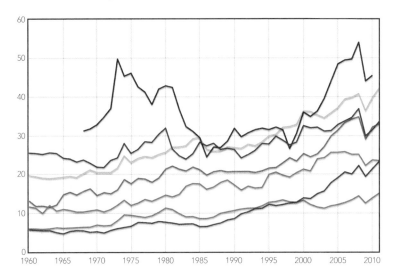

FIGURE 2-11: *Plotting multiple data sets on a single chart can be confusing for users.*

There are a couple of ways this chart falls short. First, many of the series have similar values, forcing some of the chart's lines to cross back and forth over each other. That crisscrossing makes it hard for users to follow a single series closely to see detailed trends. Second, it's hard for users to compare specific values for all of the regions at a single point in time. Most chart libraries, including Flot, have options to display values as users mouse over the chart, but that approach shows only one value at a time. We'd like to give our users a chance to compare the values of multiple regions.

In this example we'll use a two-phase approach to solve both of those problems. First, we'll change the visualization from a single chart with multiple series to multiple charts, each with a single series. That will isolate each region's data, making it easier to see a particular region's trends. Then we'll add an advanced mouse tracking feature that spans all of the charts. This feature will let users see individual values in all of the charts at once.

Step 1: Set Aside a <div> Element to Hold the Charts

Within our document, we need to create a <div> element to contain the charts we'll construct. This element won't contain the charts directly; rather, we'll be placing other <div>s within it, which will each contain a chart.

```
<!DOCTYPE html>
<html lang="en">
  <head>
    <meta charset="utf-8">
    <title></title>
  </head>
  <body>
❶   <div id="charts"></div>
    <!--[if lt IE 9]><script src="js/excanvas.min.js"></script><![endif]-->
    <script src="//cdnjs.cloudflare.com/ajax/libs/jquery/1.8.3/jquery.min.js">
    </script>
    <script src="//cdnjs.cloudflare.com/ajax/libs/flot/0.7/jquery.flot.min.js">
    </script>
  </body>
</html>
```

The "charts" `<div>` is added at ❶. We've also included the required JavaScript libraries here, just as in the previous examples.

We'll use JavaScript to create the `<div>`s for the charts themselves. These elements must have an explicit height and width, or Flot won't be able to construct the charts. You can indicate the element's size in a CSS style sheet, or you can define it when we create the `<div>` (as in the following example). This creates a new `<div>`, sets its width and height, saves a reference to it, and then appends it to the containing `<div>` already in our document.

```
$.each(exports, function(idx,region) {
    var div = $("<div>").css({
        width: "600px",
        height: "60px"
    });
    region.div = div;
    $("#charts").append(div);
});
```

To iterate through the array of regions, we use the jQuery `.each()` function. That function accepts two parameters: an array of objects (**exports**) and a function. It iterates through the array one object at a time, calling the function with the individual object (**region**) and its index (**idx**) as parameters.

Step 2: Prepare the Data

We'll see how to get data directly from the World Bank's web service in the next section, but for now we'll keep things simple again and assume we have the data downloaded and formatted for JavaScript already. (Once again, only excerpts are shown here. The book's source code includes the full data set.)

```
var exports = [
    { label: "East Asia & Pacific",
      data: [[1960,13.2277],[1961,11.7964], // Data continues...
    { label: "Europe & Central Asia",
```

```
          data: [[1960,19.6961],[1961,19.4264], // Data continues...
    { label: "Latin America & Caribbean",
          data: [[1960,11.6802],[1961,11.3069], // Data continues...
    { label: "Middle East & North Africa",
          data: [[1968,31.1954],[1969,31.7533], // Data continues...
    { label: "North America",
          data: [[1960,5.9475],[1961,5.9275], // Data continues...
    { label: "South Asia",
          data: [[1960,5.7086],[1961,5.5807], // Data continues...
    { label: "Sub-Saharan Africa",
          data: [[1960,25.5083],[1961,25.3968], // Data continues...
];
```

The `exports` array contains an object for each region, and each object contains a label and a data series.

Step 3: Draw the Charts

With the `<div>`s for each chart now in place on our page, we can draw the charts using Flot's `plot()` function. That function takes three parameters: the containing element (which we just created), the data, and chart options. To start, let's look at the charts without any decoration—such as labels, grids, or checkmarks—just to make sure the data is generally presented the way we want.

```
$.each(exports, function(idx,region) {
    region.plot = $.plot(region.div, [region.data], {
        series: {lines: {fill: true, lineWidth: 1}, shadowSize: 0},
        xaxis:  {show: false, min:1960, max: 2011},
        yaxis:  {show: false, min: 0, max: 60},
        grid:   {show: false},
    });
});
```

The preceding code uses several `plot()` options to strip the chart of all the extras and set the axes the way we want. Let's consider each option in turn.

series Tells Flot how we want it to graph the data series. In our case we want a line chart (which is the default type), but we want to fill the area from the line down to the x-axis, so we set `fill` to `true`. This option creates an area chart instead of a line chart. Because our charts are so short, an area chart will keep the data visible. For the same reason, we want the line itself to be as small as possible to match, so we set `lineWidth` to `1` (pixel), and we can dispense with shadows by setting `shadowSize` to `0`.

xaxis Defines the properties of the x-axis. We don't want to include one on these charts, so we set `show` to `false`. We do, however, need to explicitly set the range of the axis. If we don't, Flot will create one automatically, using the range of each series. Since our data doesn't have consistent values for all years (the Middle East & North Africa data set, for example, doesn't include data before 1968), we need to make Flot use the exact same x-axis range on all charts, so we specify a range from **1960** to **2011**.

yaxis Works much like the **xaxis** options. We don't want to show one, but we do need to specify an explicit range so that all of the charts are consistent.

grid Tells Flot how to add grid lines and checkmarks to the charts. For now, we don't want anything extra, so we turn off the grid completely by setting **show** to **false**.

We can check the result in Figure 2-12 to make sure the charts appear as we want.

FIGURE 2-12: *Separating individual data sets into multiple charts can make it easier to see the details of each set.*

Next we turn to the decoration for the chart. We're obviously missing labels for each region, but adding them takes some care. Your first thought might be to include a legend along with each chart in the same **<div>**. Flot's event handling, however, will work much better if we can keep all the charts—and only the charts—in their own **<div>**. That's going to require some restructuring of our markup. We'll create a wrapper **<div>** and then place separate **<div>**s for the charts and the legends within it. We can use the CSS **float** property to position them side by side.

```
<div id="charts-wrapper">
    <div id="charts" style="float:left;"></div>
    <div id="legends" style="float:left;"></div>
    <div style="clear:both;"></div>
</div>
```

When we create each legend, we have to be sure it has the exact same height as the chart. Because we're setting both explicitly, that's not hard to do.

```
$.each(exports, function(idx,region) {
    var legend = $("<p>").text(region.label).css({
```

```
        "height":         "17px",
        "margin-bottom": "0",
        "margin-left":    "10px",
        "padding-top":    "33px"
    });
    $("#legends").append(legend);
});
```

Once again we use .each, this time to append a legend for each region to the legends element.

Now we'd like to add a continuous vertical grid that spans all of the charts. Because the charts are stacked, grid lines in the individual charts can appear as one continuous line as long as we can remove any borders or margins between charts. It takes several plot() options to achieve that, as shown here.

```
$.plot(region.div, [region.data], {
    series: {lines: {fill: true, lineWidth: 1}, shadowSize: 0},
    xaxis:  {show: true, labelHeight: 0, min:1960, max: 2011,
             tickFormatter: function() {return "";}},
    yaxis:  {show: false, min: 0, max: 60},
    grid:   {show: true, margin: 0, borderWidth: 0, margin: 0,
             labelMargin: 0, axisMargin: 0, minBorderMargin: 0},
});
```

We enable the grid by setting the grid option's show property to true. Then we remove all the borders and padding by setting the various widths and margins to 0. To get the vertical lines, we also have to enable the x-axis, so we set its show property to true as well. But we don't want any labels on individual charts, so we specify a labelHeight of 0. To be certain that no labels appear, we also define a tickFormatter() function that returns an empty string.

The last bits of decoration we'd like to add are x-axis labels below the bottom chart. To do that, we can create a dummy chart with no visible data, position that dummy chart below the bottom chart, and enable labels on its x-axis. The following three sections create an array of dummy data, create a <div> to hold the dummy chart, and plot the dummy chart.

```
var dummyData = [];
for (var yr=1960; yr<2012; yr++) dummyData.push([yr,0]);

var dummyDiv = $("<div>").css({ width: "600px", height: "15px" });
$("#charts").append(dummyDiv);

var dummyPlot = $.plot(dummyDiv, [dummyData], {
    xaxis:  {show: true, labelHeight: 12, min:1960, max: 2011},
    yaxis:  {show: false, min: 100, max: 200},
    grid:   {show: true, margin: 0, borderWidth: 0, margin: 0,
             labelMargin: 0, axisMargin: 0, minBorderMargin: 0},
});
```

With the added decoration, our chart in Figure 2-13 looks great.

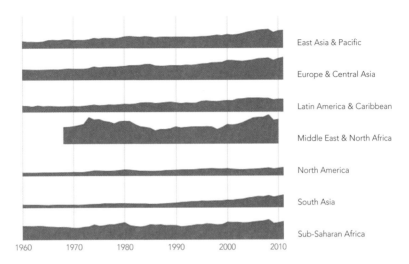

FIGURE 2-13: *Carefully stacking multiple charts creates the appearance of a unified chart.*

Step 4: Implement the Interaction

For our visualization, we want to track the mouse as it hovers over any of our charts. The Flot library makes that relatively easy. The `plot()` function's **grid** options include the **hoverable** property, which is set to **false** by default. If you set this property to **true**, Flot will trigger **plothover** events as the mouse moves over the chart area. It sends these events to the `<div>` that contains the chart. If there is code listening for those events, that code can respond to them. If you use this feature, Flot will also highlight the data point nearest the mouse. That's a behavior we don't want, so we'll disable it by setting **autoHighlight** to **false**.

```
$.plot(region.div, [region.data], {
    series: {lines: {fill: true, lineWidth: 1}, shadowSize: 0},
    xaxis:  {show: true, labelHeight: 0, min: 1960, max: 2011,
             tickFormatter: function() {return "";}},
    yaxis:  {show: false, min: 0, max: 60},
    grid:   {show: true, margin: 0, borderWidth: 0, margin: 0,
             labelMargin: 0, axisMargin: 0, minBorderMargin: 0,
             hoverable: true, autoHighlight: false},
});
```

Now that we've told Flot to trigger events on all of our charts, you might think we would have to set up code to listen for events on all of them. There's an even better approach, though. We structured our markup so that all the charts—and only the charts—are inside the containing **charts** `<div>`. In JavaScript, if no code is listening for an event on a specific document element, those events automatically "bubble up" to the containing elements. So if we just set up an event listener on the charts `<div>`, we can capture the plothover events on all of the individual charts. We'll also need to know when the mouse leaves the chart area. We can catch those events using the standard mouseout event as follows:

```
$("charts").on("plothover", function() {
    // The mouse is hovering over a chart
}).on("mouseout", function() {
    // The mouse is no longer hovering over a chart
});
```

To respond to the plothover events, we want to display a vertical line across all of the charts. We can construct that line using a `<div>` element with a border. In order to move it around, we use absolute positioning. It also needs a positive z-index value to make sure the browser draws it on top of the chart. The marker starts off hidden with a display property of none. Since we want to position the marker within the containing `<div>`, we set the containing `<div>`'s position property to relative.

```
<div id="charts-wrapper" style="position:relative;">
    <div id="marker" style="position:absolute;z-index:1;display:none;
                            width:1px;border-left: 1px solid black;"></div>
    <div id="charts" style="float:left;"></div>
    <div id="legends" style="float:left;"></div>
    <div style="clear:both;"></div>
</div>
```

When Flot calls the function listening for plothover events, it passes that function three parameters: the JavaScript event object, the position of the mouse expressed as x- and y-coordinates, and, if a chart data point is near the mouse, information about that data point. In our example we need only the x-coordinate. We can round it to the nearest integer to get the year. We also need to know where the mouse is relative to the page. Flot will calculate that for us if we call the pointOffset() of any of our plot objects. Note that we can't reliably use the third parameter, which is available only if the mouse is near an actual data point, so we can ignore it.

```
$("charts").on("plothover", function(ev, pos) {
    var year = Math.round(pos.x);
    var left = dummyPlot.pointOffset(pos).left;
});
```

Once we've calculated the position, it's a simple matter to move the marker to that position, make sure it's the full height of the containing `<div>`, and turn it on.

```
$("#charts").on("plothover", function(ev, pos) {
    var year = Math.round(pos.x);
    var left = dummyPlot.pointOffset(pos).left;
```

```
❶      var height = $("#charts").height();
       $("#marker").css({
           "top":     0,
❷          "left":    left,
           "width":   "1px",
❸          "height":  height
       }).show();
   });
```

In this code, we calculate the marker height at ❶, set its position at ❷, and set the height at ❸.

We also have to be a little careful on the mouseout event. If a user moves the mouse so that it is positioned directly on top of the marker, that will generate a mouseout event for the charts <div>. In that special case, we want to leave the marker displayed. To tell where the mouse has moved, we check the relatedTarget property of the event. We hide the marker only if the related target isn't the marker itself.

```
$("#charts").on("mouseout", function(ev) {
    if (ev.relatedTarget.id !== "marker") {
        $("#marker").hide();
    }
});
```

There's still one hole in our event processing. If the user moves the mouse directly over the marker, and then moves the mouse off the chart area entirely (without moving it off the marker), we won't catch the fact that the mouse is no longer hovering on the chart. To catch this event, we can listen for mouseout events on the marker itself. There's no need to worry about the mouse moving off the marker and back onto the chart area; the existing plothover event will cover that scenario.

```
$("#marker").on("mouseout", function(ev) {
    $("#marker").hide();
});
```

The last part of our interaction shows the values of all charts corresponding to the horizontal position of the mouse. We can create <div>s to hold these values back when we create each chart. Because these <div>s might extend beyond the chart area proper, we'll place them in the outer charts-wrapper <div>.

```
$.each(exports, function(idx,region) {
    var value = $("<div>").css({
        "position":  "absolute",
        "top":       (div.position().top - 3) + "px",
❶       "display":   "none",
        "z-index":   1,
        "font-size": "11px",
        "color":     "black"
```

```
    });
    region.value = value;
    $("#charts-wrapper").append(value);
});
```

Notice that as we create these <div>s, we set all the properties except the left position, since that will vary with the mouse. We also hide the elements with a display property of none at ❶.

With the <div>s waiting for us in the document, our event handler for plothover sets the text for each, positions them horizontally, and shows them on the page. To set the text value, we can use the jQuery .grep() function to search through the data for a year that matches. If none is found, the text for the value <div> is emptied.

```
$("#charts").on("plothover", function(ev, pos) {
    $.each(exports, function(idx, region) {
        matched = $.grep(region.data, function(pt) { return pt[0] === year; });
        if (matched.length > 0) {
            region.value.text(year + ": " + Math.round(matched[0][1]) + "%");
        } else {
            region.value.text("");
        }
        region.value.css("left", (left+4)+"px").show();
    });
});
```

Finally, we need to hide these <div>s when the mouse leaves the chart area. We should also handle the case of the mouse moving directly onto the marker, just as we did before.

```
$("#charts").on("plothover", function(ev, pos) {

    // Handle plothover event

}).on("mouseout", function(ev) {
    if (ev.relatedTarget.id !== "marker") {
        $("#marker").hide();
        $.each(exports, function(idx, region) {
            region.value.hide();
        });
    }
});

$("#marker").on("mouseout", function(ev) {
    $("#marker").hide();
    $.each(exports, function(idx, region) {
        region.value.hide();
    });
});
```

We can now enjoy the results of our coding, in Figure 2-14. Our visualization clarifies the trends in exports for each region, and it lets users interact with the charts to compare regions and view detailed values.

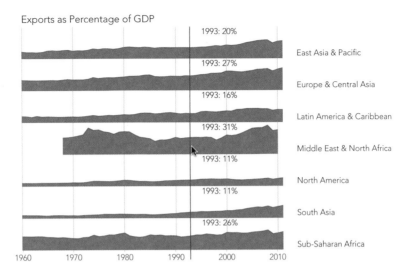

FIGURE 2-14: *The final visualization combines multiple charts with mouse tracking to more clearly present the data.*

As users move their mouse across the charts, the vertical bar moves as well. The values corresponding to the mouse position also appear to the right of the marker for each chart. The interaction makes it easy and intuitive to compare values for any of the regions.

The chart we've created in this example is similar to the *small multiples* approach for letting users compare many values. In our example the chart takes up the full page, but it could also be designed as one element in a larger presentation such as a table. Chapter 3 gives examples of integrating charts in larger web page elements.

Retrieving Data Using AJAX

Most of the examples in this book emphasize the final product of data visualization: the graphs, charts, or images that our users see. But effective visualizations often require a lot of work behind the scenes. After all, effective data visualizations need *data* just as much as they need the visualization. This example focuses on a common approach for accessing data—*Asynchronous JavaScript and XML*, more commonly known as *AJAX*. The example here details AJAX interactions with the World Bank, but both the general approach and the specific techniques shown here apply equally well to many other data sources on the Web.

Step 1: Understand the Source Data

Often, the first challenge in working with remote data is to understand its format and structure. Fortunately, our data comes from the World Bank, and its website thoroughly documents its *application programming interface (API)*. We won't spend too much time on the particulars in this example, since you'll likely be using a different data source. But a quick overview is helpful.

The first item of note is that the World Bank divides the world into several regions. As with all good APIs, the World Bank API allows us to issue a query to get a list of those regions.

```
http://api.worldbank.org/regions/?format=json
```

Our query returns the full list as a JSON array, which starts as follows:

```
[ { "page": "1",
    "pages": "1",
    "per_page": "50",
    "total": "22"
  },
  [ { "id": "",
      "code": "ARB",
      "name": "Arab World"
    },
    { "id": "",
      "code": "CSS",
      "name": "Caribbean small states"
    },
    { "id": "",
      "code": "EAP",
      "name": "East Asia & Pacific (developing only)"
    },
    { "id": "1",
      "code": "EAS",
      "name": "East Asia & Pacific (all income levels)"
    },
    { "id": "",
      "code": "ECA",
      "name": "Europe & Central Asia (developing only)"
    },
    { "id": "2",
      "code": "ECS",
      "name": "Europe & Central Asia (all income levels)"
    },
```

The first object in the array supports paging through a large data set, which isn't important for us now. The second element is an array with the information we need: the list of regions. There are 22 regions in total, but many overlap. We'll want to pick from the total number of regions so that we both include all the world's countries and don't have any country in multiple regions. The regions that meet these criteria are conveniently marked with an **id** property, so we'll select from the list only those regions whose **id** property is not **null**.

Step 2: Get the First Level of Data via AJAX

Now that you understand the data format (so far), let's write some code to retrieve the data. Since we have jQuery loaded, we'll take advantage of many of its utilities. Let's start at the simplest level and work up to a full implementation.

As you might expect, the **$.getJSON()** function will do most of the work for us. The simplest way to use that function might be something like the following:

```
$.getJSON(
    "http://api.worldbank.org/regions/",
❶   {format: "json"},
    function(response) {
        // Do something with response
    }
);
```

Note that we're adding **format: "json"** to the query at ❶ to tell the World Bank what format we want. Without that parameter, the server returns XML, which isn't at all what **getJSON()** expects.

Unfortunately, that code won't work with the current web servers supplying the World Bank data. In fact, this problem is very common today. As is often the case with the Web, security concerns are the source of the complication. Consider the information flow we're establishing, shown in Figure 2-15.

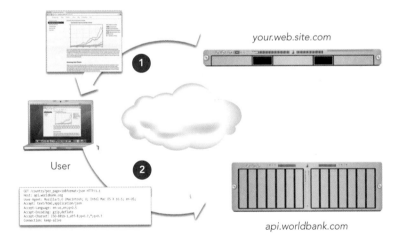

FIGURE 2-15: *Our server (your.web.site.com) sends a web page— including scripts—to the user, and those scripts, executing in the user's browser, query the World Bank site (api.worldbank.com).*

Getting data using AJAX often requires the cooperation of three different systems.

The script's communication with the World Bank is invisible to users, so they have no chance to approve or refuse the exchange. In the case of the World Bank, it's hard to imagine any reason for users to reject the query, but what if our script were accessing users' social network profile or, more seriously, their online banking site? In such cases user concerns would be justified. Because the communication is invisible to the user, and because the web browser cannot guess which communications might be sensitive, the browser simply prohibits all such communications. The technical term for this is *same-origin policy*. This policy means that web pages that our server provides cannot directly access the World Bank's JSON interface.

Some websites address this problem by adding an HTTP header in their responses. The header tells the browser that it's safe for any web page to access this data:

`Access-Control-Allow-Origin: *`

Unfortunately, as of this writing, the World Bank has not implemented this header. The option is relatively new, so it's missing from many web servers. To work within the constraints of the same-origin policy, therefore, we rely on jQuery's help and a small bit of trickery. The trick relies on the one exception to the same-origin policy that all browsers recognize: third-party JavaScript files. Browsers do allow web pages to request JavaScript files from third-party servers (that is, after all, how services such as Google Analytics can work). We just need to make the response data from the World Bank look like regular JavaScript instead of JSON. Fortunately, the World Bank cooperates with us in this minor deception. We simply add two query parameters to our request:

`?format=jsonP&prefix=Getdata`

The `format` parameter with a value of `jsonP` tells the World Bank that we want the response formatted as *JSON with padding*, which is a variant of JSON that is also regular JavaScript. The second parameter, `prefix`, tells the World Bank the name of the function that will accept the data. (Without that information, the JavaScript that the World Bank constructs wouldn't know how to communicate with our code.) It's a bit messy, but jQuery handles most of the details for us. The only catch is that we have to add `?something=?` to the URL we pass to `.getJSON()`, where *something* is whatever the web service requires for its JSONP response. The World Bank expects `prefix`, but a more common value is `callback`.

Now we can put together some code that will work with the World Bank and many other web servers, although the parameter `prefix` is specific to the World Bank.

```
$.getJSON(
❶    "http://api.worldbank.org/regions/?prefix=?",
❷    {format: "jsonp"},
     function(response) {
```

```
        // Do something with response
    }
);
```

We've added the **prefix** directly in the URL at ❶, and we've changed the format to **jsonp** at ❷.

JSONP does suffer from one major shortcoming: there is no way for the server to indicate an error. That means we should spend extra time testing and debugging any JSONP requests, and we should be vigilant about any changes in the server that might cause previously functioning code to fail. Eventually the World Bank will update the HTTP headers in its responses (perhaps even by the time of this book's publication), and we can switch to the more robust JSON format.

✳ **NOTE:** At the time of this writing, the World Bank has a significant bug in its API. The server doesn't preserve the case (uppercase versus lowercase) of the callback function. The full source code for this example includes a workaround for the bug, but you're unlikely to need that for other servers. Just in case, though, you can look at the comments in the source code for a complete documentation of the fix.

Now let's get back to the code itself. In the preceding snippet, we're defining a callback function directly in the call to `.getJSON()`. You'll see this code structure in many implementations. This certainly works, but if we continue along these lines, things are going to get quite messy very soon. We've already added a couple of layers of indentation before we even start processing the response. As you can guess, once we get this initial response, we'll need to make several more requests for additional data. If we try to build our code in one monolithic block, we'll end up with so many levels of indentation that there won't be any room for actual code. More significantly, the result would be one massive interconnected block of code that would be challenging to understand, much less debug or enhance.

Fortunately, jQuery gives us the tool for a much better approach: the `$.Deferred` object. A `Deferred` object acts as a central dispatcher and scheduler for events. Once the `Deferred` object is created, different parts of our code indicate that they want to know when the event completes, while other parts of our code signal the event's status. `Deferred` coordinates all those different activities, letting us separate how we trigger and manage events from dealing with their consequences.

Let's see how to improve our AJAX request with `Deferred` objects. Our main goal is to separate the initiation of the event (the AJAX request) from dealing with its consequences (processing the response). With that separation, we won't need a success function as a callback parameter to the request itself. Instead, we'll rely on the fact that the `.getJSON()` call returns a `Deferred` object. (Technically, the function returns a restricted form of the `Deferred` object known as a `promise`; the differences aren't important for us now, though.) We want to save that returned object in a variable.

```
// Fire off the query and retain the deferred object tracking it
deferredRegionsRequest = $.getJSON(
    "http://api.worldbank.org/regions/?prefix=?",
    {format: "jsonp"}
);
```

That's simple and straightforward. Now, in a different part of our code, we can indicate our interest in knowing when the AJAX request is complete.

```
deferredRegionsRequest.done(function(response) {
    // Do something with response
});
```

The done() method of the Deferred object is key. It specifies a new function that we want to execute whenever the event (in this case the AJAX request) successfully completes. The Deferred object handles all the messy details. In particular, if the event is already complete by the time we get around to registering the callback via done(), the Deferred object executes that callback immediately. Otherwise, it waits until the request is complete. We can also express an interest in knowing if the AJAX request fails; instead of done(), we use the fail() method for this. (Even though JSONP doesn't give the server a way to report errors, the request itself could still fail.)

```
deferredRegionsRequest.fail(function() {
    // Oops, our request for region information failed
});
```

We've obviously reduced the indentation to a more manageable level, but we've also created a much better structure for our code. The function that makes the request is separate from the code that handles the response. That's much cleaner, and it's definitely easier to modify and debug.

Step 3: Process the First Level of Data

Now let's tackle processing the response. The paging information isn't relevant, so we can skip right to the second element in the returned response. We want to process that array in two steps.

1. Filter out any elements in the array that aren't relevant to us. In this case we're interested only in regions that have an id property that isn't null.
2. Transform the elements in the array so that they contain only the properties we care about. For this example, we need only the code and name properties.

This probably sounds familiar. In fact, it's exactly what we needed to do in this chapter's first example. As we saw there, jQuery's $.map() and $.grep() functions are a big help.

Taking these steps one at a time, here's how to filter out irrelevant data from the response.

```
filtered = $.grep(response[1], function(regionObj) {
    return (regionObj.id !== null);
});
```

And here's how to transform the elements to retain only relevant properties. And as long as we're doing that, let's get rid of the parenthetical "(all income levels)" that the World Bank appends to some region names. All of our regions (those with an **id**) include all income levels, so this information is superfluous.

```
regions = $.map(filtered, function(regionObj) {
        return {
            code: regionObj.code,
            name: regionObj.name.replace(" (all income levels)","")
        };
    }
);
```

There's no need to make these separate steps. We can combine them in a nice, concise expression.

```
deferredRegionsRequest.done(function(response) {
    regions = $.map(
        $.grep(response[1], function(regionObj) {
            return (regionObj.id !== null);
        }),
        function(regionObj) {
            return {
                code: regionObj.code,
                name: regionObj.name.replace(" (all income levels)","")
            };
        }
    );
});
```

Step 4: Get the Real Data

At this point, of course, all we've managed to retrieve is the list of regions. That's not the data we want to visualize. Usually, getting the real data through a web-based interface requires (at least) two request stages. The first request just gives you the essential information for subsequent requests. In this case, the real data we want is the GDP, so we'll need to go through our list of regions and retrieve that data for each one.

Of course we can't just blindly fire off the second set of requests, in this case for the detailed region data. First, we have to wait until we have the list of regions. In Step 2 we dealt with a similar situation by using .getJSON() with a Deferred object to separate event management from processing. We can use the same technique here; the only difference is that we'll have to create our own Deferred object.

```
var deferredRegionsAvailable = $.Deferred();
```

Later, when the region list is available, we indicate that status by calling the object's resolve() method.

```
deferredRegionsAvailable.resolve();
```

The actual processing is handled by the done() method.

```
deferredRegionsAvailable.done(function() {
    // Get the region data
});
```

The code that gets the actual region data needs the list of regions, of course. We could pass that list around as a global variable, but that would be polluting the global namespace. (And even if you've properly namespaced your application, why pollute your own namespace?) This problem is easy to solve. Any arguments we provide to the resolve() method are passed straight to the done() function.

Let's take a look at the big picture so we can see how all the pieces fit together.

```
    // Request the regions list and save status of the request in a Deferred object
❶ var deferredRegionsRequest = $.getJSON(
        "http://api.worldbank.org/regions/?prefix=?",
        {format: "jsonp"}
    );

    // Create a second Deferred object to track when list processing is complete
❷ var deferredRegionsAvailable = $.Deferred();

    // When the request finishes, start processing
❸ deferredRegionsRequest.done(function(response) {
        // When we finish processing, resolve the second Deferred with the results
❹      deferredRegionsAvailable.resolve(
            $.map(
                $.grep(response[1], function(regionObj) {
                    return (regionObj.id != "");
                }),
                function(regionObj) {
                    return {
                        code: regionObj.code,
                        name: regionObj.name.replace(" (all income levels)","")
                    };
                }
            )
        );
    });
```

```
deferredRegionsAvailable.done(function(regions) {
```
❺   `// Now we have the regions, go get the data`
```
});
```

First, starting at ❶, we request the list of regions. Then, at ❷, we create a second `Deferred` object to track our processing of the response. In the block starting at ❸, we handle the response from our initial request. Most importantly, we resolve the second `Deferred` object, at ❹, to signal that our processing is complete. Finally, starting at ❺, we can begin processing the response.

Retrieving the actual GDP data for each region requires a new AJAX request. As you might expect, we'll save the `Deferred` objects for those requests so we can process the responses when they're available. The jQuery `.each()` function is a convenient way to iterate through the list of regions to initiate these requests.

```
deferredRegionsAvailable.done(function(regions) {
    $.each(regions, function(idx, regionObj) {
        regionObj.deferredDataRequest = $.getJSON(
            "http://api.worldbank.org/countries/"
            + regionObj.code
            + "/indicators/NY.GDP.MKTP.CD"
            + "?prefix=?",
            { format: "jsonp", per_page: 9999 }
        );
    });
});
```

The "`NY.GDP.MKTP.CD`" part of each request URL at ❶ is the World Bank's code for GDP data.

As long as we're iterating through the regions, we can include the code to process the GDP data. By now it won't surprise you that we'll create a `Deferred` object to track when that processing is complete. The processing itself will simply store the returned response (after skipping past the paging information) in the region object.

```
deferredRegionsAvailable.done(function(regions) {
    $.each(regions, function(idx, regionObj) {
        regionObj.deferredDataRequest = $.getJSON(
            "http://api.worldbank.org/countries/"
            + regionObj.code
            + "/indicators/NY.GDP.MKTP.CD"
            + "?prefix=?",
            { format: "jsonp", per_page: 9999 }
        );
        regionObj.deferredDataAvailable = $.Deferred();
        regionObj.deferredDataRequest.done(function(response) {
            regionObj.rawData = response[1] || [];
            regionObj.deferredDataAvailable.resolve();
        });
    });
});
```

Note that we've also added a check at ❶ to make sure the World Bank actually returns data in its response. Possibly due to internal errors, it may return a `null` object instead of the array of data. When that happens, we'll set the `rawData` to an empty array instead of `null`.

Step 5: Process the Data

Now that we've requested the real data, it's almost time to process it. There is a final hurdle to overcome, and it's a familiar one. We can't start processing the data until it's available, which calls for defining one more `Deferred` object and resolving that object when the data is complete. (By now it's probably sinking in just how handy `Deferred` objects can be.)

There is one little twist, however. We've now got multiple requests in progress, one for each region. How can we tell when all of those requests are complete? Fortunately, jQuery provides a convenient solution with the `.when()` function. That function accepts a list of `Deferred` objects and indicates success only when all of the objects have succeeded. We just need to pass that list of `Deferred` objects to the `.when()` function.

We could assemble an array of `Deferred` objects using the `.map()` function, but `.when()` expects a parameter list, not an array. Buried deep in the JavaScript standard is a technique for converting an array to a list of function parameters. Instead of calling the function directly, we execute the `.when()` function's `apply()` method. That method takes, as its parameters, the context (`this`) and an array.

Here's the `.map()` function that creates the array.

```
$.map(regions, function(regionObj) {
    return regionObj.deferredDataAvailable
})
```

And here's how we pass it to `when()` as a parameter list.

```
$.when.apply(this,$.map(regions, function(regionObj) {
    return regionObj.deferredDataAvailable
}));
```

The `when()` function returns its own `Deferred` object, so we can use the methods we already know to process its completion. Now we finally have a complete solution for retrieving the World Bank data.

With our data safely in hand, we can now coerce it into a format that Flot accepts. We extract the `date` and `value` properties from the raw data. We also have to account for gaps in the data. The World Bank doesn't have GDP data for every region for every year. When it's missing data for a particular year, it returns `null` for `value`. The same combination of `.grep()` and `.map()` that we used before will serve us once again.

```
deferredAllDataAvailable.done(function(regions) {
❶    $.each(regions, function(idx, regionObj) {
❷        regionObj.flotData = $.map(
```

```
❸          $.grep(regionObj.rawData, function(dataObj) {
               return (dataObj.value !== null);
           }),
❹          function(dataObj) {
               return [[
❺                  parseInt(dataObj.date),
❻                  parseFloat(dataObj.value)/1e12
               ]];
           }
       )
    })
});
```

As you can see, we're iterating through the list of regions with the `.each()` function at ❶. For each region, we create an object of data for the Flot library. (No points for originality in naming that object `flotData` at ❷.) Then we filter the data starting at ❸ to eliminate any data points with `null` values. The function that creates our Flot data array starts at ❹. It takes, as input, a single data object from the World Bank, and returns the data as a two-dimensional data point. The first value is the date, which we extract as an integer at ❺, and the second value is the GDP data, which we extract as a floating-point number at ❻. Dividing by `1e12` converts the GDP data to trillions.

Step 6: Create the Chart

Since we've made it this far with a clear separation between code that handles events and code that processes the results, there's no reason not to continue the approach when we actually create the chart. Yet another `Deferred` object creates that separation.

```
var deferredChartDataReady = $.Deferred();

deferredAllDataAvailable.done(function(regions) {
    $.each(regions, function(idx, regionObj) {
        regionObj.flotData = $.map(
            $.grep(regionObj.rawData, function(dataObj) {
                return (dataObj.value !== null);
            }),
            function(dataObj) {
                return [[
                    parseInt(dataObj.date),
                    parseFloat(dataObj.value)/1e12
                ]];
            }
        )
    })
❶   deferredChartDataReady.resolve(regions);
});
```

```
deferredChartDataReady.done(function(regions) {
    // Draw the chart
});
```

Here we've taken the preceding code fragments and wrapped them in
`Deferred` object handling. Once all of the data has been processed, we resolve
that `Deferred` object at ❶.

The entire process is reminiscent of a frog hopping between lily pads in a
pond. The pads are the processing steps, and `Deferred` objects are the bridges
between them (Figure 2-16).

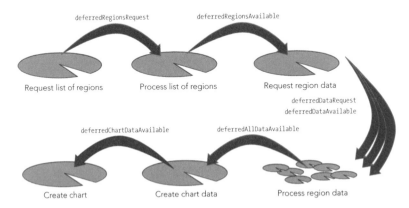

FIGURE 2-16: *Deferred objects help keep each bit of code isolated to
its own pad.*

The real benefit to this approach is its separation of concerns. Each processing step remains independent of the others. Should any step require changes,
there's no need to look at the others. Each lily pad, in effect, remains its own island
without concern for the rest of the pond.

Once we're at the final step, we can use any or all of the techniques from this
chapter's other examples to draw the chart. Once again, the `.map()` function can
easily extract relevant information from the region data. Here is a basic example:

```
deferredChartDataReady.done(function(regions) {
    $.plot($("#chart"),
        $.map(regions, function(regionObj) {
            return {
                label: regionObj.name,
                data:  regionObj.flotData
            };
        })
        ,{ legend: { position: "nw"} }
    );
});
```

Our basic chart now gets its data directly from the World Bank. We no longer have to manually process its data, and our charts are updated automatically whenever the World Bank updates its data (Figure 2-17).

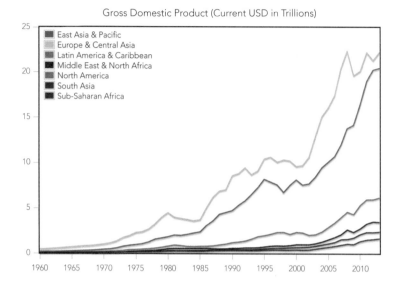

Gross Domestic Product (Current USD in Trillions)

FIGURE 2-17: *With AJAX we can graph live data from another site in the user's browser.*

In this example you've seen how to access the World Bank's application programming interface. The same approach works for many other organizations that provide data on the Internet. In fact, there are so many data sources available today that it can be difficult to keep track of them all.

Here are two helpful websites that serve as a central repository for both public and private APIs accessible on the Internet:

▸ APIhub (*http://www.apihub.com/*)

▸ ProgrammableWeb (*http://www.programmableweb.com/*)

Many governments also provide a directory of available data and APIs. The United States, for example, centralizes its resources at the Data.gov website (*http://www.data.gov/*).

This example focuses on the AJAX interaction, so the resulting chart is a simple, static line chart. Any of the interactions described in the other examples from this chapter could be added to increase the interactivity of the visualization.

Summing Up

As the examples in this chapter show, we don't have to be satisfied with static charts on our web pages. A little JavaScript can bring charts to life by letting users interact with them. These interactions give users a chance to see a "big picture" view of the data and, on the same page, look into the specific aspects that are most interesting and relevant to them. We've considered techniques that let users select which data series appear on our charts, zoom in on specific chart areas, and use their mouse to explore details of the data without losing sight of the overall view. We've also looked at how to get interactive data directly from its source using AJAX and asynchronous programming.

3

Integrating Charts on a Page

You might expect a data visualization for the Web to be featured very prominently on the page, or even make up the entire web page. That's not always the right approach, though. The best visualizations are effective because they help the user understand the data, not because they "look pretty" on the page.

Some data may be straightforward enough to present without context, but meaningful data probably isn't. And if our presentation requires context, its visualizations are likely sharing the page with other content. When we design web pages, we should take care to balance any individual component with the page as a whole. If a single visualization is not the entire story, it shouldn't take up all (or even most) of the space on the page. It can be challenging, however, to minimize the space a traditional chart requires. There are, after all, axes, labels, titles, legends, and more to place.

Edward Tufte considered this problem in his groundbreaking work *The Visual Display of Quantitative Information* (Graphics Press, 1983), and he proposed a novel solution he called sparklines. *Sparklines* are charts stripped to their bare essentials, presented without the aforementioned elements we often see in a chart. Sparklines can present a lot of information in very little space, even to the point where it is possible to include a chart right in the middle of a sentence. There is no need for "See figure below" or "Click for larger view." One of Tufte's earliest examples presents the glucose level of a medical patient; Figure 3-1 shows a reproduction.

128 Glucose

FIGURE 3-1: *Tufte's classic sparkline example shows a lot of information in a small space.*

In a mere 154×20 pixels, we've shown the patient's current glucose level, its trend for more than two months, high and low values, and the range of normal values. This high information density makes sparklines effective anytime space is a premium—inline in textual paragraphs, as cells in tables, or as part of information dashboards. Sparklines do have disadvantages, of course. They cannot provide as much fine-grained detail as a full-size chart with axes and labels. They also cannot support significant interactivity, so we can't give users a lot of flexibility in selecting data or zooming in for detail. But for many visualizations, these aren't major concerns. Plus, as we'll see in this chapter's examples, the Web gives us the chance to augment sparklines in ways that aren't possible in print. There are a few JavaScript libraries and toolkits for creating sparklines, but we'll focus on the most popular of them: jQuery sparklines (*http://omnipotent.net/jquery.sparkline/*). As the name implies, this open source library is an extension to jQuery. The examples in this chapter look closely at how to use these tools to incorporate dense visualizations into your web page. Here's what you'll learn:

▸ How to create a classic sparkline for integration directly into text

▸ How to combine multiple sparklines to show comparisons

▸ How to annotate sparklines with additional details

▸ How to create composite charts

▸ How to respond to click events on the page

▸ How to update charts in real time

Creating a Classic Sparkline

As later examples will demonstrate, the sparklines library is both flexible and powerful, and we can use it in many different contexts. As a start, though, we'll use the library to create a sparkline exactly as Edward Tufte first defined it. The process is quite straightforward and takes only four simple steps.

Step 1: Include the Required JavaScript Libraries

Since we're using the jQuery sparklines library to create the chart, we need to include that library in our web pages, along with jQuery. Both jQuery and sparklines are available on public CDNs. For this example (and the others in this chapter), we'll use the CloudFlare CDN. For some notes on the advantages and disadvantages of using CDNs, see page 49.

Here's the skeleton with which we start:

```
<!DOCTYPE html>
<html lang="en">
  <head>
    <meta charset="utf-8">
    <title></title>
  </head>
  <body>
    <!-- Content goes here -->
    <!--[if lt IE 9]><script src="js/excanvas.min.js"></script><![endif]-->
    <script src="//cdnjs.cloudflare.com/ajax/libs/jquery/1.8.3/jquery.min.js">
    </script>
    <script src="//cdnjs.cloudflare.com/ajax/libs/jquery-sparklines/2.0.0/
jquery.sparkline.min.js"></script>
  </body>
</html>
```
❶

As you can see, we're including the JavaScript libraries at the end of the document. This approach lets the browser load all of the document's HTML markup and begin laying out the page while waiting for the server to provide the JavaScript libraries.

In addition to the jQuery library, sparklines rely on the HTML *canvas* feature. Since Internet Explorer didn't support canvas until version 9, we use some special markup at ❶ to ensure that IE 8 and earlier will load an additional library (excanvas .min.js), just like we did in Chapter 2.

Step 2: Create the HTML Markup for the Sparkline

Because we're closely integrating the sparkline chart with other elements, we simply use a `<span>` tag to hold the HTML markup for our visualization, rather than using a `<div>`. In addition to the chart itself, we include the final value and a label as standard HTML. Here is the HTML for the glucose sparkline:

```
<p>
  <span class="sparkline">
```

```
      170,134,115,128,168,166,122,81,56,39,97,114,114,130,151,
      184,148,145,134,145,145,145,143,148,224,181,112,111,129,
      151,131,131,131,114,112,112,112,124,187,202,200,203,237,
      263,221,197,184,185,203,290,330,330,226,113,148,169,148,
      78,96,96,96,77,59,22,22,70,110,128
    </span>
    128 Glucose
</p>
```

Compared to other visualizations, two characteristics of our sparkline chart are unusual.

▸ We include the data right in the HTML itself, not in the JavaScript that creates the chart.

▸ The <span> for the chart does not have a unique id attribute.

Both of these differences are optional; we could construct the chart as in other visualizations by passing data to a JavaScript function and identifying its container with a unique id. For sparklines, however, the approach we're using here often makes more sense. By including the chart data directly in the HTML, we can easily see the data's relation to other content on the page. It's clear, for example, that the final value of our chart (128) is the same as the value we're using for the label. If we had made a mistake and used a different value for the label, the error would be much easier to spot and correct. Using a common class for all sparklines instead of unique ids simplifies how we might use the library to create multiple charts on one page. With unique ids, we would have to call a library function for every chart. With a common class, on the other hand, we need only call a single library function to create multiple charts. That's especially helpful when a web page contains a lot of sparklines.

Step 3: Draw the Sparkline

Now that we've included the necessary libraries and set up our HTML, it's remarkably easy to draw the charts. In fact, a single line of JavaScript is sufficient. We simply select the containing element(s) using jQuery—$(".sparkline")—and call the sparklines plug-in.

```
$(function() {
    $(".sparkline").sparkline();
}
```

As you can see in Figure 3-2, the sparklines library creates a standard sparkline from our data.

 128 Glucose

FIGURE 3-2: *The default sparkline options differ slightly from the classic example.*

The library's default options differ from Tufte's classic sparkline in color, chart type, and density. We'll tweak those next.

Step 4: Adjust the Chart Style

To make our sparkline match Tufte's definition exactly, we can specify new values for some of the default options. To pass these options to sparklines, we construct a JavaScript object and include it as the second parameter in the `sparkline` function call. The function's first parameter is the data itself, which here we specify with `"html"` because our data is included in the HTML markup.

```
$(".sparkline").sparkline("html",{
❶    lineColor: "dimgray",
❷    fillColor: false,
❸    defaultPixelsPerValue: 1,
❹    spotColor: "red",
     minSpotColor: "red",
     maxSpotColor: "red",
❺    normalRangeMin: 82,
     normalRangeMax: 180,
});
```

To complete our transformation to Tufte's original, we can style the HTML content as well. Making the final value the same color as the key data points clarifies that connection, and making the chart label bold emphasizes it as a title.

```
<p>
  <span class="sparkline">
    170,134,115,128,168,166,122,81,56,39,97,114,114,130,151,
    184,148,145,134,145,145,145,143,148,224,181,112,111,129,
    151,131,131,131,114,112,112,112,124,187,202,200,203,237,
    263,221,197,184,185,203,290,330,330,226,113,148,169,148,
    78,96,96,96,77,59,22,22,70,110,128
  </span>
  <span style="color:red"> 128 </span>
  <strong> Glucose </strong>
</p>
```

Let's walk through the changes we just made:

▶ Tufte's classic sparklines are black and white except for key data points (minimum, maximum, and final values). His color scheme adds extra emphasis to those points. To change the library's default (blue), we can set a `lineColor`. For screen displays, we might choose a dark gray rather than pure black. That's what we're using at ❶.

▶ Tufte doesn't fill the area below the line so that he can use shading to indicate a normal range. To eliminate the library's light blue shading, we set `fillColor` to `false` ❷.

- By default, the library uses 3 pixels as the width for each data point. To maximize information density, Tufte would likely suggest using only a single pixel. Setting the `defaultPixelsPerValue` option at ❸ makes that change.

- Tufte uses red for key data points. To change the library's default (orange), we set `spotColor`, `minSpotColor`, and `maxSpotColor` at ❹.

- Finally, Tufte's sparklines can include shading to mark the normal range for a value. To show, for example, a range of 82–180 mg/dL, we set the `normalRangeMin` and `normalRangeMax` options at ❺.

With these changes, we have the classic Tufte sparkline on our web page. We can even include it within a text paragraph, like this 〜〜〜 128 **Glucose**, so that the visualization enhances the content of the text.

Charting Many Variables

By design, sparklines take up very little space on a page, and that makes them ideal for another visualization challenge: showing many variables at once. Of course, regular line charts and bar charts can plot multiple data sets simultaneously; however, these multiple-series charts rapidly grow unwieldy if the number of data sets exceeds four or five. Some visualization projects show dozens of different variables, far beyond what a multiple-series chart can accommodate. A *small-multiples* approach turns the standard chart approach completely around. Instead of showing one chart with multiple data sets, we can show multiple charts, each with a single data set. Placing lots of charts on a page means that each individual chart cannot take up much space. That is exactly the problem that sparklines solve.

We won't go too crazy here, to keep the code examples manageable, but it's easy to extend this approach to many more variables. In our case, we'll construct a visualization for analyzing stock market performance. The companies in our analysis will include the 10 largest American companies in 2012 (*http://money.cnn.com/magazines/fortune/fortune500/2012/full_list/*), also known as the Fortune 500 Top 10; Barclay's best technology stocks for 2012 (*http://www.marketwatch.com/story/barclays-best-tech-stocks-for-2012-2011-12-20/*), as identified in December 2011; and Bristol-Myers Squibb, which *CR Magazine* named the top company in America for corporate responsibility (*http://www.thecro.com/files/100Best2012_List_3.8.pdf/*). Those selections are completely arbitrary, but the example is designed to include three different cases that we will style differently in our visualization. We'll treat one as a general case (the Fortune 500 Top 10 list), one as a special class (the Barclay's list), and one as a unique variable (Bristol-Myers Squibb). Just as in this chapter's first example, we need to include the sparklines and jQuery libraries in our web page.

Step 1: Prepare the HTML Markup

The sparklines library makes it easy to embed the data directly inside the HTML markup. For this example, an HTML table is the most appropriate structure for the data. Here's how such a table could begin. (For brevity's sake, the following excerpt doesn't include the full HTML, but the complete example is available in the book's source code at *http://jsDataV.is/source/*.)

```
<table>
    <thead>
        <tr>
            <th>Symbol</th>
            <th>Company</th>
            <th>2012 Performance</th>
            <th>Gain</th>
        </tr>
    </thead>
    <tbody>
        <tr class="barclays">
            <td>AAPL</td>
            <td>Apple Inc.</td>
            <td class="sparkline">
                418.68,416.11,416.6,443.34,455.63,489.08,497.7,517.81,...
            </td>
            <td>27%</td>
        </tr>
        <tr class="barclays">
            <td>ALTR</td>
            <td>Altera Corporation</td>
            <td class="sparkline">
                37.1,36.92,39.93,39.81,40.43,39.76,39.73,38.55,36.89,...
            </td>
            <td>-7%</td>
        </tr>
        // Markup continues...
    </tbody>
</table>
```

The table has three important characteristics relevant to our visualization.

▶ Each stock is a single table row (<tr>).

▶ Stocks from Barclay's technology list have the class attribute "barclays" added to that <tr> element.

▶ The top corporate responsibility stock has no special attributes or characteristics (yet).

Step 2: Draw the Charts

Just as in this chapter's first example, creating the sparklines using default options is amazingly simple: it takes only a single line of JavaScript. We use jQuery to select all the elements that contain sparkline data, and we call the sparkline() function to generate the charts.

```
$(function() {
    $(".sparkline").sparkline();
}
```

Notice that we only have to make one call to sparkline(), even though each chart has unique data. That's a major benefit of placing the data within the HTML itself.

The resulting charts, shown in Figure 3-3, all have identical styles, but we'll fix that in the next few steps.

Symbol	Company	2012 Performance	Gain
AAPL	Apple Inc.		27%
ALTR	Altera Corporation		(7%)
BMY	Bristol Meyers Squibb Co.		(2%)
BRKA	Berkshire Hathaway Inc.		17%
COP	ConocoPhillips		10%
CTXS	Citrix Systems, Inc.		6%
CVX	Chevron Corporation		3%
F	Ford Motor Company		13%
FNMA	Federal National Mortgage Association		30%
GE	General Electric Company		16%
GLW	Corning Incorporated		(4%)

FIGURE 3-3: *Sparklines can be a good visualization to include within page elements such as tables.*

Step 3: Establish a Default Style for the Charts

If we don't like the sparklines library's default style, it's easy to change it using an options object, as shown next.

```
$(".sparkline").sparkline("html",{
    lineColor: "#006363",
    fillColor: "#2D9999",
    spotColor: false,
    minSpotColor: false,
    maxSpotColor: false
});
```

The object is the second parameter to the sparkline() function, and here it changes the color for the charts and disables the highlights on the minimum, maximum, and final values. The first parameter, the string "html", indicates to the library that the data is already present in our HTML.

Figure 3-4 shows the result for one row. We'll use this style as the default for all our charts.

Symbol	Company	2012 Performance	Gain
AAPL	Apple Inc.		27%

FIGURE 3-4: *The sparkline options let us adjust the chart styles.*

Step 4: Modify the Default Style for Special Classes

With a default style in place, we can turn our attention to the special class of charts for stocks in Barclay's technology list. For our example, let's change the color of the chart without any other changes to our default style. That final clause is important. We could just copy and paste the options, but that would be setting ourselves up for problems in the future. You can see why in the following example code.

```
$("tr:not(.barclays) .sparkline").sparkline("html",{
    lineColor: "#006363",
    fillColor: "#2D9999",
    spotColor: false,
    minSpotColor: false,
    maxSpotColor: false
});
$("tr.barclays .sparkline").sparkline("html",{
    lineColor: "#A50000",
    fillColor: "#FE4C4C",
    spotColor: false,
    minSpotColor: false,
    maxSpotColor: false
});
```

Notice that the second call to `sparklines()` duplicates options from the first call that haven't changed, specifically for the spot colors. This makes the code harder to maintain if, in the future, we decide to turn spot colors back on for all our charts, since we would have to make changes to our code in two places. There is a better way.

To avoid duplication, we first define a variable that holds our default options.

```
var sparkline_default = {
    lineColor: "#006363",
    fillColor: "#2D9999",
    spotColor: false,
    minSpotColor: false,
    maxSpotColor: false
};
```

Next we create a new variable for the Barclay's styles. To create this new variable, we can use the jQuery `.extend()` function to avoid duplication.

```
var sparkline_barclays = $.extend( {}, sparkline_default, {
    lineColor: "#A50000",
    fillColor: "#FE4C4C"
});
```

In this code, we pass three parameters to .extend(). The first parameter is the target. It's an object that the function will modify, and we start with an empty object ({}). The next parameters are objects that .extend() will merge into the target. The merge process adds new properties to the target and updates any properties in the target object with new values. Since we're passing two additional parameters, we're asking for two merges.

You can think of the call to .extend() as a two-stage process.

1. Since our target is initially empty, the first merge will add all of the properties from sparkline_default to the target.

2. Our target now has the same properties as sparkline_default, and the second merge will modify it by updating the two properties in the last parameter, lineColor and fillColor.

The resulting object will hold the options we want for charts of Barclay's technology stocks. Here's a complete code listing, using these objects to create the charts.

```
var sparkline_default = {
    lineColor: "#006363",
    fillColor: "#2D9999",
    spotColor: false,
    minSpotColor: false,
    maxSpotColor: false
};
var sparkline_barclays = $.extend( {}, sparkline_default, {
    lineColor: "#A50000",
    fillColor: "#FE4C4C"
});
❶ $("tr:not(.barclays) .sparkline").sparkline("html",sparkline_default);
❷ $("tr.barclays .sparkline").sparkline("html",sparkline_barclays);
```

Notice at ❶ that we create the nontechnology sparklines by selecting table rows (<tr>) that don't have the "barclays" class. At ❷ we create the technology sparklines. Because we've defined the technology options based on the default, we have an easy way to maintain both default styles and styles for special classes. The chart colors in Figure 3-5 clearly distinguish the stock types in our table.

Symbol	Company	2012 Performance	Gain
TSLA	Tesla Motors Inc		26%
WMT	Wal-Mart Stores, Inc.		18%

FIGURE 3-5: *Different visual styles distinguish different types of data.*

Step 5: Create a Unique Style for a Specific Chart

For the final step in this example, let's consider the single stock at the top of *CR Magazine*'s list. Suppose we want to add distinct styles to its chart, and we know those styles only when we're generating the HTML, not when we're writing the JavaScript. How can we adjust the chart style if we can't modify any JavaScript?

Sparklines let you add special attributes directly to the HTML element containing a chart. To set the line color, for example, you need to specify the attribute sparkLineColor. The problem is that if we were to enter this attribute directly in the HTML, the result wouldn't be valid HTML, because the HTML specification doesn't recognize the sparkLineColor attribute. To conform to the HTML standard, custom attributes must have names that begin with the prefix data-.

```
<tr>
    <td>BMY</td>
    <td>Bristol Meyers Squibb Co.</td>
❶   <td class="sparkline" data-LineColor="#679A00"
        data-FillColor="#B6ED47">32.86,32.46,31.36,...</td>
    <td>(2%)</td>
</tr>
```

To use HTML-compliant names to refer to sparklines' custom attributes, we just need to tell the sparklines library how to find those names. For our HTML, we use the standard data- prefix instead of spark in at ❶.

Now we have to add a couple more options in our call to sparkline(). First we set enableTagOptions to true to tell the library that we're including options directly in the HTML. Then we set tagOptionsPrefix to "data-" to specify the prefix we're using for those attributes.

✳ **NOTE:** As of this writing, the jQuery sparklines documentation for tagOptionsPrefix is not correct. The documentation lists the option as tagOptionPrefix, where *option* is singular instead of plural. The library's code, however, expects the plural form.

If we use these options correctly, one of our charts will have the distinct color in Figure 3-6.

BMY	Bristol Meyers Squibb Co.		(2%)

FIGURE 3-6: *The sparklines library supports unique styling options for individual charts.*

To pass the appropriate options to **sparkline()**, we can take advantage of the work we did in Step 5. Since we created a special object for default options, that's the only object we have to change.

```
var sparkline_default = {
    lineColor: "#006363",
    fillColor: "#2D9999",
    spotColor: false,
    minSpotColor: false,
    maxSpotColor: false,
    enableTagOptions: true,
    tagOptionsPrefix: "data-"
};
```

We only need to make the change in one place, and all of our calls to sparkline() use the new options. Here is the final, complete JavaScript code for this example.

```
$(function() {
    var sparkline_default = {
        lineColor: "#006363",
        fillColor: "#2D9999",
        spotColor: false,
        minSpotColor: false,
        maxSpotColor: false,
        enableTagOptions: true,
        tagOptionsPrefix: "data-"
    };
    var sparkline_barclays = $.extend( {}, sparkline_default, {
        lineColor: "#A50000",
        fillColor: "#FE4C4C"
    });
    $("tr:not(.barclays) .sparkline").sparkline("html",sparkline_default);
    $("tr.barclays .sparkline").sparkline("html",sparkline_barclays);
}
```

Figure 3-7 shows the final result. We have a table that integrates text and charts, and we can style those charts appropriately and efficiently for the default case, for a special class, and for a unique value.

Symbol	Company	2012 Performance	Gain
AAPL	Apple Inc.		27%
ALTR	Altera Corporation		(7%)
BMY	Bristol Meyers Squibb Co.		(2%)
BRKA	Berkshire Hathaway Inc.		17%
COP	ConocoPhillips		10%
CTXS	Citrix Systems, Inc.		6%
CVX	Chevron Corporation		3%
F	Ford Motor Company		13%
FNMA	Federal National Mortgage Association		30%
GE	General Electric Company		16%
GLW	Corning Incorporated		(4%)

FIGURE 3-7: *A complete example distinguishes different individual data sets in a larger collection.*

"Tracking Data Values" on page 65 uses a full-featured charting package for a similar result. If you don't need the space efficiency of sparklines, consider that approach as an alternative.

Annotating Sparklines

Because they're designed to maximize information density, sparklines omit many traditional chart components such as axes and labels. This approach certainly focuses on the data itself, but it can sometimes leave users without enough context to understand the data. Print versions usually rely on traditional text to supply this context, but on the Web we have more flexibility. We can present the data by itself in a sparkline, and we can give users the chance to explore the data's context through interactions. *Tool tips*, which show additional information as a user hovers their mouse pointer over sections of a web page, can be an effective way to annotate a sparkline, so long as the users are accessing the page from a desktop computer. (Touch-based devices such as smartphones and tablets don't typically support the concept of hover.) We'll walk through a visualization that includes tool tips in this example; other examples in the chapter consider alternative approaches that may be more effective for touch devices. Let's see how we can use a customized form of tool tips by enhancing the charts in the previous example. Just as in this chapter's first example, we need to include the sparklines and jQuery libraries in our web page.

Step 1: Prepare the Data

In the previous examples, we've embedded the data directly in the HTML markup. That's convenient since it lets us separate the data from our code. In this example, however, the JavaScript code will need more-detailed knowledge of the data so it can present the right tool tip information. This time we'll use a JavaScript array to store our data so that all the relevant information is in one place. For this example, we can focus on a single stock. And even though we're graphing only the adjusted closing price, the array will track additional data that we can include in the tool tips. Here's an excerpt of the data for one of the stocks.

```
var stock = [
    { date: "2012-01-03", open: 409.40, high: 422.75, low: 409.00, close: 422.40,
      volume: 10283900, adj_close: 416.26 },
    { date: "2012-01-09", open: 425.50, high: 427.75, low: 418.66, close: 419.81,
      volume:  9327900, adj_close: 413.70 },
    { date: "2012-01-17", open: 424.20, high: 431.37, low: 419.75, close: 420.30,
      volume: 10673200, adj_close: 414.19 },
    // Data set continues...
```

Step 2: Prepare the HTML Markup

Our visualization will include three distinct areas, each in a `<div>` element.

```
<div id="stock">
    <div style="float:left">
❶        <div class="chart"></div>
❷        <div class="info"></div>
    </div>
    <div style="float:left">
❸        <div class="details"></div>
    </div>
</div>
```

The primary `<div>` created at ❶ will hold the chart. Underneath the chart we'll add the primary tool tip information in its own `<div>` ❷, and we'll include supplementary details to the right ❸. This example uses inline styles for clarity; a production site might prefer to use CSS style sheets.

Step 3: Add the Chart

Adding the chart to our markup is easy with the sparklines library. We can use the jQuery `.map()` function to extract the adjusted close value from our `stock` array. The `minSpotColor` and `maxSpotColor` options tell the library how to highlight the lowest and highest values for the year.

```
$("#stock .chart").sparkline(
    $.map(stock, function(wk) { return wk.adj_close; }),
    {
        lineColor: "#006363",
```

```
        fillColor: "#2D9999",
        spotColor: false,
        minSpotColor: "#CA0000",
        maxSpotColor: "#CA0000"
    }
);
```

The static chart of Figure 3-8 shows the stock performance nicely.

FIGURE 3-8: *A static sparkline shows the change in the data set over time.*

Step 4: Add the Primary Annotation

The sparklines library adds a simple tool tip to all of its charts by default. Although that tool tip shows the value over which the user's mouse is hovering, the presentation isn't particularly elegant, and, more importantly, it doesn't provide as much information as we would like. Let's enhance the default behavior to meet our needs.

Looking at the library's defaults, we can retain the vertical marker, but we don't want the default tool tip. Adding the option **disableTooltips** with a value of **true** will turn off the undesired tool tip.

For our own custom tool tip, we can rely on a handy feature of the sparklines library. The library generates a custom event whenever the user's mouse moves over a chart region. That event is the **sparklineRegionChange** event. The library attaches a custom property, **sparklines**, to those events. By analyzing that property, we can determine the mouse's location relative to the data.

```
$(".chart")
    .on("sparklineRegionChange", function(ev) {
        var idx = ev.sparklines[0].getCurrentRegionFields().offset;
❶       /* If it's defined, idx has the index into the
           data array corresponding to the mouse pointer */
    });
```

As the comment at ❶ indicates, the library sometimes generates the event when the mouse leaves the chart area. In those cases, a defined value for the offset will not exist.

Once we have the mouse position, we can place our tool tip information in the `<div>` we set aside for it.

```
    if (idx) {
        $(".info").html(
❶          "Week of " + stock[idx].date
        + "    "
❷      + "Close: $" + stock[idx].adj_close);
    }
```

We get the information at ❶ and ❷ from the stock array using the index value from the sparklineRegionChange event.

The sparklines library isn't completely reliable in generating events when the mouse leaves the chart area. Instead of using the custom event, therefore, we can use the standard JavaScript mouseout event. When the user moves the mouse off the chart, we'll turn off the custom tool tip by setting its content to a blank space. We use the HTML nonbreaking space ( ) so the browser doesn't think the <div> is completely empty. If we used a standard space character, the browser would treat the <div> as empty and recalculate the height of the page, causing an annoying jump in the page contents. (For the same reason, we should initialize that <div> with   instead of leaving it blank.)

```
.on("mouseout", function() {
    $(".info").html(" ");
});
```

For the cleanest implementation, we combine all of these steps using method chaining. (To keep it concise, I've omitted the chart styling options in the following excerpt.)

```
$("#stock .chart")
    .sparkline(
        $.map(stock, function(wk) { return wk.adj_close; }),
        { disableTooltips: true }
    ).on("sparklineRegionChange", function(ev) {
        var idx = ev.sparklines[0].getCurrentRegionFields().offset;
        if (idx) {
            $(".info").html(
                "Week of " + stock[idx].date
                + "    "
                + "Close: $" + stock[idx].adj_close);
        }
    }).on("mouseout", function() {
        $(".info").html(" ");
    });
```

Now with Figure 3-9 we have a nice, interactive tool tip that tracks the user's mouse as it moves across the chart.

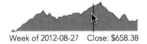

Week of 2012-08-27   Close: $658.38

FIGURE 3-9: *An interactive sparkline tracks the user's mouse and provides information relevant to the mouse position.*

Step 5: Provide Additional Information

The tool tip information we've added so far shows the immediately relevant information to the user: the week and the adjusted closing price of the stock. Our data, however, contains additional information that might be useful to the user. We can expand on the original tool tip by displaying that as well.

At the same time we update the primary tool tip region, let's add the extra data.

```
$(".details").html(
    "Open: $" + stock[idx].open + "<br/>"
  + "High: $" + stock[idx].high + "<br/>"
  + "Low: $"  + stock[idx].low  + "<br/>"
  + "Volume: " + stock[idx].volume
);
```

When we clear the primary tool tip region, we'll clear this area as well.

```
$(".details").html("");
```

Because it won't affect the vertical size of the page, we don't need to fill this `<div>` with a dummy ` `.

With Figure 3-10 we have the visualization we want. The chart clearly shows the overall trend for the stock during the year, but it takes up only a small amount of space on the web page. At first glance the chart is also free of distracting elements such as labels and axes. For users who just want a general sense of the stock's performance, those elements are superfluous. Users who want the full details need only hover their mouse over the chart, and it reveals the complete market information.

FIGURE 3-10: *Interactive sparklines can show additional information in many ways.*

Because we've managed to display the information while retaining the compact nature of sparklines, the technique in this example works well when combined with the small-multiples approach of this chapter's second example. The next example includes an alternate method for showing the extra details.

Drawing Composite Charts

So far in this chapter, we've seen how sparklines can provide a lot of visual information in a very small space. That characteristic makes them perfect for integrating charts in a complete web page that includes text, tables, and other elements. We haven't yet exhausted the capabilities of sparklines, however. We can increase the information density of our visualizations still further by creating composite charts—in effect, drawing multiple charts in the same space.

To see an example of this technique, we can build on the previous example. In that example we used a sparkline to show the closing price of a stock over an entire year. Price is indeed the most relevant data about a stock, but there's another quantity that many investors like to see: the stock's trading volume. And just as with price, it can be important to understand the trend for trading volume at a glance. That makes the value an excellent candidate for a chart.

Just as in this chapter's first example, we need to include the sparklines and jQuery libraries in our web page. Because we're visualizing the same data as in the previous example, we'll also want to set up the data array and the HTML markup exactly as in that example.

Step 1: Draw the Trading Volume Chart

Even though we're including a chart of trading volume, the most important quantity is the stock price. To keep the emphasis on stock price, we want to draw that chart *on top of* the chart for trading volume. That means we need to draw the trading volume chart first.

The code for trading volume is very similar to that of the stock price from the previous example. Instead of an area chart, however, we'll use a bar chart.

```
$("#stock .chart").sparkline(
    $.map(stock, function(wk) { return wk.volume; }),
❶   { type: "bar" }
);
```

We use the jQuery .map() function to extract the volume property from our data array. Setting the type option to "bar" at ❶ is all it takes to tell the sparklines library to create a bar chart.

Figure 3-11 shows the results.

FIGURE 3-11: *The sparklines library can create bar charts as well as line charts.*

Step 2: Add the Closing Price Chart

To add the price chart on top of the volume chart, we can call the sparklines library once again.

```
$("#stock .chart")
    .sparkline(
        $.map(stock, function(wk) { return wk.volume; }),
```

```
        {
            type: "bar"
        }
    ).sparkline(
        $.map(stock, function(wk) { return wk.adj_close; }),
        {
❶          composite: true,
            lineColor: "#006363",
            fillColor: "rgba(45, 153, 153, 0.3)",
            disableTooltips: true
        }
    );
```

We give it the same containing element and, most importantly, set the
composite option to **true** at ❶. This parameter tells the library not to erase any
existing chart in the element but to simply draw over it.

Notice the way we specify the fill color for the second chart. We set a transparency (or *alpha*) value of 0.3. This value makes the chart area nearly transparent,
so the volume chart will show through. Note, though, that some older web browsers,
notably IE8 and earlier, do not support the transparency standard. If your site has a
significant number of users with those browsers, you might consider simply setting
the **fillColor** option to **false**, which will disable filling the area entirely.

As Figure 3-12 shows, the result combines both charts in the same space.

FIGURE 3-12: *Multiple charts may be
combined in the same space.*

Step 3: Add the Annotations

We can add annotations to the chart using the same approach as in the previous
example. Because our charts now include the trading volume, it's appropriate to
move that value from the details area into the primary annotation **<div>**. The code
to do that is a simple adjustment from the prior example.

```
    .on("sparklineRegionChange", function(ev) {
❶      var idx = ev.sparklines[1].getCurrentRegionFields().offset;
        if (idx) {
            $(".info").html(
                "Week of " + stock[idx].date
            + "    Close: $" + stock[idx].adj_close
❷          + "    Volume: "
            + Math.round(stock[idx].volume/10000)/100 + "M"
            );
            $(".details").html(
                "Open: $" + stock[idx].open + "<br/>"
            + "High: $" + stock[idx].high + "<br/>"
```

```
        + "Low: $"  + stock[idx].low
    );
  }
```

In addition to moving the text from one area to the other, we've made two significant changes.

▶ We get the `idx` value from the second element of the event's `sparklines` array (`sparklines[1]`) at ❶. That's because the first element of that array is the first chart. The sparklines library doesn't really return any useful information about bar charts in the `sparklineRegionChange` event. Fortunately, we can get all the information we need from the line bchart.

▶ We show the trading volume in millions, rounded to two decimal places. The calculation is in at ❷. It's much easier for users to quickly grasp "24.4M" than "24402100."

As in the previous example, the annotations in our chart (shown in Figure 3-13) provide additional details.

Open: $679.99
High: $680.87
Low: $657.25
Week of 2012-08-27   Close: $658.38   Volume: 10.99M

FIGURE 3-13: *Tracking the mouse position makes it possible to interactively annotate the charts.*

Step 4: Show Details as a Chart

So far we've shown the additional details for the stock (open, close, high, and low) as text values. As long as we're drawing multiple charts, we can show those values graphically as well. The statistical box plot serves as a useful model for us. Traditionally, that plot type shows the range of a distribution, including deviations, quartiles, and medians. Visually, however, it provides a perfect model of a stock's trading performance. We can use it to show the opening and closing prices, as well as the high and low values during the period.

The sparklines library can draw a box plot for us, but normally it calculates the values to display given the distribution as input data. In our case we don't want to use the standard statistical calculations. Instead, we can use an option that tells the library to use precomputed values. The library expects at least five values:

▶ The lowest sample value

▶ The first quartile

▶ The median

▶ The third quartile

▶ The highest sample value

For our example, we'll provide the following values instead:

▶ The lowest price

▶ Whichever is less of the opening and closing prices

▶ The adjusted closing price

▶ Whichever is greater of the opening and closing prices

▶ The highest price

We'll also color the median bar red or green depending on whether the stock gained or lost value during the period.

This code creates that chart in response to the **sparklineRegionChange** event:

```
$("#composite-chart4 .details")
    .sparkline([
❶        stock[idx].low,
        Math.min(stock[idx].open,stock[idx].close),
        stock[idx].adj_close,
        Math.max(stock[idx].open,stock[idx].close),
        stock[idx].high
    ], {
        type: "box",
        showOutliers: false,
❷        medianColor: (stock[idx].open < stock[idx].close)
❸            ? "green" : "red"
    });
```

The data for the chart (shown at ❶) is simply the five values extracted from the stock data for the appropriate week. As ❷ and ❸ demonstrate, we can change the color of the median bar depending on whether the stock finished higher or lower for the day.

When the mouse leaves the chart region, we can remove the box plot by emptying its container.

```
$(".details").empty();
```

Now as our users mouse over the chart area, they can see a visual representation of the stock's price range during each period (Figure 3-14).

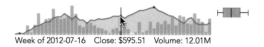

Week of 2012-07-16   Close: $595.51   Volume: 12.01M

FIGURE 3-14: *Interactive annotations can be charts themselves in addition to text.*

Responding to Click Events

Throughout this chapter we've looked at how to include a lot of visual information in a small space, making it easier to integrate a visualization within a web page. The basic sparkline by itself is very efficient, and previous examples have added annotations and composites to increase the information density further. Sometimes, however, there's just no way to fit all the possible data in a small enough space. Even in these cases, though, the interactive nature of the Web can help us out. Our web page can start with a compact visualization but expand to a different view—one with richer details—with a simple click or tap.

Indeed, the compact quality of sparklines seems to invite interaction. In every usability test I've performed that included sparklines on a web page, the participants invariably clicked on the chart. That was true even when there were no other details that the page could provide and the participants had no idea what to expect in response to their clicks. They clicked just to see what would happen.

This example continues our stock market example. We'll begin with the same basic stock price chart we've seen before, but enhance it to provide details when users click on the chart region.

Just as in this chapter's first example, we need to include the sparklines and jQuery libraries in our web page. Because we're visualizing the same data as in the previous example, we'll also want to set up the data array exactly as in that example. The HTML markup, however, can be much simpler. All we need is a `<div>` to hold the chart.

```
<div id="stock"></div>
```

Step 1: Add the Chart

Adding the chart to our markup is easy with the sparklines library. We can use the jQuery `.map()` function to extract the adjusted close value from our **stock** array.

```
$("#stock").sparkline($.map(stock, function(wk) { return wk.adj_close; }));
```

The static chart of Figure 3-15, which shows the stock performance, probably looks familiar by now.

FIGURE 3-15: *Starting with a static chart ensures that the visualization is sound.*

Step 2: Handle Click Events

The sparklines library makes it easy for us to handle click events. When users click on a chart region, the library generates a custom **sparklineClick** event. The event data includes all of the normal click properties, plus information about where on the chart the user clicked. To be notified of clicks, we define a handler for that custom event.

```
$("#stock")
    .sparkline($.map(stock, function(wk) { return wk.adj_close; }))
    .on("sparklineClick", function(ev) {
        var sparkline = ev.sparklines[0],
        region = sparkline.getCurrentRegionFields();
        /* region.x and region.y are the coordinates of the click */
    });
```

Now that we're set up to receive **sparklineClick** events, we can write the code to respond to them. For our example, let's reveal a detailed financial analysis widget. Many web services, including Yahoo and Google, have similar widgets, but we'll use one from WolframAlpha. As is typical, WolframAlpha provides code for the widget as an HTML **<iframe>**. We can wrap that **<iframe>** in our own **<div>** and place it immediately after the chart. We set a **display** property of **none** so that the contents are initially hidden. (The following snippet omits the details of the **<iframe>** element for clarity.)

```
<div id="stock"></div>
<div id="widget" style="display:none"><iframe></iframe></div>
```

Now our event handling code can reveal the widget using the jQuery **show()** function.

```
    .on("sparklineClick", function(ev) {
      $("#widget").show();
    });
```

That works to reveal the details, but as Figure 3-16 shows, the resulting presentation isn't as elegant as it could be since the details appear so abruptly.

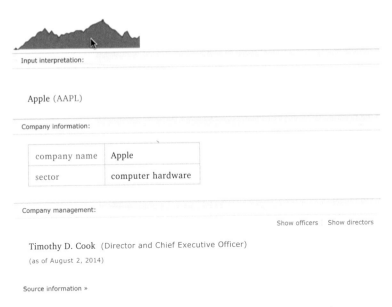

FIGURE 3-16: *Mouse clicks can reveal more details for a chart.*

Step 3: Improve the Transitions

Instead of simply revealing the widget beneath the chart, it would be better to have the widget replace the chart. And if we're going to do that, we'll also want to give users a chance to restore the chart and hide the widget.

```
<div id="stock"></div>
❶ <div id="widget-control" style="width:600px;display:none">
    <a href="#" style="float:right">&times;</a>
</div>
<div id="widget" style="width:600px;display:none">
    <iframe></iframe>
</div>
```

Here, we include a `"widget-control"` `<div>` ❶ for controlling the widget's visibility. The only content we need for this controller is a close symbol floated right. Just like the widget itself, the controller is initially hidden.

Now when the user clicks on the chart, we reveal the widget, reveal the controller, and hide the chart.

```
.on("sparklineClick", function(ev) {
    $("#widget").show();
    $("#widget-control").show();
    $("#stock").hide();
});
```

Next we intercept clicks on the close symbol in the widget controller. We first prevent default event handling; otherwise, the browser will jump disconcertingly to the top of the page. Then we hide the widget and its controller while revealing the chart again.

```
$("#widget-control a").click(function(ev) {
    ev.preventDefault();
    $("#widget").hide();
    $("#widget-control").hide();
    $("#stock").show();
})
```

Finally, we need to give the user some indication that this interaction is possible.

```
$("#stock")
    .sparkline(
        $.map(stock, function(wk) { return wk.adj_close; }),
❶      { tooltipFormatter: function() {return "Click for details"; } }
    );
```

On the chart, we override the sparklines library's default tool tip at ❶ to let users know that more details are available.

And now for the widget controller:

```
<div id="stock"></div>
<div id="widget-control" style="width:600px;display:none">
❶    <a href="#" title="Click to hide" style="float:right;">&times;</a>
</div>
<div id="widget" style="width:600px;display:none">
    <iframe></iframe>
</div>
```

Here, we simply add a title attribute at ❶ to tell users how to hide the widget.

These additions give us the simple sparkline chart in Figure 3-17, which expands to offer a wealth of details with a single click. The close symbol in the upper-right corner lets users return to the more compact sparkline.

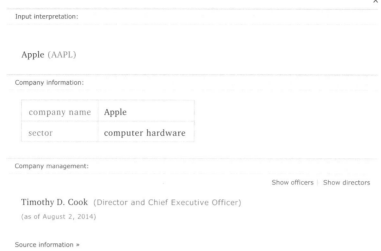

Input interpretation:

Apple (AAPL)

Company information:

company name	Apple
sector	computer hardware

Company management:

Show officers | Show directors

Timothy D. Cook (Director and Chief Executive Officer)
(as of August 2, 2014)

Source information »

FIGURE 3-17: *Mouse clicks can reveal more details for a chart.*

Step 4: Animate

For the final touch to our visualization, let's do something about the abrupt hiding and revealing of the visualization components. A smoother animation will help our users follow the transition, and jQuery makes it easy enough to implement. There are lots of animation effects available in the jQuery UI library, but the basic functionality of jQuery's core is fine for this example. We simply replace the show() and hide() functions with slideDown() and slideUp(), respectively.

```
.on("sparklineClick", function(ev) {
    $("#widget").slideDown();
    $("#widget-control").slideDown();
    $("#stock").slideUp();
});
$("#widget-control a").click(function(ev) {
    ev.preventDefault();
    $("#widget").slideUp();
    $("#widget-control").slideUp();
    $("#stock").slideDown();
})
```

At this point we can call our visualization complete; the final product is shown in Figure 3-18. The compact sparkline smoothly transitions to reveal detailed information when the user clicks, and those details transition back to the sparkline when the user closes them.

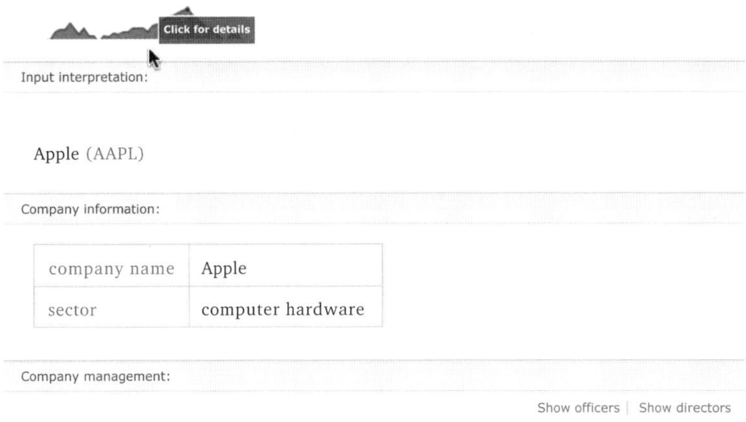

Input interpretation:

Apple (AAPL)

Company information:

company name	Apple
sector	computer hardware

Company management:

Show officers │ Show directors

FIGURE 3-18: *Animating transitions can make the visualization less jarring to users.*

Updating Charts in Real Time

As we've seen in this chapter's other examples, sparklines are great for integrating visualizations in a complete web page. They can be embedded in text content or used as table elements. Another application that suits sparklines well is an information dashboard. Effective dashboards summarize the health of the underlying system *at a glance*. When users don't have the time to read through pages of texts or detailed graphics, the information density of sparklines makes them an ideal tool.

In addition to high information density, most dashboards have another requirement: they must be up-to-date. For web-based dashboards, that means the contents should be continuously updated, even while users are viewing the page. There is no excuse for requiring users to refresh their browsers. Fortunately, the sparklines library makes it easy to accommodate this requirement as well.

Just as in this chapter's first example, we need to include the sparklines and jQuery libraries in our web page. For this visualization we'll show both a chart and the most recent value of the data. We define `<div>` elements for each and place both in a containing `<div>`. The following code includes some styles inline, but you could place them in an external style sheet. Here the styles are just meant to position the value immediately to the right of the chart rather than on a separate line.

```
<div id="dashboard">
    <div id="chart" style="float:left"></div>
    <div id="value" style="float:left"></div>
</div>
```

Step 1: Retrieve the Data

In a real dashboard example, the server would provide the data to display and updates to that data. As long as the frequency of the updates was modest (not faster than once every five seconds or so), we could simply poll the server for updates on a regular interval. It's probably not a good idea, however, to use the JavaScript `setInterval()` function to control the polling interval. That may seem strange at first because `setInterval()` executes a function periodically, which would seem to meet the requirements exactly. The situation is not quite that simple, however. If the server or network encounters a problem, then requests triggered by `setInterval()` will continue unabated, stacking up in a queue. Then, when communication with the server is restored, all of the pending requests will immediately finish, and we'd have a flood of data to handle.

To avoid this problem, we can use the `setTimeout()` function instead. That function executes only once, so we'll have to keep calling it explicitly. By doing that, though, we can make sure that we send a request to the server only after the current one finishes. This approach avoids stacking up a queue of requests.

```
(function getData(){
    setTimeout(function(){
        // Request the data from the server
        $.ajax({ url: "/api/data", success: function(data) {

            // Data has the response from the server

            // Now prepare to ask for updated data
❶          getData();
        }, dataType: "json"});
    }, 30000);  // 30000: wait 30 seconds to make the request
❷ })();
```

Notice that the structure of the code defines the `getData()` function and immediately executes it. The closing pair of parentheses at ❷ triggers the immediate execution.

Within the **success** callback, we set up a recursive call to `getData()` at ❶ so the function executes again whenever the server responds with data.

Step 2: Update the Visualization

Whenever we receive updated information from the server, we can simply update the chart and value.

```
(function getData(){
    setTimeout(function(){
        // Request the data from the server
        $.ajax({ url: "/api/data", success: function(data) {

❶          $("#chart").sparkline(data);
❷          $("#value").text(data.slice(-1));
```

```
        getData();
    }, dataType: "json"});
}, 30000);  // 30000: wait 30 seconds to make the request
})();
```

The code needs only a straightforward call to the sparklines library and a jQuery function to update the value. We've added that to the code here at ❶ and ❷.

Figure 3-19 shows what a default chart looks like. Of course, you can specify both the chart and text styles as appropriate for your own dashboard.

 254

FIGURE 3-19: *A live updating chart can show real-time data.*

Summing Up

In this chapter, we've considered various techniques for integrating visualizations within a web page. We've seen that sparklines are an excellent tool. Because they provide a lot of visual information in a small space, they leave room for other elements of the page, including text blocks, tables, and dashboards. We've considered several ways to increase the information density even further with annotations, composite charts, and click events. Finally, we looked at how to create charts that update in real time, accurately visualizing the up-to-the-minute status of an underlying system.

4

Creating Specialized Graphs

The first three chapters looked at different ways to create many common types of charts with JavaScript. But if your data has unique properties or if you want to show it in an unusual way, a more specialized chart might be more appropriate than a typical bar, line, or scatter chart.

Fortunately, there are many JavaScript techniques and plug-ins to expand our visualization vocabulary beyond the standard charts. In this chapter, we'll look at approaches for several specialized chart types, including the following:

▶ How to combine hierarchy and dimension with tree maps

▶ How to highlight regions with heat maps

▶ How to show links between elements with network graphs

▶ How to reveal language patterns with word clouds

Visualizing Hierarchies with Tree Maps

Data that we want to visualize can often be organized into a hierarchy, and in many cases that hierarchy is itself an important aspect of the visualization. This chapter considers several tools for visualizing hierarchical data, and we'll begin the examples with one of the simplest approaches: tree maps. Tree maps represent numeric data with two-dimensional areas, and they indicate hierarchies by nesting subordinate areas within their parents.

There are several algorithms for constructing tree maps from hierarchical data; one of the most common is the squarified algorithm developed by Mark Bruls, Kees Huizing, and Jarke J. van Wijk (*http://www.win.tue.nl/~vanwijk/stm.pdf*). This algorithm is favored for many visualizations because it usually generates visually pleasing proportions for the tree map area. To create the graphics in our example, we can use Imran Ghory's treemap-squared library (*https://github.com/imranghory/treemap-squared*). That library includes code for both calculating and drawing tree maps.

Step 1: Include the Required Libraries

The treemap-squared library itself depends on the Raphaël library (*http://raphaeljs.com/*) for low-level drawing functions. Our markup, therefore, must include both libraries. The Raphaël library is popular enough for public CDNs to support.

```
<!DOCTYPE html>
<html lang="en">
  <head>
    <meta charset="utf-8">
    <title></title>
  </head>
  <body>
    <div id="treemap"></div>
❶   <script src="//cdnjs.cloudflare.com/ajax/libs/raphael/2.1.0/raphael-min.js">
    </script>
❷   <script src="js/treemap-squared-0.5.min.js"></script>
  </body>
</html>
```

As you can see, we've set aside a `<div>` to hold our tree map. We've also included the JavaScript libraries as the last part of the `<body>` element, as that provides the best browser performance. In this example, we're relying on Cloud-Flare's CDN ❶. We'll have to use our own resources, however, to host the treemap-squared library ❷.

✳ *NOTE: See page 49 for a more extensive discussion of CDNs and the trade-offs involved in using them.*

Step 2: Prepare the Data

For our example we'll show the population of the United States divided by region and then, within each region, by state. The data is available from the US Census Bureau (*http://www.census.gov/popest/data/state/totals/2012/index.html*). We'll follow its convention and divide the country into four regions. The resulting JavaScript array could look like the following snippet.

```
census = [
    { region: "South", state: "AL", pop2010: 4784762, pop2012: 4822023 },
    { region: "West",  state: "AK", pop2010:  714046, pop2012:  731449 },
    { region: "West",  state: "AZ", pop2010: 6410810, pop2012: 6553255 },
    // Data set continues...
```

We've retained both the 2010 and the 2012 data.

To structure the data for the treemap-squared library, we need to create separate data arrays for each region. At the same time, we can also create arrays to label the data values using the two-letter state abbreviations.

```
var south = {};
south.data = [];
south.labels = [];
for (var i=0; i<census.length; i++) {
    if (census[i].region === "South") {
        south.data.push(census[i].pop2012);
        south.labels.push(census[i].state);
    }
}
```

This code steps through the **census** array to build data and label arrays for the **"South"** region. The same approach works for the other three regions as well.

Step 3: Draw the Tree Map

Now we're ready to use the library to construct our tree map. We need to assemble the individual data and label arrays and then call the library's main function.

```
var data = [ west.data, midwest.data, northeast.data, south.data ];
var labels = [ west.labels, midwest.labels, northeast.labels, south.labels ];
❶ Treemap.draw("treemap", 600, 450, data, labels);
```

The first two parameters at ❶ are the width and height of the map.

The resulting chart, shown in Figure 4-1, provides a simple visualization of the US population. Among the four regions, it is clear where most of the population resides. The bottom-right quadrant (the South) has the largest share of the population. And within the regions, the relative size of each state's population is also clear. Notice, for example, how California dominates the West.

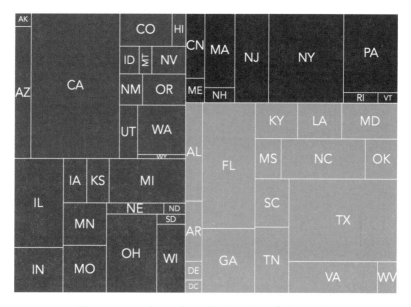

FIGURE 4-1: *Tree maps show the relative size of data values using rectangular area.*

Step 4: Vary the Shading to Show Additional Data

The tree map in Figure 4-1 does a nice job of showing the US population distribution in 2012. The population isn't static, however, and we can enhance our visualization to indicate trends by taking advantage of the 2010 population data that's still lurking in our data set. When we iterate through the **census** array to extract individual regions, we can also calculate a few additional values.

Here's an expanded version of our earlier code fragment that includes these additional calculations.

```
var total2010 = 0;
var total2012 = 0;
var south = {
    data: [],
```

```
        labels: [],
        growth: [],
        minGrowth: 100,
        maxGrowth: -100
    };
    for (var i=0; i<census.length; i++) {
❶      total2010 += census[i].pop2010;
❷      total2012 += census[i].pop2012;
❸      var growth = (census[i].pop2012 - census[i].pop2010)/census[i].pop2010;
        if (census[i].region === "South") {
            south.data.push(census[i].pop2012);
            south.labels.push(census[i].state);
            south.growth.push(growth);
❹          if (growth > south.maxGrowth) { south.maxGrowth = growth; }
❺          if (growth < south.minGrowth) { south.minGrowth = growth; }
        }
        // Code continues...
    }
```

Let's walk through those additional calculations:

▶ We accumulate the total population for all states, both in 2010 and in 2012, at ❶ and ❷, respectively. These values let us calculate the average growth rate for the entire country.

▶ For each state, we can calculate its growth rate at ❸.

▶ For each region, we save both the minimum and maximum growth rates at ❹ and ❺.

In the same way that we created a master object for the data and the labels, we create another master object for the growth rates. Let's also calculate the total growth rate for the country.

```
var growth = [ west.growth, midwest.growth, northeast.growth, south.growth ];
var totalGrowth = (total2012 - total2010)/total2010;
```

Now we need a function to calculate the color for a tree-map rectangle. We start by defining two color ranges, one for growth rates higher than the national average and another for lower growth rates. We can then pick an appropriate color for each state, based on that state's growth rate. As an example, here's one possible set of colors.

```
var colorRanges = {
  positive: [ "#FFFFBF","#D9EF8B","#A6D96A","#66BD63","#1A9850","#006837" ],
  negative: [ "#FFFFBF","#FEE08B","#FDAE61","#F46D43","#D73027","#A50026" ]
};
```

Next is the pickColor() function that uses these color ranges to select the right color for each box. The treemap-squared library will call it with two parameters—the coordinates of the rectangle it's about to draw, and the index into the data set. We don't need the coordinates in our example, but we will use the index to find the value to model. Once we find the state's growth rate, we can subtract the national average. That calculation determines which color range to use. States that are growing faster than the national average get the positive color range; states growing slower than the average get the negative range.

The final part of the code calculates where on the appropriate color range to select the color.

```
function pickColor(coordinates, index) {
    var regionIdx = index[0];
    var stateIdx  = index[1];
    var growthRate = growth[regionIdx][stateIdx];
    var deltaGrowth = growthRate - totalGrowth;
    if (deltaGrowth > 0) {
        colorRange = colorRanges.positive;
    } else {
        colorRange = colorRanges.negative;
        deltaGrowth = -1 * deltaGrowth;
    }
    var colorIndex = Math.floor(colorRange.length*(deltaGrowth-minDelta)/
(maxDelta-minDelta));
    if (colorIndex >= colorRange.length) { colorIndex = colorRange.length - 1;
}

    color = colorRange[colorIndex];
    return{ "fill" : color };
}
```

The code uses a linear scale based on the extreme values from among all the states. So, for example, if a state's growth rate is halfway between the overall average and the maximum growth rate, we'll give it a color that's halfway in the positive color range array.

Now when we call TreeMap.draw(), we can add this function to its parameters, specifically by setting it as the value for the box key of the options object. The treemap-squared library will then defer to our function for selecting the colors of the regions.

```
Treemap.draw("treemap", 600, 450, data, labels, {"box" : pickColor});
```

The resulting tree map of Figure 4-2 still shows the relative populations for all of the states. Now, through the use of color shades, it also indicates the rate of population growth compared to the national average. The visualization clearly shows the migration from the Northeast and Midwest to the South and West.

FIGURE 4-2: *Tree maps can use color as well as area to show data values.*

Highlighting Regions with a Heat Map

If you work in the web industry, heat maps may already be a part of your job. Usability researchers often use heat maps to evaluate site designs, especially when they want to analyze which parts of a web page get the most attention from users. Heat maps work by overlaying values, represented as semitransparent colors, over a two-dimensional area. As the example in Figure 4-3 shows, different colors represent different levels of attention. Users focus most on areas colored red, and less on yellow, green, and blue areas.

For this example, we'll use a heat map to visualize an important aspect of a basketball game: from where on the court the teams are scoring most of their points. The software we'll use is the heatmap.js library from Patrick Wied (*http://www.patrick-wied.at/static/heatmapjs/*). If you need to create traditional website heat maps, that library includes built-in support for capturing mouse movements and mouse clicks on a web page. Although we won't use those features for our example, the general approach is much the same.

FIGURE 4-3: *Heat maps traditionally show where web users focus their attention on a page.*

Step 1: Include the Required JavaScript

For modern browsers, the heatmap.js library has no additional requirements. The library includes optional additions for real-time heat maps and for geographic integration, but we won't need these in our example. Older browsers (principally IE8 and older) can use heatmap.js with the *explorer canvas* library. Since we don't need to burden all users with this library, we'll use conditional comments to include it only when it's needed. Following current best practices, we include all script files at the end of our `<body>`.

```
<!DOCTYPE html>
<html lang="en">
  <head>
    <meta charset="utf-8">
    <title></title>
  </head>
  <body>
    <!--[if lt IE 9]><script src="js/excanvas.min.js"></script><![endif]-->
    <script src="js/heatmap.js"></script>
  </body>
</html>
```

Step 2: Define the Visualization Data

For our example, we'll visualize the NCAA Men's Basketball game on February 13, 2013, between Duke University and the University of North Carolina. Our data set (*http://www.cbssports.com/collegebasketball/gametracker/live/NCAAB_20130213_ UNC@DUKE*) contains details about every point scored in the game. To clean the data, we convert the time of each score to minutes from the game start, and we define the position of the scorer in x- and y-coordinates. We've defined these coordinates using several important conventions:

▶ We'll show North Carolina's points on the left side of the court and Duke's points on the right side.

▶ The bottom-left corner of the court corresponds to position (0,0), and the top-right corner corresponds to (10,10).

▶ To avoid confusing free throws with field goals, we've given all free throws a position of (−1, −1).

Here's the beginning of the data; the full data is available with the book's source code (*http://jsDataV.is/source/*).

```
var game = [
  { team: "UNC",  points: 2, time: 0.85, unc: 2, duke: 0, x: 0.506, y: 5.039 },
  { team: "UNC",  points: 3, time: 1.22, unc: 5, duke: 0, x: 1.377, y: 1.184 },
  { team: "DUKE", points: 2, time: 1.65  unc: 5, duke: 2, x: 8.804, y: 7.231 },
  // Data set continues...
```

Step 3: Create the Background Image

A simple diagram of a basketball court, like that in Figure 4-4, works fine for our visualization. The dimensions of our background image are 600×360 pixels.

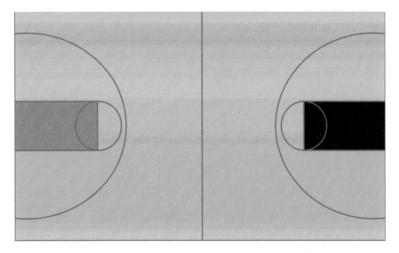

FIGURE 4-4: A background image sets the context for the visualization.

Step 4: Set Aside an HTML Element to Contain the Visualization

In our web page, we need to define the element (generally a `<div>`) that will hold the heat map. When we create the element, we specify its dimensions, and we define the background. The following fragment does both of those using inline styles to keep the example concise. You might want to use a CSS style sheet in an actual implementation.

```
<div id="heatmap"
    style="position:relative;width:600px;height:360px;
            background-image:url('img/basketball.png');">
</div>
```

Notice that we've given the element a unique `id`. The heatmap.js library needs that `id` to place the map on the page. Most importantly, we also set the `position` property to `relative`. The heatmap.js library positions its graphics using absolute positioning, and we want to contain those graphics within the parent element.

Step 5: Format the Data

For our next step, we must convert the game data into the proper format for the library. The heatmap.js library expects individual data points to contain three properties:

▸ The x-coordinate, measured in pixels from the left of the containing element

▸ The y-coordinate, measured in pixels from the top of the containing element

▸ The magnitude of the data point (specified by the **count** property)

The library also requires the maximum magnitude for the entire map, and here things get a little tricky. With standard heat maps, the magnitudes of all the data points for any particular position sum together. In our case, that means that all the baskets scored from layups and slam dunks—which are effectively from the same position on the court—are added together by the heat-map algorithm. That one position, right underneath the basket, dominates the rest of the court. To counteract that effect, we specify a maximum value far less than what the heat map would expect. In our case, we'll set the maximum value to 3, which means that any location where at least three points were scored will be colored red, and we'll easily be able to see all the baskets.

We can use JavaScript to transform the **game** array into the appropriate format.

```
❶ var docNode = document.getElementById("heatmap");
❷ var height = docNode.clientHeight;
❸ var width  = docNode.clientWidth;
❹ var dataset = {};
❺ dataset.max = 3;
❻ dataset.data = [];
```

```
for (var i=0; i<game.length; i++) {
    var currentShot = game[1];
    if ((currentShot.x !== -1) && (currentShot.y !== -1)) {
        var x = Math.round(width  * currentShot.x/10);
        var y = height - Math.round(height * currentShot.y/10);
        dataset.data.push({"x": x, "y": y, "count": currentShot.points});
    }
}
```
❼

We start by fetching the height and width of the containing element at ❶, ❷, and ❸. If those dimensions change, our code will still work fine. Then we initialize the **dataset** object ❹, with a **max** property ❺ and an empty **data** array ❻. Finally, we iterate through the game data and add relevant data points to this array. Notice that we're filtering out free throws at ❼.

Step 6: Draw the Map

With a containing element and a formatted data set, it's a simple matter to draw the heat map. We create the heat-map object (the library uses the name h337 in an attempt to be clever) by specifying the containing element, a radius for each point, and an opacity. Then we add the data set to this object.

```
var heatmap = h337.create({
    element: "heatmap",
    radius: 30,
    opacity: 50
});
heatmap.store.setDataSet(dataset);
```

The resulting visualization in Figure 4-5 shows where each team scored its points.

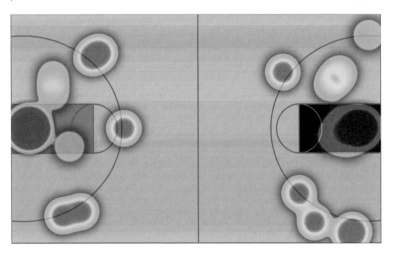

FIGURE 4-5: *The heat map shows successful shots in the game.*

Step 7: Adjust the Heat Map z-index

The heatmap.js library is especially aggressive in its manipulation of the `z-index` property. To ensure that the heat map appears above all other elements on the page, the library explicitly sets this property to a value of **10000000000**. If your web page has elements that you don't want the heat map to obscure (such as fixed-position navigation menus), that value is probably too aggressive. You can fix it by modifying the source code directly. Or, as an alternative, you can simply reset the value after the library finishes drawing the map.

If you're using jQuery, the following code will reduce the `z-index` to a more reasonable value.

```
$("#heatmap canvas").css("z-index", "1");
```

Showing Relationships with Network Graphs

Visualizations don't always focus on the actual data values; sometimes the most interesting aspects of a data set are the relationships among its members. The relationships between members of a social network, for example, might be the most important feature of that network. To visualize these types of relationships, we can use a *network graph*. Network graphs represent objects, generally known as *nodes*, as points or circles. Lines or arcs (technically called *edges*) connect these nodes to indicate relationships.

Constructing network graphs can be a bit tricky, as the underlying mathematics is not always trivial. Fortunately, the Sigma library (*http://sigmajs.org/*) takes care of most of the complicated calculations. By using that library, we can create full-featured network graphs with just a little bit of JavaScript. For our example, we'll consider one critic's list of the top 25 jazz albums of all time (*http://www.thejazzresource.com/top_25_jazz_albums.html*). Several musicians performed on more than one of these albums, and a network graph lets us explore those connections.

Step 1: Include the Required Libraries

The Sigma library does not depend on any other JavaScript libraries, so we don't need any other included scripts. It is not, however, available on common content distribution networks. Consequently, we'll have to serve it from our own web host.

```
<!DOCTYPE html>
<html lang="en">
  <head>
    <meta charset="utf-8">
    <title></title>
  </head>
```

```
    <body>
❶     <div id="graph"></div>
❷     <script src="js/sigma.min.js"></script>
    </body>
</html>
```

As you can see, we've set aside a `<div>` to hold our graph at ❶. We've also included the JavaScript library as the last part of the `<body>` element at ❷, as that provides the best browser performance.

✳ **NOTE: In most of the examples in this book, I included steps you can take to make your visualizations compatible with older web browsers such as IE8. In this case, however, those approaches degrade performance so severely that they are rarely workable. To view the network graph visualization, your users will need a modern browser.**

Step 2: Prepare the Data

Our data on the top 25 jazz albums looks like the following snippet. I'm showing only the first couple of albums, but you can see the full list in the book's source code (*http://jsDataV.is/source/*).

```
var albums = [
  {
    album: "Miles Davis - Kind of Blue",
    musicians: [
      "Cannonball Adderley",
      "Paul Chambers",
      "Jimmy Cobb",
      "John Coltrane",
      "Miles Davis",
      "Bill Evans"
    ]
  },{
    album: "John Coltrane - A Love Supreme",
    musicians: [
      "John Coltrane",
      "Jimmy Garrison",
      "Elvin Jones",
      "McCoy Tyner"
    ]
  // Data set continues...
```

That's not exactly the structure that Sigma requires. We could convert it to a Sigma JSON data structure in bulk, but there's really no need. Instead, as we'll see in the next step, we can simply pass data to the library one element at a time.

Step 3: Define the Graph's Nodes

Now we're ready to use the library to construct our graph. We start by initializing the library and indicating where it should construct the graph. That parameter is the `id` of the `<div>` element set aside to hold the visualization.

```
var s = new sigma("graph");
```

Now we can continue by adding the nodes to the graph. In our case, each album is a node. As we add a node to the graph, we give it a unique identifier (which must be a string), a label, and a position. Figuring out an initial position can be a bit tricky for arbitrary data. In a few steps, we'll look at an approach that makes the initial position less critical. For now, though, we'll simply spread our albums in a circle using basic trigonometry.

```
for (var idx=0; idx<albums.length; idx++) {
    var theta = idx*2*Math.PI / albums.length;
    s.graph.addNode({
        id: ""+idx,    // Note: 'id' must be a string
        label: albums[idx].album,
        x: radius*Math.sin(theta),
        y: radius*Math.cos(theta),
        size: 1
    });
}
```

Here, the **radius** value is roughly half of the width of the container. We can also give each node a different size, but for our purposes it's fine to set every album's size to 1.

Finally, after defining the graph, we tell the library to draw it.

```
s.refresh();
```

With Figure 4-6, we now have a nicely drawn circle of the top 25 jazz albums of all time. In this initial attempt, some of the labels may get in one another's way, but we'll address that shortly.

If you try out this visualization in the browser, you'll notice that the Sigma library automatically supports panning the graph, and users can move their mouse pointer over individual nodes to highlight the node labels.

FIGURE 4-6: *Sigma draws graph nodes as small circles.*

Step 4: Connect the Nodes with Edges

Now that we have the nodes drawn in a circle, it's time to connect them with edges. In our case, an edge—or connection between two albums—represents a musician who performed on both of the albums. Here's the code that finds those edges.

```
❶ for (var srcIdx=0; srcIdx<albums.length; srcIdx++) {
      var src = albums[srcIdx];
❷     for (var mscIdx=0; mscIdx<src.musicians.length; mscIdx++) {
          var msc = src.musicians[mscIdx];
❸         for (var tgtIdx=srcIdx+1; tgtIdx<albums.length; tgtIdx++) {
              var tgt = albums[tgtIdx];
❹             if (tgt.musicians.some(function(tgtMsc) {return tgtMsc === msc;}))
  {
                  s.graph.addEdge({
                      id: srcIdx + "." + mscIdx + "-" + tgtIdx,
                      source: ""+srcIdx,
                      target: ""+tgtIdx
                  })
              }
          }
      }
  }
```

To find the edges, we iterate through the albums in four stages.

1. Loop through each album as a potential source of a connection at ❶.
2. For the source album, loop through all musicians at ❷.
3. For each musician, loop through all of the remaining albums as potential targets for a connection at ❸.
4. For each target album, loop through all the musicians at ❹, looking for a match.

For the last step we're using the .some() method of JavaScript arrays. That method takes a function as a parameter, and it returns **true** if that function itself returns **true** for any element in the array.

We'll want to insert this code before we refresh the graph. When we've done that, we'll have a connected circle of albums, as shown in Figure 4-7.

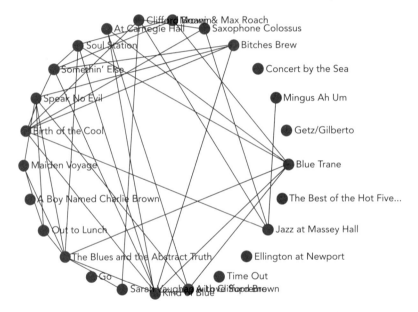

FIGURE 4-7: *Sigma can then connect graph nodes using lines to represent edges.*

Again, you can pan and zoom in on the graph to focus on different parts.

Step 5: Automate the Layout

So far we've manually placed the nodes in our graph in a circle. That's not a terrible approach, but it can make it hard to discern some of the connections. It would be better if we could let the library calculate a more optimal layout than the simple circle. That's exactly what we'll do now.

The mathematics behind this approach is known as *force-directed graphing*. In a nutshell, the algorithm proceeds by treating the graph's nodes and edges as physical objects subject to real forces such as gravity and electromagnetism. It simulates the effect of those forces, pushing and prodding the nodes into new positions on the graph.

The underlying algorithm may be complicated, but Sigma makes it easy to employ. First we have to add the optional `forceAtlas2` plug-in to the Sigma library.

```html
<!DOCTYPE html>
<html lang="en">
    <head>
        <meta charset="utf-8">
        <title></title>
    </head>
    <body>
        <div id="graph"></div>
        <script src="js/sigma.min.js"></script>
        <script src="js/sigma.layout.forceAtlas2.min.js"></script>
    </body>
</html>
```

Mathieu Jacomy and Tommaso Venturini developed the specific force-direction algorithm employed by this plug-in; they document the algorithm, known as *ForceAtlas2*, in the 2011 paper "ForceAtlas2, A Graph Layout Algorithm for Handy Network Visualization" (*http://webatlas.fr/tempshare/ForceAtlas2_Paper.pdf*). Although we don't have to understand the mathematical details of the algorithm, knowing how to use its parameters does come in handy. There are three parameters that are important for most visualizations that use the plug-in:

gravity This parameter determines how strongly the algorithm tries to keep isolated nodes from drifting off the edges of the screen. Without any gravity, the only force acting on isolated nodes will be one that repels them from other nodes; undeterred, that force will push the nodes off the screen entirely. Since our data includes several isolated nodes, we'll want to set this value relatively high to keep those nodes on the screen.

scalingRatio This parameter determines how strongly nodes repel each other. A small value draws connected nodes closer together, while a large value forces all nodes farther apart.

slowDown This parameter decreases the sensitivity of the nodes to the repulsive forces from their neighbors. Reducing the sensitivity (by increasing this value) can help reduce the instability that may result when nodes face competing forces from multiple neighbors. In our data there are many connections that will tend to draw the nodes together and compete with the force pulling them apart. To dampen the wild oscillations that might otherwise ensue, we'll set this value relatively high as well.

The best way to settle on values for these parameters is to experiment with the actual data. The values we've settled on for this data set are shown in the following code.

```
s.startForceAtlas2({gravity:100,scalingRatio:70,slowDown:100});
setTimeout(function() { s.stopForceAtlas2(); }, 10000);
```

Now, instead of simply refreshing the graph when we're ready to display it, we start the force-directed algorithm, which periodically refreshes the display while it performs its simulation. We also need to stop the algorithm after it's had a chance to run for a while. In our case, 10 seconds (**10000** milliseconds) is plenty of time.

As a result, our albums start out in their original circle, but quickly migrate to a position that makes it much easier to identify the connections. Some of the top albums are tightly connected, indicating that they have many musicians in common. A few, however, remain isolated. Their musicians make the list only once.

As you can see in Figure 4-8, the labels for the nodes still get in the way of one another; we'll fix that in the next step. What's important here, however, is that it's much easier to identify the albums with lots of connections. The nodes representing those albums have migrated to the center of the graph, and they have many links to other nodes.

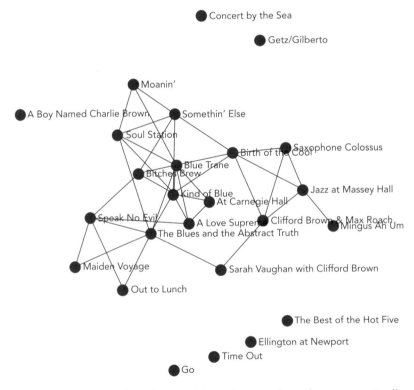

FIGURE 4-8: *Force direction positions the graph nodes automatically.*

Step 6: Add Interactivity

To keep the labels from interfering with one another, we can add some interactivity to the graph. By default, we'll hide the labels entirely, giving users the chance to appreciate the structure of the graph without distractions. We'll then allow them to click on individual nodes to reveal the album title and its connections.

```
for (var idx=0; idx<albums.length; idx++) {
    var theta = idx*2*Math.PI / albums.length;
    s.graph.addNode({
        id: ""+idx,      // Note: 'id' must be a string
❶      label: "",
❷      album: albums[idx].album,
        x: radius*Math.sin(theta),
        y: radius*Math.cos(theta),
        size: 1
    });
}
```

To suppress the initial label display, we modify the initialization code at ❶ so that nodes have blank labels. We save a reference to the album title, though, at ❷.

Now we need a function that responds to clicks on the node elements. The Sigma library supports exactly this sort of function with its interface. We simply bind to the **clickNode** event.

```
s.bind("clickNode", function(ev) {
    var nodeIdx = ev.data.node.id;
    // Code continues...
});
```

Within that function, the **ev.data.node.id** property gives us the index of the node that the user clicked. The complete set of nodes is available from the array returned by **s.graph.nodes()**. Since we want to display the label for the clicked node (but not for any other), we can iterate through the entire array. At each iteration, we either set the **label** property to an empty string (to hide it) or to the **album** property (to show it).

```
s.bind("clickNode", function(ev) {
    var nodeIdx = ev.data.node.id;
    var nodes = s.graph.nodes();
    nodes.forEach(function(node) {
❶      if (nodes[nodeIdx] === node) {
            node.label = node.album;
        } else {
            node.label = "";
        }
    });
});
```

Now that users have a way to show the title of an album, let's give them a way to hide it. A small addition at ❶ is all it takes to let users toggle the album display with subsequent clicks.

```
if (nodes[nodeIdx] === node && node.label !== node.album) {
```

As long as we're making the graph respond to clicks, we can also take the opportunity to highlight the clicked node's connections. We do that by changing their color. Just as `s.graph.nodes()` returns an array of the graph nodes, `s.graph.edges()` returns an array of edges. Each edge object includes `target` and `source` properties that hold the index of the relevant node.

```
  s.graph.edges().forEach(function(edge) {
      if ((nodes[nodeIdx].label === nodes[nodeIdx].album) &&
❶        ((edge.target === nodeIdx) || (edge.source === nodeIdx))) {
❷          edge.color = "blue";
      } else {
❸          edge.color = "black";
      }
  });
```

Here we scan through all the graph's edges to see if they connect to the clicked node. If the edge does connect to the node, we change its color at ❷ to something other than the default. Otherwise, we change the color back to the default at ❸. You can see that we're using the same approach to toggle the edge colors as we did to toggle the node labels on successive clicks at ❶.

Now that we've changed the graph properties, we have to tell Sigma to redraw it. That's a simple matter of calling `s.refresh()`.

```
s.refresh();
```

Now we have a fully interactive network graph in Figure 4-9.

Revealing Language Patterns with Word Clouds

Data visualizations don't always focus on numbers. Sometimes the data for a visualization centers on words instead, and a *word cloud* is often an effective way to present this kind of data. Word clouds can associate any quantity with a list of words; most often that quantity is a relative frequency. This type of word cloud, which we'll create for our next example, reveals which words are common and which are rare.

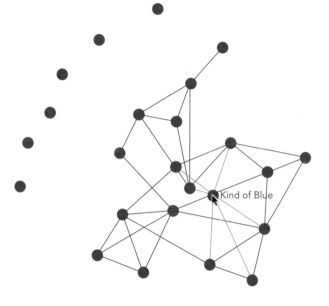

Kind of Blue

FIGURE 4-9: *An interactive graph gives users the chance to highlight specific nodes.*

To create this visualization, we'll rely on the wordcloud2 library (*http:// timdream.org/wordcloud2.js*), a spin-off from author Tim Dream's HTML5 Word Cloud project (*http://timc.idv.tw/wordcloud/*).

✳ **NOTE:** As is the case with a few of the more advanced libraries we've examined, wordcloud2 doesn't function very well in older web browsers such as IE8 and earlier. Since wordcloud2 itself requires a modern browser, for this example we won't worry about compatibility with older browsers. This will free us to use some other modern JavaScript features, too.

Step 1: Include the Required Libraries

The wordcloud2 library does not depend on any other JavaScript libraries, so we don't need any other included scripts. It is not, however, available on common content distribution networks, so we'll have to serve it from our own web host.

```
<!DOCTYPE html>
<html lang="en">
  <head>
    <meta charset="utf-8">
    <title></title>
  </head>
  <body>
    <script src="js/wordcloud2.js"></script>
  </body>
</html>
```

To keep our example focused on the visualization, we'll use a word list that doesn't need any special preparation. If you're working with natural language as spoken or written, however, you might wish to process the text to identify alternate forms of the same word. For example, you might want to count *hold*, *holds*, and *held* as three instances of *hold* rather than three separate words. This type of processing obviously depends greatly on the particular language. If you're working in English and Chinese, though, the same developer that created wordcloud2 has also released the WordFreq JavaScript library (*http://timdream.org/wordfreq/*), which performs exactly this type of analysis.

Step 2: Prepare the Data

For this example, we'll look at the different tags users associate with their questions on the popular Stack Overflow (*http://stackoverflow.com/*). That site lets users pose programming questions that the community tries to answer. Tags provide a convenient way to categorize the questions so that users can browse other posts related to the same topic. By constructing a word cloud (perhaps better named a *tag cloud*), we can quickly show the relative popularity of different programming topics.

If you wanted to develop this example into a real application, you could access the Stack Overflow data in real time using the site's API. For our example, though, we'll use a static snapshot. Here's how it starts:

```
var tags = [
    ["c#", 601251],
    ["java", 585413],
    ["javascript", 557407],
    ["php", 534590],
    ["android", 466436],
    ["jquery", 438303],
    ["python", 274216],
    ["c++", 269570],
    ["html", 259946],
    // Data set continues...
```

In this data set, the list of tags is an array, and each tag within the list is also an array. These inner arrays have the word itself as the first item and a count for that word as the second item. You can see the complete list in the book's source code (*http://jsDataV.is/source/*).

The format that wordcloud2 expects is quite similar to how our data is already laid out, except that in each word array, the second value needs to specify the drawing size for that word. For example, the array element ["javascript", 56] would tell wordcloud2 to draw *javascript* with a height of 56 pixels. Our data, of course, isn't set up with pixel sizes. The data value for *javascript* is 557407, and a word 557,407 pixels high wouldn't even fit on a billboard. As a result, we must convert counts to drawing sizes. The specific algorithm for this conversion will depend both on the size of the visualization and on the raw values. A simple approach that works in this case is to divide the count values by 10,000 and round to the nearest integer.

```
var list = tags.map(function(word) {
    return [word[0], Math.round(word[1]/10000)];
});
```

In Chapter 2, we saw how jQuery's .map() function makes it easy to process all the elements in an array. It turns out that modern browsers have the same functionality built in, so here we use the native version of .map() even without jQuery. (This native version won't work on older browsers like jQuery will, but we're not worrying about that for this example.)

After this code executes, our list variable will contain the following:

```
[
    ["c#", 60],
    ["java", 59],
    ["javascript", 56],
    ["php", 53],
    ["android", 47],
    ["jquery", 44],
    ["python", 27],
    ["c++", 27],
    ["html", 26],
    // Data set continues...
```

Step 3: Add the Required Markup

The wordcloud2 library can build its graphics either using the HTML <canvas> interface or in pure HTML. As we've seen with many graphing libraries, <canvas> is a convenient interface for creating graphic elements. For word clouds, however, there aren't many benefits to using <canvas>. Native HTML, on the other hand, lets us use all the standard HTML tools (such as CSS style sheets or JavaScript event handling). That's the approach we'll take in this example.

```
<!DOCTYPE html>
<html lang="en">
  <head>
    <meta charset="utf-8">
    <title></title>
  </head>
  <body>
```

```
❶    <div id="cloud" style="position:relative;"></div>
     <script src="js/wordcloud2.js"></script>
   </body>
</html>
```

When using native HTML, we do have to make sure that the containing element has a `position: relative` style, because wordcloud2 relies on that when placing the words in their proper location in the cloud. You can see that here we've set that style inline at ❶.

Step 4: Create a Simple Cloud

With these preparations in place, creating a simple word cloud is about as easy as it can get. We call the wordcloud2 library and tell it the HTML element in which to draw the cloud, and the list of words for the cloud's data.

```
WordCloud(document.getElementById("cloud"), {list: list});
```

Even with nothing other than default values, wordcloud2 creates the attractive visualization shown in Figure 4-10.

The wordcloud2 interface also provides many options for customizing the visualization. As expected, you can set colors and fonts, but you can also change the shape of the cloud (even providing a custom polar equation), rotation limits, internal grid sizing, and many other features.

FIGURE 4-10: *A word cloud can show a list of words with their relative frequency.*

Step 5: Add Interactivity

If you ask wordcloud2 to use the `<canvas>` interface, it gives you a couple of callback hooks that your code can use to respond to user interactions. With native HTML, however, we aren't limited to just the callbacks that wordcloud2 provides. To demonstrate, we can add a simple interaction to respond to mouse clicks on words in the cloud.

First we'll let users know that interactions are supported by changing the cursor to a pointer when they hover the mouse over a cloud word.

```
#cloud span {
    cursor: pointer;
}
```

Next let's add an extra element to the markup where we can display information about any clicked word.

```
<!DOCTYPE html>
<html lang="en">
  <head>
    <meta charset="utf-8">
    <title></title>
  </head>
  <body>
    <div id="cloud" style="position:relative;"></div>
❶   <div id="details"><div>
    <script src="js/wordcloud2.js"></script>
  </body>
</html>
```

Here we've added the `<div>` with the `id details` at ❶.

Then we define a function that can be called when the user clicks within the cloud.

```
var clicked = function(ev) {
❶   if (ev.target.nodeName === "SPAN") {
        // A <span> element was the target of the click
    }
}
```

Because our function will be called for any clicks on the cloud (including clicks on empty space), it first checks to see if the target of the click was really a word. Words are contained in `<span>` elements, so we can verify that by looking at the `nodeName` property of the click target. As you can see at ❶, JavaScript node names are always uppercase.

If the user did click on a word, we can find out which word by looking at the `textContent` property of the event target.

```
var clicked = function(ev) {
    if (ev.target.nodeName === "SPAN") {
➊       var tag = ev.target.textContent;
    }
}
```

After ➊, the variable **tag** will hold the word on which the user clicked. So, for example, if a user clicks on the word *javascript*, then the tag variable will have the value "`javascript`".

Since we'd like to show users the total count when they click on a word, we're going to need to find the word in our original data set. We have the word's value, so that's simply a matter of searching through the data set to find a match. If we were using jQuery, the **.grep()** function would do just that. In this example, we're sticking with native JavaScript, so we can look for an equivalent method in pure JavaScript. Unfortunately, although there is such a native method defined—**.find()**—very few browsers, even modern ones, currently support it. We could resort to a standard **for** or **forEach** loop, but there is an alternative that many consider an improvement over that approach. It relies on the **.some()** method, an array method that modern browsers support. The **.some()** method passes every element of an array to an arbitrary function and stops when that function returns **true**. Here's how we can use it to find the clicked tag in our **tags** array.

```
var clicked = function(ev) {
    if (ev.target.nodeName === "SPAN") {
        var tag = ev.target.textContent;
        var clickedTag;
➊       tags.some(function(el) {
➋           if (el[0] === tag) {
                clickedTag = el;
                return true;  // This ends the .some() loop
            }
➌           return false;
➍       });
    }
}
```

The function that's the argument to **.some()** is defined beginning at ➊ and ending at ➍. It is called with the parameter **el**, short for an *element* in the **tags** array. The conditional statement at ➋ checks to see if that element's word matches the clicked node's text content. If so, the function sets the **clickedTag** variable and returns **true** to terminate the **.some()** loop.

If the clicked word doesn't match the element we're checking in the **tags** array, then the function supplied to .some() returns **false** at ➌. When .some() sees a **false** return value, it continues iterating through the array.

We can use the return value of the **.some()** method to make sure the clicked element was found in the array. When that's the case, **.some()** itself returns **true**.

```
var clicked = function(ev) {
  var details = "";
```

```
    if (ev.target.nodeName === "SPAN") {
        var tag = ev.target.textContent,
            clickedTag;
        if (tags.some(function(el) {
            if (el[0] === tag) {
                clickedTag = el;
                return true;
            }
            return false;
        })) {
❶          details = "There were " + clickedTag[1] +
❷                  " Stack Overflow questions tagged \"" + tag + "\"";
        }
    }
❸   document.getElementById("details").innerText = details;
}
```

At ❶ and ❷ we update the **details** variable with extra information. At ❸ we update the web page with those details.

And finally we tell the browser to call our handler when a user clicks on anything in the cloud container.

```
document.getElementById("cloud").addEventListener("click", clicked)
```

With these few lines of code, our word cloud is now interactive, as shown in Figure 4-11.

There were 557407 Stack Overflow questions tagged "javascript".

FIGURE 4-11: *Because our word cloud consists of standard HTML elements, we can make it interactive with simple JavaScript event handlers.*

Summing Up

In this chapter, we've looked at several different special-purpose visualizations and some JavaScript libraries that can help us create them. Tree maps are handy for showing both hierarchy and dimension in a single visualization. Heat maps can highlight varying intensities throughout a region. Network graphs reveal the connections between objects. And word clouds show relative relationships between language properties in an attractive and concise visualization.

5

Displaying Timelines

The most compelling visualizations often suc-
ceed because they tell a story; they extract a
narrative from data and reveal that narrative to
their users. And as with any narrative, time is a
critical component. If the data consists solely of
numbers, a standard bar or line chart can easily show its evolution over time. If the data is
not numerical, however, standard charts probably won't work. This chapter considers several
alternatives for time-based visualizations.

All are based on some variation of a timeline; one linear dimension represents time, and events are places along that dimension based on when they occurred. In all of the examples, we'll consider the same underlying data: a possible chronology of the plays of William Shakespeare (*http://en.wikipedia.org/wiki/Chronology_of_Shakespeare%27s_plays*).

We'll look at three very different approaches for adding timelines to web pages. One option relies on a JavaScript library, and it follows a process similar to many other visualizations in the book. The other two techniques, however, offer a different perspective. In one, we won't use a visualization library at all. Instead, we'll build a timeline with basic JavaScript, HTML, and CSS, and we'll see how to do that both with and without jQuery. The final example shows the other extreme. It relies on a full-featured web component available from an external website. In short, we'll look at the following:

▶ How to use a library to create timelines

▶ How to create timelines without a library using only JavaScript, HTML, and CSS

▶ How to integrate a timeline component in a web page

Building Timelines with a Library

First, we'll build the timeline using the Chronoline.js library (*http://stoicloofah.github.io/chronoline.js/*), which works a lot like most of the other JavaScript libraries we've used in the book. You include the library in your page, define your data, and let the library create the visualization.

Step 1: Include the Required Libraries

The Chronoline.js library itself depends on a few other libraries, and we'll need to include all of them in our pages.

▶ jQuery (*http://jquery.com/*)

▶ qTip2, including its style sheet (*http://qtip2.com/*)

▶ Raphaël (*http://raphaeljs.com/*)

All of these libraries are popular enough for public content distribution networks to support, so we'll use CloudFlare's CDN in the following markup. We'll have to use our own resources, however, to host Chronoline.js itself. That library also defines its own style sheet.

```
<!DOCTYPE html>
<html lang="en">
  <head>
    <meta charset="utf-8">
    <title></title>
    <link rel="stylesheet" type="text/css"
        href="//cdnjs.cloudflare.com/ajax/libs/qtip2/2.2.0/jquery.qtip.css">
    <link rel="stylesheet" type="text/css"
        href="css/chronoline.css">
```

```
  </head>
  <body>
❶ <div id="timeline"></div>
    <script src="//cdnjs.cloudflare.com/ajax/libs/jquery/2.0.3/jquery.min.js">
    </script>
    <script src="//cdnjs.cloudflare.com/ajax/libs/qtip2/2.2.0/jquery.qtip.min.js">
    </script>
    <script src="//cdnjs.cloudflare.com/ajax/libs/raphael/2.1.2/raphael-min.js">
    </script>
    <script src="js/chronoline.js"></script>
  </body>
</html>
```

As you can see at ❶, we've set aside a `<div>` to hold our timeline. We've also included the JavaScript libraries as the last part of the `<body>` element, as that provides the best browser performance.

Step 2: Prepare the Data

The data for our timeline comes from Wikipedia (*http://en.wikipedia.org/wiki/Chronology_of_Shakespeare%27s_plays*). As a JavaScript object, that data might be structured like the following excerpt:

```
[
  {
    "play": "The Two Gentlemen of Verona",
    "date": "1589-1591",
    "record": "Francis Meres'...",
    "published": "First Folio (1623)",
    "performance": "adaptation by Benjamin Victor...",
    "evidence": "The play contains..."
  }, {
    "play": "The Taming of the Shrew",
    "date": "1590-1594",
    "record": "possible version...",
    "published": "possible version...",
    "performance": "According to Philip Henslowe...",
    "evidence": "Kier Elam posits..."
  }, {
    "play": "Henry VI, Part 2",
    "date": "1590-1591",
    "record": "version of the...",
    "published": "version of the...",
    "performance": "although it is known...",
    "evidence": "It is known..."
  },
  // Data set continues...
```

You can see the complete data set in the book's source code (*http://jsDataV.is/source/*).

Before we can use Chronoline.js, we have to convert the raw data into the format the library expects. Since we have jQuery available, we can take advantage of its .map() function for the conversion. (For details on .map(), see Step 7 of "Selecting Chart Content" on page 55.)

```
var events = $.map(plays, function(play) {
    var event = {};
    event.title = play.play;
❶  if (play.date.indexOf("-") !== -1) {
        var daterange = play.date.split("-");
❷      event.dates = [new Date(daterange[0], 0, 1),
                       new Date(daterange[1], 11, 31)]
    } else {
❸      event.dates = [new Date(play.date, 0, 1), new Date(play.date, 11, 31)]
    }
    return event;
});
```

As you can see from our data set, some of the plays have a single year as their date, while others have a range of years (two dates separated by a dash). To set the date range for Chronoline.js, we check for a dash at ❶. If one is present, we split the date string at that dash and set a multiyear range at ❷. Otherwise, we set the range to a single year at ❸.

> **NOTE:** Recall that the JavaScript Date object numbers months from 0 rather than 1.

Step 3: Draw the Timeline

To draw the timeline, we create a new Chronoline object, passing it the HTML container element, our event data, and any options. The HTML container element should be a native element, not a jQuery selection. To convert from a selection to a native element, we use the get() method. In this case, we want the first element, so we use the parameter 0.

```
$(function() {
    var timeline = new Chronoline($("#timeline").get(0), events, {});
}
```

If we try to use the default options of Chronoline.js with our data, however, the result is quite disappointing. (In fact, it's illegible and not worth reproducing at this point.) We can fix that in the next step with some additional options.

Step 4: Set Chronoline.js Options for the Data

The Chronoline.js library has default options that are well suited for its original application, but they don't work so well for Shakespeare's plays. Fortunately, we can change the options from the default values. As of this writing, Chronoline.js doesn't have much documentation on its options; to see the full set, you would normally have to examine the source code. We'll cover the most important options here, though.

One of the most obvious problems with the Chonoline.js defaults is the date shown in the initial view. Chronoline.js starts by displaying the current date by default. Since our timeline ends in 1613, the user would have to scroll backward for a long time to see anything meaningful. We can change this view by giving Chronoline.js a different start date for the initial view:

```
defaultStartDate: new Date(1589, 0, 1),
```

As long as we're setting the timeline to start somewhere near Shakespeare's lifetime, there's no need for Chronoline.js to add a special mark for the current date, so we use this simple option to tell it not to bother:

```
markToday: false,
```

The next major problem to address is the labeling. By default, Chronoline.js tries to label every day on the timeline. As our events span 24 years, we don't need that granularity. Instead, we can tell Chronoline.js just to label the years. For the same reason, we also need to change the checkmarks. Instead of every day, we need checkmarks only for every month.

To change both of these options, we supply Chronoline.js with a pair of functions to call.

```
hashInterval: function(date) {
    return date.getDate() === 1;
},
labelInterval: function(date) {
    return date.getMonth() === 0 && date.getDate() === 1;
},
```

Chronoline.js passes each of these functions a date object, and the functions return **true** or **false** depending on whether the date merits a checkmark or label. For checkmarks, we return **true** only on the first day of the month. We return **true** for labels only on January 1.

By default, Chronoline.js will try to show a full date for each label. Since we only want to label each year, we'll change the label format to just show the year. The details for the format specification are based on a standard C++ library (*http://www.cplusplus.com/reference/ctime/strftime/*).

```
labelFormat: "%Y",
```

For our last adjustments to the labeling, we remove the "sublabels" and "sub-sublabels" that Chronoline.js adds by default. Those labels don't provide any value in our case.

```
subLabel: null,
subSubLabel: null,
```

We also want to change the span of time that Chronoline.js displays in the timeline. For our data, showing a span of five years at a time seems good.

```
visibleSpan: DAY_IN_MILLISECONDS * 366 * 5,
```

Note that the variable `DAY_IN_MILLISECONDS` is defined by Chronoline.js itself. We're free to use it in this or any other option setting.

Now we can address the timeline scrolling. Chronoline.js normally advances the timeline by a single day with each click. That would result in some rather tedious scrolling for our users. Instead of the default behavior, we'll have Chronoline.js advance by a full year. As with the labels, we change this behavior by supplying Chronoline.js with a function. That function is passed a date object, and it should return a new date object to which Chronoline.js should scroll. In our case, we simply add or subtract one from the year value.

```
scrollLeft: function(date) {
    return new Date(date.getFullYear() - 1, date.getMonth(), date.getDate());
},
scrollRight: function(date) {
    return new Date(date.getFullYear() + 1, date.getMonth(), date.getDate());
},
```

The last few adjustments clean up the appearance and behavior of Chronoline.js. Adding some extra space (in our case, three months) before the start and after the end of the timeline gives the data a bit of room.

```
timelinePadding: DAY_IN_MILLISECONDS * 366 / 4,
```

We can also make the scrolling animate smoothly instead of jumping, enable users to drag the timeline right or left, and improve the default browser tool tips.

```
animated: true,
draggable: true,
tooltips: true,
```

For the final tweaks, we can change the appearance of the timeline. To change the color and size of the events, we use the following options:

```
eventAttrs: {  // attrs for the bars and circles of the events
    fill: "#ffa44f",
    stroke: "#ffa44f",
    "stroke-width": 1
},
eventHeight: 10,
```

To change the color of the scroll buttons, we have to modify the *chronoline.css* style sheet. The property to change is **background-color**.

```
.chronoline-left:hover,
.chronoline-right:hover {
    opacity: 1;
    filter: alpha(opacity=100);
    background-color: #97aceb;
}
```

With those changes, we finally have a timeline of Shakespeare's plays, as shown in Figure 5-1.

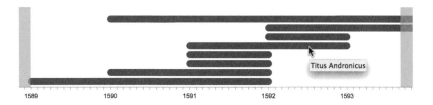

FIGURE 5-1: *The Chronoline.js library creates a simple, interactive timeline.*

The resulting timeline looks pretty good, but the limitations of the library make it difficult to customize and enhance the timeline further. Next, we'll build a new timeline from scratch without the library so we have complete control.

Building Timelines with JavaScript

If you followed the example in the previous section, you might not be completely satisfied with the results. We did end up with an accurate timeline of Shakespeare's plays, but the resulting visualization may not be communicating what you want. For example, the timeline doesn't show the names of the plays unless the user hovers a mouse over that section of the graph. Perhaps we'd rather have the plays' titles always visible. That kind of problem is a limitation of third-party libraries. The author of Chronoline.js didn't see the need for displaying titles, so he didn't offer the option. And unless we're willing to take on the potentially daunting task of modifying the library's source code, we can't make the library do exactly what we want.

Fortunately, particularly in the case of timelines, we can take a completely different approach. We can create visualizations without using any third-party library at all, which will give us total control over the result. Timelines are especially amenable to this technique because they can be created with nothing more than text and styling. All it takes is a basic understanding of HTML and CSS, plus enough JavaScript to set things up and perhaps provide simple interactions.

That's exactly what we'll do in this example. We'll start with the same data set as before. Instead of feeding that data into a third-party library, however, we'll use plain old JavaScript (with an optional dose of jQuery) to construct a pure HTML representation of the data. Then we'll use CSS to set the appearance of the timeline.

Step 1: Prepare the HTML Skeleton

Without any required libraries, the HTML page for our timeline is pretty simple. All we need is a containing `<div>` with a unique `id` attribute.

```
<!DOCTYPE html>
<html lang="en">
  <head>
    <meta charset="utf-8">
    <title></title>
  </head>
  <body>
    <div id="timeline"></div>
  </body>
</html>
```

Step 2: Start JavaScript Execution

As soon as the browser has finished loading our page, we can start processing the data. As before, we'll start with our data formatted as a JavaScript array. You can see the complete data set in the book's source code (*http://jsDataV.is/source/*).

```
window.onload = function () {
  var plays = [
    {
      "play": "The Two Gentlemen of Verona",
      "date": "1589-1591",
      "record": "Francis Meres'...",
      "published": "First Folio (1623)",
      "performance": "adaptation by Benjamin Victor...",
      "evidence": "The play contains..."
    }, {
      "play": "The Taming of the Shrew",
      "date": "1590-1594",
      "record": "possible version...",
      "published": "possible version...",
      "performance": "According to Philip Henslowe...",
      "evidence": "Kier Elam posits..."
    }, {
      "play": "Henry VI, Part 2",
      "date": "1590-1591",
      "record": "version of the...",
      "published": "version of the...",
      "performance": "although it is known...",
      "evidence": "It is known..."
    },
```

```
    // Data set continues...
}
```

Step 3: Create the Timeline in Semantic HTML

To create the timeline in HTML, we first need to decide how to represent it. If you're used to working with arbitrary `<div>` and `<span>` elements, you might think that's the best approach here as well. Instead of jumping right to these generic elements, however, we should consider other HTML structures that more accurately convey the content. HTML that more closely reflects the meaning of the underlying content is known as *semantic markup*, and it's usually preferred over generic `<div>` and `<span>` tags. Semantic markup exposes the meaning of your content to computers such as search engines and screen readers for users with visual impairments, and it can improve your site's search rank and accessibility. If we think about a timeline in the context of semantic markup, it's easy to see that the timeline is really just a list. In fact, it's a list with a specific order. We should build our HTML timeline, therefore, as an ordered list (`<ol>`) element. While we're creating the `<ol>`, we can also give it a class name for CSS style rules we'll be adding later.

```
var container = document.getElementById("timeline");
var list = document.createElement("ol");
list.className="timeline";
container.appendChild(list);
```

Next we can iterate through the plays, creating an individual list item, `<li>`, for each one. For now, we'll just insert the date and title as text.

```
plays.forEach(function(play) {
    var listItem = document.createElement("li");
    listItem.textContent = play.date + ": " + play.play;
    list.appendChild(listItem);
})
```

Figure 5-2 shows a truncated version of the resulting list. It may not look like much (yet), but it has the essential data and structure.

1. 1589-1591: The Two Gentlemen of Verona
2. 1590-1594: The Taming of the Shrew
3. 1590-1591: Henry VI, Part 2
4. 1591: Henry VI, Part 3
5. 1591: Henry VI, Part 1

FIGURE 5-2: *A pure HTML timeline can start out as a simple ordered list.*

If you look at the resulting HTML that underlies that list, it's pretty simple:

```
<ol class="timeline">
    <li>1589-1591: The Two Gentlemen of Verona</li>
```

```
    <li>1590-1594: The Taming of the Shrew</li>
    <li>1590-1591: Henry VI, Part 2</li>
    <li>1591: Henry VI, Part 3</li>
    <li>1591: Henry VI, Part 1</li>
</ol>
```

In the spirit of semantic HTML, we should stop and consider whether that markup can be improved. Since it appears first in our list items, let's consider the date or date range for a play. Although there has been some controversy around the decision, HTML5 has defined support for a `<time>` element to contain dates and times. Using that element as a wrapper will make our dates more semantic. The second part of each list item is the title of the play. As it happens, HTML5's `<cite>` element is perfect for that content. To quote the current standard (*http:// html.spec.whatwg.org*):

> The `<cite>` element represents the title of a work (e.g., a book, . . . **a play,** [emphasis added] . . . etc). This can be a work that is being quoted or referenced in detail (i.e., a citation), or it can just be a work that is mentioned in passing.

To add those elements to our code, we'll have to distinguish between dates that are single years and those that are ranges. Looking for a dash (-) in the data will tell us which we have.

```
plays.forEach(function(play) {
    var listItem = document.createElement("li");
    if (play.date.indexOf("-") !== -1) {
❶      var dates = play.date.split("-");
        var time = document.createElement("time");
        time.textContent = dates[0];
        listItem.appendChild(time);
        time = document.createElement("time");
        time.textContent = dates[1];
❷      listItem.appendChild(time);
    } else {
        var time = document.createElement("time");
        time.textContent = play.date;
        listItem.appendChild(time);
    }
    var cite = document.createElement("cite");
    cite.textContent = play.play;
    listItem.appendChild(cite);
    list.appendChild(listItem);
})
```

Notice how we handle date ranges (❶ through ❷). Since a range has a start and end time, we create two distinct `<time>` elements. We don't need to add any punctuation between the dates at this point.

Because we're no longer including the punctuation, the resulting output (shown in Figure 5-3) might look a little worse than before. Don't worry, though; we'll fix it soon.

1. 15891591 *The Two Gentlemen of Verona*
2. 15901594 *The Taming of the Shrew*
3. 15901591 *Henry VI, Part 2*
4. 1591 *Henry VI, Part 3*
5. 1591 *Henry VI, Part 1*

FIGURE 5-3: *Semantic markup simplifies the required HTML, but it may require special styling.*

What *is* much improved is the underlying HTML. The markup clearly identifies the type of content it contains: an ordered list of dates and citations.

```
<ol class="timeline">
    <li><time>1589</time><time>1591</time><cite>The Two Gentlemen of Verona
    </cite></li>
    <li><time>1590</time><time>1594</time><cite>The Taming of the Shrew
    </cite></li>
    <li><time>1590</time><time>1591</time><cite>Henry VI, Part 2</cite></li>
    <li><time>1591</time><cite>Henry VI, Part 3</cite></li>
    <li><time>1591</time><cite>Henry VI, Part 1</cite></li>
</ol>
```

Step 4: Include the Supporting Content

When we created a timeline using the Chronoline.js library, we weren't able to include the supporting content from Wikipedia, because the library did not offer that option. In this example, though, we have complete control over the content, so let's include that information in our timeline. For most plays, our data includes its first official record, its first publication, its first performance, and a discussion of the evidence. This type of content is perfectly matched to the HTML *description list* (`<dl>`), so that's how we'll add it to our page. It can follow the `<cite>` of the play's title.

```
plays.forEach(function(play) {
    // Additional code...
    listItem.appendChild(cite);
    var descList = document.createElement("dl");
    // Add terms to the list here
    listItem.appendChild(descList);
    list.appendChild(listItem);
})
```

We can define a mapping array to help add the individual terms to each play. That array maps the property name in our data set to the label we want to use in the content.

```
var descTerms = [
    { key: "record",      label: "First official record"},
    { key: "published",   label: "First published"},
    { key: "performance", label: "First recorded performance"},
    { key: "evidence",    label: "Evidence"},
];
```

With that array we can quickly add the descriptions to our content. We iterate over the array using `.forEach()`.

```
plays.forEach(function(play) {
    // Additional code...
    listItem.appendChild(cite);
    var descList = document.createElement("dl");
    descTerms.forEach(function(term) {
❶      if (play[term.key]) {
            var descTerm = document.createElement("dt");
            descTerm.textContent = term.label;
            descList.appendChild(descTerm);
            var descElem = document.createElement("dd");
            descElem.textContent = play[term.key];
            descList.appendChild(descElem);
        }
    });
    listItem.appendChild(descList);
    list.appendChild(listItem);
})
```

At each iteration, we make sure that the data has content (❶) before creating the description item. A description item contains the term(s) being described in one `<dt>` tag and the description itself in a `<dd>` tag.

Our timeline is still lacking a bit of visual appeal, but it has a much richer set of content, as you can see in Figure 5-4. In fact, even without any styling at all, it still communicates the essential data quite well.

Here's the resulting markup (truncated for brevity):

```
<ol class="timeline">
    <li>
        <time>1589</time><time>1591</time>
        <cite>The Two Gentlemen of Verona</cite>
        <dl>
            <dt>First official record</dt><dd>Francis Meres'...</dd>
            <dt>First published</dt><dd>First Folio (1623)</dd>
            <dt>First recorded performance</dt><dd>adaptation by...</dd>
            <dt>Evidence</dt><dd>The play contains...</dd>
        </dl>
    </li>
    <li>
        <time>1590</time><time>1594</time><cite>The Taming of the Shrew</cite>
        <dl>
```

```
        <dt>First official record</dt><dd>possible version...</dd>
        <dt>First published</dt><dd>possible version...</dd>
        <dt>First recorded performance</dt><dd>According to Philip...</dd>
        <dt>Evidence</dt><dd>Kier Elam posits...</dd>
      </dl>
    </li>
</ol>
```

1. 1589 1591 *The Two Gentlemen of Verona*

First official record	Francis Meres' Palladis Tamia (1598); referred to as "Gentlemen of Verona"
First published	First Folio (1623)
First recorded performance	adaptation by Benjamin Victor performed at David Garrick's Theatre Royal, Drury Lane in 1762. Earliest known performance of straight Shakespearean text at Royal Opera House in 1784, although because of the reference to the play in Palladis Tamia, we know it was definitely performed in Shakespeare's day.
Evidence	The play contains passages which seem to borrow from John Lyly's Midas (1589), meaning it could not have been written prior to 1589. Additionally, Stanley Wells argues that the scenes involving more than four characters, "betray an uncertainty of technique suggestive of inexperience." As such, the play is considered to be one of the first Shakespeare composed upon arriving in London (Roger Warren, following E.A.J. Honigmann, suggests he may have written it prior to his arrival) and, as such, he lacked theatrical experience. This places the date of composition as most likely somewhere between 1589 and 1591, by which time it is known he was working on the Henry VI plays

FIGURE 5-4: *HTML makes it easy to add extra content to the list.*

Step 5: Optionally Take Advantage of jQuery

Our code so far has used nothing but plain JavaScript. If you're using jQuery on your web pages, you can shorten the code a bit by taking advantage of some jQuery features. If your web pages aren't using jQuery already, the minor enhancements in this step don't justify adding it, but if you'd like to see a more concise version, check out the book's source code for an alternative.

Step 6: Fix Timeline Problems with CSS

Now that we've built our timeline's content in HTML, it's time to define the styles that determine its appearance. Throughout this example, we'll focus on the functional aspects of styling rather than pure visual elements such as fonts and colors, since you'll probably want those visual styles to be specific to your own website.

The first step is a simple one. We want to get rid of the numbering (1, 2, 3 . . .) that browsers normally add to ordered list items. A single rule banishes them from our timeline: by setting the `list-style-type` to `none`, we tell the browser not to add any special characters to our list items.

```
.timeline li {
    list-style-type: none;
}
```

We can also use CSS rules to add some punctuation to our semantic HTML. First we look for places where two `<time>` elements appear right after each other, while skipping isolated `<time>` tags.

```
.timeline li > time + time:before {
    content: "-";
}
```

The trick to finding `<time>` pairs is the CSS adjacent selector +. A rule with `time + time` specifies a `<time>` element that immediately follows a `<time>` element. To add the punctuation, we use the `:before` pseudoselector to specify what we want to happen *before* this second `<time>` tag, and we set the `content` property to indicate the content we want inserted.

If you haven't seen the > before in a CSS rule, it's the *direct descendant selector*. In this example, it means that the `<time>` element must be an immediate child of the `<li>` element. We're using this selector so our rules won't inadvertently apply to other `<time>` elements that may be nested deeper within the list item's content.

To finish up the punctuation, let's add a colon and space after the last of the `<time>` elements in each list item.

```
.timeline li > time:last-of-type:after {
    content: ": ";
}
```

We use two pseudoselectors for this rule. The `:last-of-type` selector targets the last `<time>` element in the list item. That's the first `<time>` if there's only one, and the second `<time>` if both are present. Then we add the `:after` pseudoselector to insert content after that `<time>` element.

With these changes, we've cleaned up all of the obvious problems with our timeline (see Figure 5-5).

1589-1591: *The Two Gentlemen of Verona*

First official record	Francis Meres'…
First published	First Folio (1623)
First recorded performance	adaptation by…
Evidence	The play contains…

1590-1594: *The Taming of the Shrew*

First official record	possible version…
First published	possible version…
First recorded performance	According to Philip…
Evidence	Kier Elam posits…

FIGURE 5-5: *CSS styles make the timeline easier to read without changing the markup.*

Now we can add a little flair to the visualization.

Step 7: Add Styles to Visually Structure the Timeline

The next set of CSS styles will improve the visual structure of the timeline. First among those improvements will be making the timeline look more like, well, a *line*. To do that, we can add a border to the left side of the <li> elements. At the same time, we'll also want to make sure that those <li> elements don't have any margins, as margins would introduce gaps in the border and break the continuity of the line.

```
.timeline li {
    border-left: 2px solid black;
}
.timeline dl,
.timeline li {
    margin: 0;
}
```

These styles add a nice vertical line on the left side of our entire timeline. Now that we have that line, we can shift the dates over to the left side of it. The shift requires rules for the parent <li> as well as the <time> elements. For the parent <li> elements, we want their position specified as relative.

```
.timeline li {
    position: relative;
}
```

By itself, this rule doesn't actually change our timeline. It does, however, establish a *positioning context* for any elements that are children of the <li>. Those children include the <time> elements that we want to move. With the <li> set to position: relative, we can now set the <time> children to position: absolute. This rule lets us specify exactly where the browser should place the time elements, *relative* to the parent <li>. We want to move all <time> elements to the left, and we want to move the second <time> element down.

```
.timeline li > time {
    position: absolute;
    left: -3.5em;
}
.timeline li > time + time {
    top: 1em;
    left: -3.85em;
}
```

In the previous code, the first selector targets both of our <time> tags, while the second selector, using the same time + time trick described earlier, targets only the second of two <time> tags.

By using em units rather than px (pixel) units for this shift, we define the shift to be relative to the current font size, regardless of what it is. That gives us the freedom to change the font size without having to go back and tweak any pixel positioning.

The specific values for the position shift may need adjustment depending on the specific font face, but, in general, we use a negative `left` position to shift content farther to the left than it would normally appear, and a positive `top` position to move the content down the page.

After moving the dates to the left of the vertical line, we'll also want to shift the main content a bit to the right so it doesn't crowd up against the line. The `padding-left` property takes care of that. And while we're adjusting the left padding, we can also add a bit of padding on the bottom to separate each play from the other.

```
.timeline li {
    padding-left: 1em;
    padding-bottom: 1em;
}
```

With the dates and the main content on opposite sides of our vertical line, we no longer need any punctuation after the date, so we'll remove the style that adds a colon after the last `<time>` element.

```
.timeline li > time:last-of-type:after {
    content: ": ";
}
```

The fact that we're able to make this change highlights one of the reasons for using CSS to add the colon in the first place. If we had included the punctuation explicitly in the markup (by, for example, generating it in the JavaScript code), then our markup would be more tightly coupled to our styles. If a style modification changed whether the colon was appropriate, we would have to go back and change the JavaScript as well. With the approach that we're using here, however, styles and markup are much more independent. Any style changes are isolated to our CSS rules; no modifications to the JavaScript are required.

To further improve its visual styling, we can make a few other changes to our timeline. We can increase the font size for each play's title to make that information more prominent. At the same time, we can add some extra spacing below the title and indent the description list a bit.

```
.timeline li > cite {
    font-size: 1.5em;
    line-height: 1em;
    padding-bottom: 0.5em;
}
.timeline dl {
    padding-left: 1.5em;
}
```

For a last bit of polish, let's add a bullet right on the vertical line to mark each play and tie the title more closely to the dates. We use a large bullet (several times the normal size) and position it right over the line.

```
.timeline li > time:first-of-type:after {
    content: "\2022";
    font-size: 3em;
    line-height: 0.4em;
    position: absolute;
    right: -0.65em;
    top: 0.1em;
}
```

As you can see, the Unicode character for a bullet can be represented as "\2022". The exact position values will depend on the specific font, but a bit of trial and error can perfect the adjustments.

Now our timeline is starting to look like an actual timeline (as shown in Figure 5-6). In your own pages, you could include additional styles to define fonts, colors, and so on, but even without those decorations the visualization is effective.

FIGURE 5-6: *Additional styles clarify the structure of the timeline elements.*

Step 8: Add Interactivity

The full details on all 40 of Shakespeare's plays might be a little overwhelming for a first view of our timeline. The visualization would be more effective if it showed only the play titles at first, but let users reveal more details through interactions. Because we're building this visualization ourselves, we have all the control necessary to make that happen.

First we'll set up a few additional styles. There are several ways to hide the play details with CSS, the most obvious being the `display:none` property. As we'll see a little later, though, a better choice for our timeline is setting the `max-height` to 0. If the maximum height of an element is 0, then, in theory, it should be invisible. In practice, we also have to set the `overflow` property to `hidden`. Otherwise, even though the `<dl>` element itself has no height, the browser will display the content that overflows from it. Since we want our description lists to start out hidden, we can set that property as the default.

```
.timeline li dl {
    max-height: 0;
    overflow: hidden;
}
```

To reveal a play's details, users click on the play's title in the `<cite>` element. To indicate to users that they can click on the title, we'll change the mouse cursor from the normal arrow to the "clickable" hand. We can also change the `display` property from the default `inline` to `block`. That change gives users a larger and more consistent area to click.

```
.timeline li > cite {
    cursor: pointer;
    display: block;
}
```

Finally, we need a way to reveal a play's details. We'll do that by adding a class of `"expanded"` to the `<li>` for the play. When that class is present, our styles should override the `max-height` of 0.

```
.timeline li.expanded dl {
    max-height: 40em;
}
```

The exact value for the expanded `max-height` will depend on the content. In general, though, it should be large enough to reveal the full details for the item. It's okay to make it a little larger than necessary "just in case." Don't go overboard, however, and make it unreasonably large. (We'll see why at the end of this step.)

With these styles in place, we can add a bit of JavaScript to control them. It won't take much. The first step is writing an event handler that will be called when users click.

```
var clicked = function(ev) {
    if (ev.target.nodeName === "CITE") {
        // Code continues...
    }
};
```

This function takes a single parameter, specifically an **Event** object, with details about the click. One of those details is the `.target` property, which will contain a reference to the specific element of the page on which the user clicked. We care only about clicks on the `<cite>` elements.

Once we know that a `<cite>` was clicked, we find its parent `<li>` element. We can then check to see if the `<li>` has the `"expanded"` class. If it doesn't, we add it. If the class is already present, we remove it.

```
var clicked = function(ev) {
    if (ev.target.nodeName === "CITE") {
```

```
        var li = ev.target.parentNode;
        if (li.className === "expanded") {
            li.className = "";
        } else {
            li.className = "expanded";
        }
    }
};
```

Our approach is a bit primitive because it allows only one class to be defined for the `<li>`. That's all we need for this example, though, so we'll stick with it.

> **✳ NOTE:** Modern browsers have a more sophisticated interface for controlling the class attributes of elements. That interface is the `classList`, and it easily supports multiple classes per element, as well as toggling the class on and off with a single function. Older browsers (namely IE9 and earlier) don't support that interface, however. Since we don't need the extra functionality, the older `className` is sufficient for this example.

With our event handling function defined, we can associate it with clicks anywhere on the timeline. The standard `addEventListener` method creates the association for any element.

```
document.getElementById("timeline").addEventListener("click", clicked);
```

You might be curious as to why we're associating an event listener with the entire timeline visualization instead of, for example, adding individual event listeners to each `<cite>`. That alternative would eliminate the need to check the event target in the handler; however, it turns out that it's much less efficient than the approach we're taking. Event listeners can consume a fair bit of JavaScript resources, and our page will perform better if we keep them to a minimum.

If you're using jQuery, the required code is even simpler:

```
$("#timeline").on("click", "cite", function() {
    $(this).parent("li").toggleClass("expanded");
})
```

We're almost ready to show our new and improved timeline to the world, but there's one final refinement we can make. Our current version shows or hides a play's details all at once. This transition can be abrupt to users, as content appears or disappears instantly. We can provide a better experience by gracefully transitioning between the two states, and a natural transition for this timeline is animating the height of the content. When the details are hidden, they have a height of 0. And when we want to show them, we will gradually animate the height to its natural value.

It's possible to add these animations using JavaScript. The jQuery library, in fact, has a fairly extensive set of animation functions. In modern browsers, however, it is much better to animate content using CSS transitions. Web browsers are optimized for CSS, often offloading the computations to special high-performance graphics coprocessors. In those cases, CSS-based animations can perform several orders of magnitude better than JavaScript. The only disadvantage to using CSS for animations is a lack of support in older browsers. But animation isn't usually *critical* to most web pages. Sure, it's nice, but if a user with an older browser misses out on the graceful transitions, it isn't the end of the world. The web page will still *function* just fine.

The CSS `transition` property is the simplest way to define a CSS animation. It specifies the actual property to animate, the duration of the animation, and the *easing function* to follow. Here's a rule we could use in our example:

```
.timeline li dl {
    transition: max-height 500ms ease-in-out;
}
```

This rule defines a transition for the timeline's `<dl>` elements. It specifies that the property to animate is `max-height`, so the transition will take effect whenever an element's `max-height` property changes (and that's precisely the property we modify when the `"expanded"` class is added or removed). The transition rule also specifies that the animation should take 500 milliseconds, and that it should "ease in" and "ease out." This last property indicates that the animation should start slowly, speed up, and then slow down again before finishing. That behavior usually looks more natural than animating at a constant speed.

CSS transitions can animate many CSS properties, but there is one important constraint. Both the starting and ending values must be explicit. That constraint explains why we're animating `max-height` instead of `height`, even though it's really just `height` that we want to change. Unfortunately, we can't animate `height`, because it has no explicit value when the description list is expanded. Every `<dl>` will have its own height based on its content, and there's no way we can predict those values in our CSS. The `max-height` property, on the other hand, gives us explicit values for both states—0 and 40em in this example—so CSS can animate its transitions. We just have to be sure that no `<dl>` has content more than 40em high. Otherwise, the extra content will be cut off. This doesn't mean, however, that we should set the `max-height` for expanded `<dl>` elements to an astronomical value. To see why, consider what would happen if we transitioned `max-height` to 1000em for a `<dl>` that needed only 10em of height. Ignoring (for simplicity) the complications of easing, it would take only 1/100 of the full transition time before the full content of the element was visible. The animation that we had planned to take 500 milliseconds is over in 5 milliseconds instead.

There is one final complication with CSS transitions. Most browsers implemented the functionality before the official standard was finalized. To make sure their implementations wouldn't conflict with potential changes in the official standards, browser vendors initially implemented transitions using a proprietary syntax. That syntax adds a prefix (`-webkit-` for Safari and Chrome, `-moz-` for Firefox, and `-o-` for Opera) to the property name. To cover all the major browsers, we must include a rule with each prefix.

```
.timeline li dl {
    -webkit-transition: max-height 500ms ease-in-out;
       -moz-transition: max-height 500ms ease-in-out;
         -o-transition: max-height 500ms ease-in-out;
            transition: max-height 500ms ease-in-out;
}
```

✳ **NOTE:** Internet Explorer doesn't need a prefix, because Microsoft didn't implement transitions until the standard was stable. Also, there's no harm in specifying multiple prefixes, since browsers simply ignore properties they don't understand.

Now our handcrafted timeline responds perfectly to user interactions. Figure 5-7 shows the complete visualization.

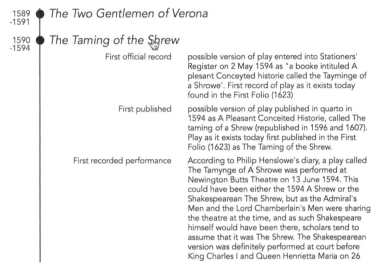

FIGURE 5-7: *A fully interactive timeline requires only HTML, CSS, and a little JavaScript.*

Using a Web Component

In this example, we'll look at another alternative approach; instead of building a timeline from scratch using low-level JavaScript, we'll integrate a full-featured timeline component: TimelineJS (*http://timeline.knightlab.com/*). In many ways this approach is the exact opposite of low-level JavaScript. At its most basic, it requires no coding at all; it can be as easy as embedding a YouTube video in a blog post. That method sacrifices a lot of control over the resulting visualization, however, so we'll also look at ways to regain some of that control.

Step 1: Preview the Standard Component

Before we spend too much time customizing the visualization, it's worthwhile to check out the component in its most basic form. Fortunately, TimelineJS makes this process very simple. The website (*http://timeline.knightlab.com/*) will walk you through the steps in detail, but in a nutshell, they are as follows:

1. Create a Google Docs spreadsheet (*http://docs.google.com/*) with data for the timeline.
2. Publish that spreadsheet for web access, which will create a URL for it.
3. Enter that URL into a form on the TimelineJS website, which will generate an HTML snippet.
4. Copy and paste the snippet into your web page.

Figure 5-8 shows what the spreadsheet (*https://docs.google.com/spreadsheet/ccc?key=0An4ME25ELRdYdDk4WmRacmxjaDM0V0tDTk9vMnQxU1E#gid=0*) looks like for Shakespeare's plays.

FIGURE 5-8: The TimelineJS component can get its data from a Google Docs spreadsheet.

The HTML snippet that TimelineJS creates for this timeline is as follows:

```
<iframe src="http://cdn.knightlab.com/libs/timeline/latest/embed/index.html?
    source=0An4ME25ELRdYdDk4WmRacmxjaDMOVOtDTk9vMnQxU1E&font=Bevan-PotanoSans&
    maptype=toner&lang=en&height=650" width="100%" height="650"
frameborder="0">
</iframe>
```

When included in a page, that snippet results in fully interactive timeline for the chronology, as shown in Figure 5-9.

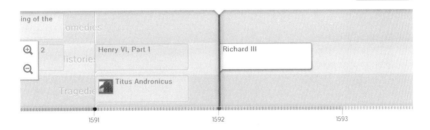

Richard III

It is known that Richard III was definitely a sequel to 3 Henry VI, which was on-stage by 25 June 1592, hence Richard III must have been written later than early 1592. Additionally, it has been argued that the play contains evidence suggesting it was originally written for Strange's Men, but then rewritten for Pembroke's Men, a company which formed in mid-1592. Also, with the closure of the theatres due to an outbreak of plague in June 1592, the play was unlikely to have been written any later than that, all of which suggests a date of composition as sometime in early-1592.

FIGURE 5-9: *TimelineJS builds a complete timeline component within an `<iframe>`.*

If the result meets the needs of your visualization, you may not have to go any further. Many web pages that use TimelineJS do so in exactly this manner. There are some potential problems with the simplest approach, however:

▸ The data for the visualization must be available in a public Google Docs spreadsheet, so the approach may not be appropriate for confidential data.

▸ The data source is a spreadsheet, so it may be difficult to update it often or show more real-time events. This problem doesn't really affect our Shakespeare chronology, but if the timeline you're creating shows real-time data such as trending topics on a social network, a static spreadsheet won't be practical.

▸ The embedded component has few styling options. Although the default styles and options that TimelineJS offers are quite attractive, they are very limited and may not be appropriate for your web page.

- The timeline is embedded as an `<iframe>`, which gives TimelineJS complete control over what is displayed in that section of your page. While there is *absolutely no indication* that the organizations supporting TimelineJS would do so, *in theory* they could alter the content (for example, by including ads) in ways that your site might not find appropriate.

Fortunately, none of these possible concerns need prevent us from adding beautiful TimelineJS visualizations to our web pages. The folks behind TimelineJS make all of the software available as open source, giving us the flexibility to address all of the aforementioned issues. We'll see how in the rest of this example.

Step 2: Include the Required Components

To use TimelineJS, our web pages must include CSS style sheets and JavaScript code. For now we'll stick with the default styles, so we need only a single additional style sheet. The main JavaScript is contained in timeline.js.

It's not obvious, but TimelineJS also requires jQuery. When you embed a TimelineJS `<iframe>`, your main web page doesn't have to include jQuery, because the `<iframe>` will include it. To integrate the timeline directly in our page, though, we have to include jQuery explicitly. We can, however, use a content distribution network instead of hosting it ourselves. (See Chapter 2 for more details on the advantages and disadvantages of content distribution networks.)

```html
<!DOCTYPE html>
<html lang="en">
  <head>
    <meta charset="utf-8">
    <title></title>
    <link rel="stylesheet" type="text/css" href="css/timeline.css">
  </head>
  <body>
    <script src="//cdnjs.cloudflare.com/ajax/libs/jquery/2.0.3/jquery.min.js">
    </script>
    <script src="js/timeline-min.js"></script>
  </body>
</html>
```

The HTML at this point doesn't include the element in which we'll place the timeline. There are some special constraints on that element, which we'll consider when we add it to the page.

Step 3: Prepare the Data

Because TimelineJS supports several features that we haven't used in the earlier examples, we'll add a few additional properties to our data set. The overall format, though, looks the same as before:

```javascript
var plays = [
  {
    "play": "The Two Gentlemen of Verona",
```

```
      "genre": "Comedies",
      "date": "1589-1591",
      "record": "Francis Meres'...",
      "published": "First Folio (1623)",
      "performance": "adaptation by Benjamin Victor...",
      "evidence": "The play contains..."
    }, {
      "play": "The Taming of the Shrew",
      "genre": "Comedies",
      "date": "1590-1594",
      "record": "possible version...",
      "published": "possible version...",
      "performance": "According to Philip Henslowe...",
      "evidence": "Kier Elam posits..."
    }, {
      "play": "Henry VI, Part 2",
      "genre": "Histories",
      "date": "1590-1591",
      "record": "version of the...",
      "published": "version of the...",
      "performance": "although it is known...",
      "evidence": "It is known..."
      "media": "http://upload.wikimedia.org/wikipedia/commons/9/96/
FirstFolioHenryVI2.jpg",
      "credit": "Wikimedia Commons",
      "caption": "Photo of the first page..."
    // Data set continues...
},
```

As you can see, we've added genre information to the plays, as well as optional multimedia links, and text for credits and captions. With that starting point, we can rearrange the data to match what TimelineJS expects. The basic structure of that object, shown next, includes some overall properties (such as the headline), and an array of events. We can initialize it to an empty array.

```
var timelineData = {
    headline: "Chronology of Shakespeare's Plays",
    type: "default",
    date: []
};
```

Note that the type property is required and should be set to "default".

Now we iterate through the data set, adding events to timelineData. For the following code, we'll use forEach for this iteration, but there are plenty of alternatives we could use here (including for loops, array .map() methods, or jQuery's $.each() and $.map() functions).

```
plays.forEach(function(play) {
    var start = play.date;
    var end = "";
    if (play.date.indexOf("-") !== -1) {
        var dates = play.date.split("-");
        start = dates[0];
        end = dates[1];
    }
});
```

The first step in each iteration is parsing the date information. It can take one of two forms: either a single year ("1591") or a range of years ("1589-1591"). Our code assumes a single date and makes adjustments if it finds two.

Now we can provide the full entry for the event in TimelineJS format by pushing the new object into the `timelineData.date` array.

```
timelineData.date.push({
    startDate: start,
    endDate: end,
    headline: play.play,
    text: play.evidence,
    tag: play.genre,
    asset: {
        media: play.media,
        credit: play.credit,
        caption: play.caption
    }
});
```

Step 4: Create a Default Timeline

With our HTML set up and our data set prepared, we can now call TimelineJS to create its default visualization. Figuring out exactly how to do that, however, isn't quite as simple as looking in the documentation. That's because TimelineJS assumes that it will be used primarily as an embedded and isolated component rather than an integrated part of a page. The documentation, therefore, describes how to use TimelineJS using the *storyjs_embed.js* wrapper for embedded content. That wrapper loads all the TimelineJS resources (style sheets, JavaScript, fonts, and so on), and if we use it as intended, we'll end up with most of the same problems as if we had simply embedded an `<iframe>`.

Fortunately, it's not too difficult to skip all the embedding and simply access the JavaScript code directly. It requires only three steps:

1. Set up the configuration object.
2. Create a TimelineJS object.
3. Initialize the object using the configuration object.

Here's what these steps will look like in our JavaScript, with the details omitted for now:

```
var timelineConfig = {/* Needs properties */};
var timelinejs = new VMM.Timeline(/* Needs parameters */);
timelinejs.init(timelineConfig);
```

We still need to fill in the exact configuration object and the parameters for the VMM.Timeline constructor. The configuration object is documented in the TimelineJS source (*https://github.com/NUKnightLab/TimelineJS#config-options*). We must provide a type (equal to "timeline"), dimensions, the data source, and the id of the HTML element into which the timeline should be placed. For example, we could use this:

```
var timelineConfig = {
        type:       "timeline",
        width:      "100%",
        height:     "600",
        source:     {timeline: timelineData},
        embed_id:   "timeline"
};
```

We have to pass many of those same parameters to the constructor. In particular, we provide the container's id and the dimensions.

```
var timelinejs = new VMM.Timeline("timeline","100%","600px");
```

Finally, we have to build our HTML markup with care. TimelineJS styles its HTML appropriately for an embedded <iframe>, but those styles aren't as compatible with a timeline that's integrated in the page. In particular, it positions the timeline absolutely and sets its z-index. If we don't compensate, the timeline will float out of the flow of the page content, which is almost certainly not desirable. There are several ways to adjust for this issue, and we'll use a simple one in this example. Instead of a single <div>, we use two nested <div> elements. The inner <div> will contain the timeline, and the outer <div> establishes both a positioning context and size for the timeline.

```
<div style="position:relative;height:600px;">
    <div id="timeline"></div>
</div>
```

Now when our JavaScript executes, it produces the integrated timeline shown in Figure 5-10 with the default TimelineJS styling.

Before we leave this step, it's worth considering how we've reached this point. We've taken a complete web component with explicit instructions for its use, and ignored those instructions. Instead, we've included only part of the component (albeit a major part). Figuring out how to use an isolated part of a web component (in a way that it isn't necessarily intended for) can involve some guesswork and trial and error, and there is clearly some risk in this approach. Even if you manage to get it working now, a future update might invalidate your implementation. If you adopt this approach with your website, it's a good idea to test the implementation thoroughly and to take extra care with any updates.

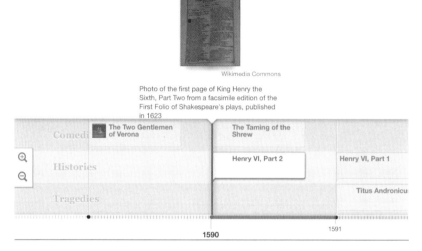

FIGURE 5-10: *With a little extra work, we can embed a TimelineJS timeline directly in the page without an `<iframe>`.*

Step 5: Adjust the Timeline Styles

Now that we've addressed the issues that an `<iframe>` can cause, we can turn our attention to the timeline's appearance. The *timeline.css* stylesheet determines that appearance, and there are several alternatives for adjusting it.

Modify *timeline.css* directly   Although this approach might seem the most obvious, it's probably not what we should do. If you look at the file, you'll notice that it's compressed CSS that's difficult to read and understand. Making the appropriate modifications will be challenging. Furthermore, if we later update to a new version of TimelineJS, that new version may well have a new *timeline.css* file, and we'd have to start all over again.

Work with the source code   TimelineJS authors its styles using the LESS (*http://lesscss.org/*) CSS preprocessor. If you're comfortable using a CSS preprocessor, you could modify the source and build your own custom version of *timeline.css*. LESS has support for variables and mixins that make it easier to accommodate updates in the future. There are many applications that compile LESS into CSS; TimelineJS uses CodeKit (*https://incident57.com/ codekit/*), which is available only for Apple's Mac OS X, and the source code includes all of the appropriate application settings.

Supersede *timeline.css* styles   Instead of changing the TimelineJS style sheet, leave it *as is* and add custom styles with a higher priority than the default styles. This approach takes advantage of the *cascade* in Cascading Style Sheets.

For this example, we'll use the last approach. We'll identify the *timeline.css* styles that we want to change and add new rules to our style sheet to take precedence over those styles. When CSS finds that multiple, conflicting rules apply to an element, it resolves the conflict by considering the specificity of the rules and their order in the document. We can give our rules priority by making them more specific than the *timeline.css* rules, or by making them equally specific but including them after *timeline.css*.

First we'll tackle the fonts that TimelineJS uses. There's nothing wrong with the default or optional fonts, but they may not match the style of our web page. In addition, downloading extra fonts will slow the performance of the page. The quickest way to find the styles that affect fonts is to look at one of the optional font selections that TimelineJS offers on its website. For example, if you select the "Merriweather & News Cycle" option, you'll see that TimelineJS adds an additional style sheet to the visualization, *NewsCycle-Merriweather.css*, which defines all the font rules for this option:

```
.vco-storyjs {
    font-family: "News Cycle", sans-serif;
}

/* Additional styles... */

.timeline-tooltip {
    font-family: "News Cycle", sans-serif
}
```

To use our own fonts, all we need to do is copy that file and replace "News Cycle" and "Merriweather" with our own choice—in this case, Avenir.

```
.vco-storyjs {
    font-family: "Avenir","Helvetica Neue",Helvetica,Arial,sans-serif;
    font-weight: 700;
}

/* Additional styles... */

.timeline-tooltip {
    font-family: "Avenir", sans-serif;
}
```

Customizing other aspects of the TimelineJS visualization is more challenging but not impossible. These customizations are rather fragile, however, as even the slightest change in the TimelineJS implementation could render them ineffective. If it's important for your page, though, it can be done.

For our example, we'll change the blue color that TimelineJS uses in the bottom section of the visualization. It uses that color to highlight the active item, to show the timeline marker, and for the event line. Finding the specific rules to override takes a bit of detective work with your browser's developer tools, but here's how to change the color from blue to green:

```
.vco-timeline .vco-navigation .timenav .content .marker.active .flag
.flag-content h3,
.vco-timeline .vco-navigation .timenav .content .marker.active .flag-small
.flag-content h3 {
    color: green;
}
.vco-timeline .vco-navigation .timenav-background .timenav-line {
    background-color: green;
}
.vco-timeline .vco-navigation .timenav .content .marker .line .event-line,
.vco-timeline .vco-navigation .timenav .content .marker.active .line
.event-line,
.vco-timeline .vco-navigation .timenav .content .marker.active .dot,
.vco-timeline .vco-navigation .timenav .content .marker.active .line {
    background: green;
}
```

Combining font changes with the alternative color scheme helps the visualization integrate more seamlessly in an overall web page, as Figure 5-11 shows.

1590 — 1591 `Histories`

Henry VI, Part 2

It is known that 3 Henry VI was on stage by June 1592, and it is also known that 3 Henry VI was definitely a sequel to 2 Henry VI, meaning 2 Henry VI must also have been on stage by early 1592. This places the likely date of composition as 1590-1591.

Wikimedia Commons

Photo of the first page of King Henry the Sixth, Part Two from a facsimile edition of the First Folio of Shakespeare's plays, published in 1623

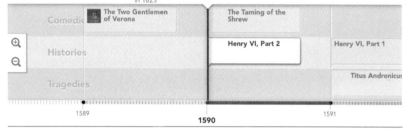

FIGURE 5-11: *Adjusting the CSS for TimelineJS can help match its styles with the rest of the web page.*

Summing Up

In this chapter, we've looked at a wide range of approaches for creating timeline visualizations. The most familiar approach relies on an open source library, but we also considered two other options. In one, we developed the code for a timeline from scratch, which gave us complete control over its appearance and behavior. For the other extreme, we examined a popular open source web component. Pages normally use that component by embedding `<iframe>` elements in the page, but we also saw that it's possible to take the open source code and integrate it more seamlessly in our pages, even altering the visual styles if necessary.

6
Visualizing Geographic Data

Humans crave context when evaluating data, so it's important to provide that context when it's available. In the previous chapter, we saw how timelines can provide one frame of reference; now we'll examine another equally important context: place. If a data set includes geographic coordinates or has values that correspond to different geographic regions, you can provide geographic context using a map-based visualization. The examples in this chapter consider two types of map-based visualizations.

In the first two examples, we want to show how data varies by region. The resulting visualizations, known as choropleth maps, use color to highlight different characteristics of the different regions. For the next two examples, the visualization data doesn't itself vary by region directly, but the data does have a geographic component. By showing the data on a map, we can help our users understand it.

More specifically, we'll see the following:

▸ How to use special map fonts to create maps with minimal JavaScript

▸ How to manipulate Scalable Vector Graphic (SVG) image maps with JavaScript

▸ How to use a simple mapping library to add maps to web pages

▸ How to integrate a full-featured map library into a visualization

Using Map Fonts

One technique for adding maps to web pages is surprisingly simple but often overlooked—map fonts. Two examples of these fonts are Stately (*http://intridea .github.io/stately/*) for the United States and Continental (*http://contfont.net/*) for Europe. Map fonts are special-purpose web fonts whose character sets contain map symbols instead of letters and numbers. In just a few easy steps, we'll create a visualization of Europe using the symbols from Continental.

Step 1: Include the Fonts in the Page

The main websites for both Stately and Continental include more detailed instructions for installing the fonts, but all that's really necessary is including a single CSS style sheet. In the case of Continental, that style sheet is called, naturally, *continental.css*. No JavaScript libraries are required.

```
<!DOCTYPE html>
<html lang="en">
  <head>
    <meta charset="utf-8">
    <title></title>
    <link rel="stylesheet" type="text/css" href="css/continental.css">
  </head>
  <body>
    <div id="map"></div>
  </body>
</html>
```

* **NOTE:** For a production website, you might want to combine *continental.css* with your site's other style sheets to minimize the number of network requests the browser has to make.

Step 2: Display One Country

To show a single country, all we have to do is include an HTML `<span>` element with the appropriate attributes. We can do this right in the markup, adding a class attribute set to `map-` followed by a two-letter country abbreviation. (*fr* is the international two-letter abbreviation for France.)

```
<div id="map">
    <span class="map-fr"></span>
</div>
```

For this example, we'll use JavaScript to generate the markup.

```
var fr = document.createElement("span");
fr.className = "map-fr";
document.getElementById("map").appendChild(fr);
```

Here we've created a new `<span>` element, giving it a class name of `"map-fr"`, and appending it to the map `<div>`.

One last bit of housekeeping is setting the size of the font. By default, any map font character will be the same size as a regular text character. For maps we want something much larger, so we can use standard CSS rules to increase the size.

```
#map {
    font-size: 200px;
}
```

That's all it takes to add France to a web page, as you can see in Figure 6-1.

FIGURE 6-1: *Map fonts make it very easy to add a map to a web page.*

Step 3: Combine Multiple Countries into a Single Map

For this example we want to show more than a single country. We'd like to visualize the median age for all of Europe's countries, based on United Nations population data (*http://www.un.org/en/development/desa/population/*) from 2010. To do that, we'll create a map that includes all European countries, and we'll style each country according to the data.

The first step in this visualization is putting all of the countries into a single map. Since each country is a separate character in the Continental font, we want to overlay those characters on top of one another rather than spread them across the page. That requires setting a couple of CSS rules.

```
#map {
❶    position: relative;
}
#map > [class*="map-"] {
❷    position: absolute;
❸    top: 0;
     left: 0;
}
```

First we set the position of the outer container to **relative** ❶. This rule doesn't change the styling of the outer container at all, but it does establish a *positioning context* for anything within the container. Those elements will be our individual country symbols, and we set their position to be **absolute** ❷. We then place each one at the top and left ❸, respectively, of the map so they'll overlay one another. Because we've positioned the container **relative**, the country symbols will be positioned relative to that container rather than to the page as a whole.

Note that we've used a couple of CSS tricks to apply this positioning to all of the individual symbols within this element. We start by selecting the element with an **id** of **map**. Nothing fancy there. The direct descendent selector (>), however, says that what follows should match only elements that are immediate children of that element, not arbitrary descendants. Finally, the attribute selector [**class*="map-"**] specifies only children that have a class containing the characters **map-**. Since all the country symbols will be **<span>** elements with a class of **map-xx** (where *xx* is the two-letter country abbreviation), this will match all of our countries.

In our JavaScript, we can start with an array listing all of the countries and iterate through it. For each country, we create a **<span>** element with the appropriate class and insert it in the map **<div>**.

```
var countries = [
  "ad", "al", "at", "ba", "be", "bg", "by", "ch", "cy", "cz",
  "de", "dk", "ee", "es", "fi", "fo", "fr", "ge", "gg", "gr",
  "hr", "hu", "ie", "im", "is", "it", "je", "li", "lt", "lu",
  "lv", "mc", "md", "me", "mk", "mt", "nl", "no", "pl", "pt",
  "ro", "rs", "ru", "se", "si", "sk", "sm", "tr", "ua", "uk",
  "va"
];
```

```
var map = document.getElementById("map");
countries.forEach(function(cc) {
    var span = document.createElement("span");
    span.className = "map-" + cc;
    map.appendChild(span);
});
```

With these style rules defined, inserting multiple `<span>` elements within our map `<div>` creates the complete, if somewhat uninteresting, map of Europe shown in Figure 6-2.

FIGURE 6-2: *Overlaying map characters on top of one another creates a complete map.*

Step 4: Vary the Countries Based on the Data

Now we're ready to create the actual data visualization. Naturally, we'll start with the data, in this case from the United Nations. Here's how we could format that data in a JavaScript array. (The full data set can be found with the book's source code at *http://jsDataV.is/source/.*)

```
var ages = [
    { "country": "al", "age": 29.968 },
    { "country": "at", "age": 41.768 },
    { "country": "ba", "age": 39.291 },
    { "country": "be", "age": 41.301 },
    { "country": "bg", "age": 41.731 },
    // Data set continues...
```

There are several ways we could use this data to modify the map. We could use JavaScript code to set the visualization properties directly by, for example, changing the **color** style for each country symbol. That would work, but it forgoes one of the big advantages of map fonts. With map fonts, our visualization is standard HTML, so we can use standard CSS to style it. If, in the future, we want to change the styles on the page, they'll all be contained within the style sheets, and we won't have to hunt through our JavaScript code to adjust colors.

To indicate which styles are appropriate for an individual country symbol, we can attach a **data-** attribute to each.

```
❶ var findCountryIndex = function(cc) {
      for (var idx=0; idx<ages.length; idx++) {
          if (ages[idx].country === cc) {
              return idx;
          }
      }
      return -1;
  }
  var map = document.getElementById("map");
  countries.forEach(function(cc) {
      var idx = findCountryIndex(cc);
      if (idx !== -1) {
          var span = document.createElement("span");
          span.className = "map-" + cc;
❷         span.setAttribute("data-age", Math.round(ages[idx].age));
          map.appendChild(span);
      }
  });
```

In this code, we set the **data-age** attribute to the mean age, rounded to the nearest whole number ❷. To find the age for a given country, we need that country's index in the **ages** array. The **findCountryIndex()** function ❶ does that in a straightforward way.

Now we can assign CSS style rules based on that **data-age** attribute. Here's the start of a simple blue gradient for the different ages, where greater median ages are colored darker blue-green.

```
#map > [data-age="44"] { color: #2d9999; }
#map > [data-age="43"] { color: #2a9493; }
#map > [data-age="42"] { color: #278f8e; }
/* CSS rules continue... */
```

Now we have the nice visualization of the age trends shown in Figure 6-3.

FIGURE 6-3: *With CSS rules, we can change the styles of individual map symbols.*

Step 5: Add a Legend

To finish off the visualization, we can add a legend to the map. Because the map itself is nothing more than standard HTML elements with CSS styling, it's easy to create a matching legend. This example covers a fairly broad range (ages 28 to 44), so a linear gradient works well as a key. Your own implementation will depend on the specific browser versions that you wish to support, but a generic style rule would be as follows:

```
#map-legend .key {
    background: linear-gradient(to bottom, #004a4a 0%,#2d9999 100%);
}
```

The resulting visualization in Figure 6-4 summarizes the median age for European countries in a clear and concise format.

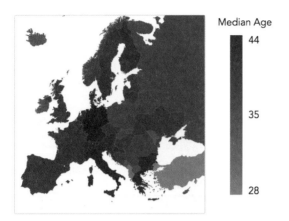

FIGURE 6-4: *Standard HTML can also provide a legend for the visualization.*

Working with Scalable Vector Graphics

Map fonts like those in the previous example are easy to use and visually effective, but only a few map fonts exist, and they definitely don't cover all the conceivable geographic regions. For visualizations of other regions, we'll have to find a different technique. Maps, of course, are ultimately images, and web browsers can display many different image formats. One format in particular, called *Scalable Vector Graphics (SVG)*, is especially well suited for interactive visualizations. That's because, as we'll see in this example, JavaScript code (as well as CSS styles) can easily and naturally interact with SVG images.

Although our example for this section deals with a map, the techniques here are by no means limited to maps. Whenever you have a diagram or illustration in SVG format, you can manipulate it directly on a web page.

✱ NOTE: **There is one important consideration for using SVG: only modern web browsers support it. More specifically, IE8 (and earlier) cannot display SVG images. If a significant number of your users are using older browsers, you might want to consider alternatives.**

For web developers, SVG is especially convenient because its syntax uses the same structure as HTML. You can use many of the same tools and techniques for working with HTML on SVG as well. Consider, for example, a skeletal HTML document.

```
<!DOCTYPE html>
<html lang="en">
  <head><!-- --></head>
  <body>
    <nav><!-- --></nav>
```

```
    <main>
      <section><!-- --></section>
    </main>
    <nav><!-- --></nav>
  </body>
</html>
```

Compare that to the next example: the universal symbol for first aid represented in an SVG document.

✳ *NOTE:* **If you have worked with HTML before HTML5, the similarities might be especially striking, as the SVG header text follows the same format as HTML4.**

```
<?xml version="1.0" encoding="UTF-8"?>
<!DOCTYPE svg PUBLIC "-//W3C//DTD SVG 1.1//EN"
    "http://www.w3.org/Graphics/SVG/1.1/DTD/svg11.dtd">
<svg id="firstaid" version="1.1" xmlns="http://www.w3.org/2000/svg"
    width="100" height="100">
    <rect id="background" x="0"  y="0"  width="100" height="100" rx="20" />
    <rect id="vertical"   x="39" y="19" width="22"  height="62" />
    <rect id="horizontal" x="19" y="39" width="62"  height="22" />
</svg>
```

You can even style the SVG elements using CSS. Here's how we could color the preceding image:

```
svg#firstaid {
    stroke: none;
}
svg#firstaid #background {
    fill: #000;
}
svg#firstaid #vertical,
svg#firstaid #horizontal {
    fill: #FFF;
}
```

Figure 6-5 shows how that SVG renders.

FIGURE 6-5: SVG images may be embedded directly within web pages.

The affinity between HTML and SVG is, in fact, far stronger than the similar syntax. With modern browsers, you can mix SVG and HTML in the same web page. To see how that works, let's visualize health data for the 159 counties in the US state of Georgia. The data comes from County Health Rankings (*http://www.countyhealthrankings.org/*).

Step 1: Create the SVG Map

Our visualization starts with a map, so we'll need an illustration of Georgia's counties in SVG format. Although that might seem like a challenge, there are actually many sources for SVG maps that are free to use, as well as special-purpose applications that can generate SVG maps for almost any region. The Wikimedia Commons (*http://commons.wikimedia.org/wiki/Main_Page*), for example, contains a large number of open source maps, including many of Georgia. We'll use one showing data from the National Register of Historic Places (*http://commons.wikimedia.org/wiki/File:NRHP_Georgia_Map.svg#file*).

After downloading the map file, we can adjust it to better fit our needs, removing the legend, colors, and other elements that we don't need. Although you can do this in a text editor (just as you can edit HTML), you may find it easier to use a graphics program such as Adobe Illustrator or a more web-focused app like Sketch (*http://www.bohemiancoding.com/sketch/*). You might also want to take advantage of an SVG optimization website (*http://petercollingridge.appspot.com/svg-optimiser/*) or application (*https://github.com/svg/*), which can compress an SVG by removing extraneous tags and reducing the sometimes-excessive precision of graphics programs.

Our result will be a series of `<path>` elements, one for each county. We'll also want to assign a `class` or `id` to each path to indicate the county. The resulting SVG file might begin like the following.

```
<svg version="1.1" xmlns="http://www.w3.org/2000/svg"
    width="497" height="558">
    <path id="ck" d="M 216.65,131.53 L 216.41,131.53 216.17,131.53..." />
    <path id="me" d="M 74.32,234.01 L 74.32,232.09 74.32,231.61..." />
    <path id="ms" d="M 64.96,319.22 L 64.72,319.22 64.48,318.98..." />
    <!-- Markup continues... -->
```

To summarize, here are the steps to create the SVG map.

1. Locate a suitably licensed SVG-format map file or create one using a special-purpose map application.
2. Edit the SVG file in a graphics application to remove extraneous components and simplify the illustration.
3. Optimize the SVG file using an optimization site or application.
4. Make final adjustments (such as adding `id` attributes) in your regular HTML editor.

Step 2: Embed the Map in the Page

The simplest way to include an SVG map in a web page is to embed the SVG markup directly within the HTML markup. To include the first-aid symbol, for example, just include the SVG tags within the page itself, as shown at ❶ through ❷. You don't have to include the header tags that are normally present in a standalone SVG file.

```
<!DOCTYPE html>
<html lang="en">
  <head>
    <meta charset="utf-8">
    <title></title>
  </head>
  <body>
    <div>
      <svg id="firstaid" version="1.1"
          xmlns="http://www.w3.org/2000/svg"
        width="100" height="100">
        <rect id="background" x="0" y="0"
            width="100" height="100" rx="20" />
        <rect id="vertical" x="39" y="19"
            width="22" height="62" />
        <rect id="horizontal" x="19" y="39"
            width="62" height="22" />
      </svg>
    </div>
  </body>
</html>
```
❶ `<svg id="firstaid" ...`
❷ `</svg>`

If your map is relatively simple, direct embedding is the easiest way to include it in the page. Our map of Georgia, however, is about 1 MB even after optimization. That's not unusual for maps with reasonable resolution, as describing complex borders such as coastlines or rivers can make for large `<path>` elements. Especially if the map isn't the sole focus of the page, you can provide a better user experience by loading the rest of the page first. That will give your users something to read while the map loads in the background. You can even add a simple animated progress loader if that's appropriate for your site.

If you're using jQuery, loading the map is a single instruction. You do want to make sure, though, that your code doesn't start manipulating the map until the load is complete. Here's how that would look in the source code.

```
$("#map").load("img/ga.svg", function() {
    // Only manipulate the map inside this block
})
```

Step 3: Collect the Data

The data for our visualization is available as an Excel spreadsheet directly from County Health Rankings (*http://www.countyhealthrankings.org/*). We'll convert that to a JavaScript object in advance, and we'll add a two-letter code corresponding to each county. Here's how that array might begin.

```javascript
var counties = [
    {
      "name":"Appling",
      "code":"ap",
      "outcomes_z":0.93,
      "outcomes_rank":148,
      // Data continues...
    },
    {
      "name":"Atkinson",
      "code":"at",
      "outcomes_z":0.40,
      "outcomes_rank":118,
    // Data set continues...
];
```

For this visualization we'd like to show the variation in health outcomes among counties. The data set provides two variables for that value, a ranking and a z-score (a measure of how far a sample is from the mean in terms of standard deviation). The County Health Rankings site provides z-scores slightly modified from the traditional statistical definition. Normal z-scores are always positive; in this data set, however, measurements that are subjectively better than average are multiplied by –1 so that they are negative. A county whose health outcome is two standard deviations "better" than the mean, for example, is given a z-score of –2 instead of 2. This adjustment makes it easier to use these z-scores in our visualization.

Our first step in working with these z-scores is to find the maximum and minimum values. We can do that by extracting the outcomes as a separate array and then using JavaScript's built-in `Math.max()` and `Math.min()` functions. Note that the following code uses the `map()` method to extract the array, and that method is available only in modern browsers. Since we've chosen to use SVG images, however, we've already restricted our users to modern browsers, so we might as well take advantage of that when we can.

```javascript
var outcomes = counties.map(function(county) {return county.outcomes_z;});
var maxZ = Math.max.apply(null, outcomes);
var minZ = Math.min.apply(null, outcomes);
```

Notice how we've used the `.apply()` method here. Normally the `Math.max()` and `Math.min()` functions accept a comma-separated list of arguments. We, of course, have an array instead. The `apply()` method, which works with any JavaScript function, turns an array into a comma-separated list. The first parameter is the context to use, which in our case doesn't matter, so we set it to `null`.

To complete the data preparation, let's make sure the minimum and maximum ranges are symmetric about the mean.

```
if (Math.abs(minZ) > Math.abs(maxZ)) {
    maxZ = -minZ;
} else {
    minZ = -maxZ;
}
```

If, for example, the z-scores ranged from -2 to 1.5, this code would extend the range to [-2, 2]. This adjustment will make the color scales symmetric as well, thus making our visualization easier for users to interpret.

Step 4: Define the Color Scheme

Defining an effective color scheme for a map can be quite tricky, but fortunately there are some excellent resources available. For this visualization we'll rely on the Chroma.js library (*http://driven-by-data.net/about/chromajs/*). That library includes many tools for working with and manipulating colors and color scales, and it can satisfy the most advanced color theorist. For our example, however, we can take advantage of the predefined color scales, specifically those defined originally by Cynthia Brewer (*http://colorbrewer2.org/*).

The Chroma.js library is available on popular content distribution networks, so we can rely on a network such as CloudFlare's cdnjs (*http://cdnjs.com/*) to host it.

```
<!DOCTYPE html>
<html lang="en">
  <head>
    <meta charset="utf-8">
    <title></title>
  </head>
  <body>
    <div id="map"></div>
    <script
     src="///cdnjs.cloudflare.com/ajax/libs/chroma-js/0.5.2/chroma.min.js">
    </script>
  </body>
</html>
```

To use a predefined scale, we pass the scale's name ("BrBG" for Brewer's brown-to-blue-green scale) to the `chroma.scale()` function.

```
var scale = chroma.scale("BrBG").domain([maxZ, minZ]).out("hex");
```

At the same time, we indicate the domain for our scale (`minZ` to `maxZ`, although we're reversing the order because of the data set's z-score adjustment) and our desired output. The `"hex"` output is the common `"#012345"` format compatible with CSS and HTML markup.

Step 5: Color the Map

With our color scheme established, we can now apply the appropriate colors to each county on the map. That's probably the easiest step in the whole visualization. We iterate through all the counties, finding their `<path>` elements based on their `id` values, and applying the color by setting the `fill` attribute.

```
counties.forEach(function(county) {
    document.getElementById(county.code)
      .setAttribute("fill", scale(county.outcomes_z));
})
```

The resulting map, shown in Figure 6-6, illustrates which counties are above average and which are below average for health outcomes in 2014.

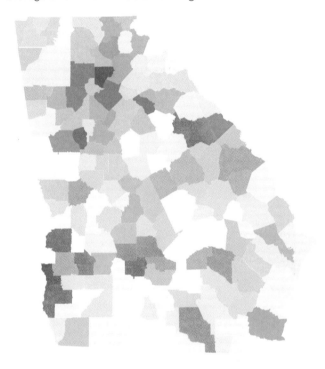

FIGURE 6-6: *CSS rules can set the styles for individual SVG elements within an SVG illustration.*

Step 6: Add a Legend

To help users interpret the map, we can add a legend to the visualization. We can take advantage of the Chroma.js scale to easily create a table that explains the variation. For the table, we'll use four increments for the colors on each side of the mean value. That gives us a total of nine colors for the legend.

```html
<table id="legend">
    <tr class="scale">
        <td></td><td></td><td></td><td></td><td></td>
        <td></td><td></td><td></td><td></td>
    </tr>
    <tr class="text">
        <td colspan="4">Worse than Average</td>
        <td>Average</td>
        <td colspan="4">Better than Average</td>
    </tr>
</table>
```

Some straightforward CSS will style the table appropriately. Because we have nine colors, we set the width of each table cell to **11.1111%** (1/9 is 0.111111).

```css
table#legend tr.scale td {
    height: 1em;
    width: 11.1111%;
}
table#legend tr.text td:first-child {
    text-align: left;
}
table#legend tr.text td:nth-child(2) {
    text-align: center;
}
table#legend tr.text td:last-child {
    text-align: right;
}
```

Finally, we use the Chroma scale created earlier to set the background color for the legend's table cells. Because the legend is a `<table>` element, we can directly access the rows and the cells within the rows. Although these elements look like arrays in the following code, they're not true JavaScript arrays, so they don't support array methods such as `forEach()`. For now, we'll iterate through them with a `for` loop, but if you'd rather use the array methods, stay tuned for a simple trick. Note that once again we're working backward because of the data set's z-score adjustments.

```
var legend = document.getElementById("legend");
var cells = legend.rows[0].cells;
for (var idx=0; idx<cells.length; idx++) {
    var td = cells[idx];
❶   td.style.backgroundColor = scale(maxZ -
        ((idx + 0.5) / cells.length) * (maxZ - minZ));
};
```

At ❶ we calculate the fraction of the current index from the total number of legend colors ((idx + 0.5) / cells.length), multiply that by the total range of the scale (maxZ - minZ), and subtract the result from the maximum value.

The result is the legend for the map in Figure 6-7.

Worse than Average   Average   Better than Average

FIGURE 6-7: An HTML <table> can serve as a legend.

Step 7: Add Interactions

To complete the visualization, let's enable users to hover their mouse over a county on the map to see more details. Of course, mouse interactions are not available for tablet or smartphone users. To support those users, you could add a similar interaction for tap or click events. That code would be almost identical to the next example.

We'll start by defining a table to show county details.

```
<table id="details">
    <tr><td>County:</td><td></td></tr>
    <tr><td>Rank:</td><td></td></tr>
    <tr><td>Health Behaviors:</td><td></td></tr>
    <tr><td>Clinical Care:</td><td></td></tr>
    <tr><td>Social & Economic Factors:</td><td></td></tr>
    <tr><td>Physical Environment:</td><td></td></tr>
</table>
```

Initially, we don't want that table to be visible.

```
table#details {
    display: none;
}
```

To show the table, we use event handler functions that track when the mouse enters or leaves an SVG path for a county. To find these <path> elements, we can use the querySelectorAll() function that modern browsers support. Unfortunately, that function doesn't return a true array of elements, so we can't use array methods such as forEach() to iterate through those elements. There's a trick, however, that will let us convert the returned list into a true array.

```
[].slice.call(document.querySelectorAll("#map path"))
    .forEach(function(path) {
        path.addEventListener("mouseenter", function(){
            document.getElementById("details").style.display = "table";
        });
        path.addEventListener("mouseleave", function(){
            document.getElementById("details").style.display = "none";
        });
    }
);
```

This code calls the [].slice.call() function with the "not quite array" object as its parameter. The result is a true array with all of its useful methods.

In addition to making the details table visible, we'll also want to update it with the appropriate information. To help with this display, we can write a function that converts a z-score into a more user-friendly explanation. The specific values in the following example are arbitrary since we're not trying for statistical precision in this visualization.

```
var zToText = function(z) {
    z = +z;
    if (z >  0.25) { return "Far Below Average"; }
    if (z >  0.1)  { return "Below Average"; }
    if (z > -0.1)  { return "Average"; }
    if (z > -0.25) { return "Above Average"; }
    return "Far Above Average";
}
```

There are a couple of noteworthy items in this function. First, the statement z = +z converts the z-score from a string to a numeric value for the tests that follow. Second, remember that because of the z-score adjustments, the negative z-scores are actually better than average, while the positive values are below average.

We can use this function to provide the data for our details table. The first step is finding the full data set for the associated <path> element. To do that, we search through the counties array looking for a code property that matches the id attribute of the path.

```
var county = null;
counties.some(function(c) {
    if (c.code === this.id) {
        county = c;
        return true;
    }
    return false;
});
```

Because indexOf() doesn't allow us to find objects by key, we've used the some() method instead. That method terminates as soon as it finds a match, so we avoid iterating through the entire array.

Once we've found the county data, it's a straightforward process to update the table. The following code directly updates the relevant table cell's text content. For a more robust implementation, you could provide class names for the cells and update based on those class names.

```
var table = document.getElementById("details");
table.rows[0].cells[1].textContent =
    county.name;
table.rows[1].cells[1].textContent =
    county.outcomes_rank + " out of " + counties.length;
table.rows[2].cells[1].textContent =
    zToText(county.health_behaviors_z);
table.rows[3].cells[1].textContent =
    zToText(county.clinical_care_z);
table.rows[4].cells[1].textContent =
    zToText(county.social_and_economic_factors_z);
table.rows[5].cells[1].textContent =
    zToText(county.physical_environment_z);
```

Now we just need a few more refinements:

```
path.addEventListener("mouseleave", function(){
    // Previous code
❶   this.setAttribute("stroke", "#444444");
});
path.addEventListener("mouseleave", function(){
    // Previous code
❷   this.setAttribute("stroke", "none");
});
```

Here we add a stroke color at ❶ for counties that are highlighted. We remove the stroke at ❷ when the mouse leaves the path.

At this point our visualization example is complete. Figure 6-8 shows the result.

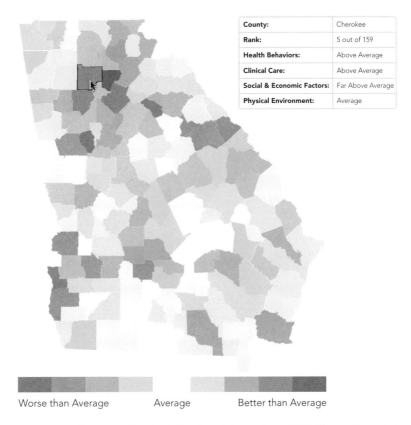

County:	Cherokee
Rank:	5 out of 159
Health Behaviors:	Above Average
Clinical Care:	Above Average
Social & Economic Factors:	Far Above Average
Physical Environment:	Average

Worse than Average   Average   Better than Average

FIGURE 6-8: *Browsers (and a bit of code) can turn SVG illustrations into interactive visualizations.*

Including Maps for Context

So far in this chapter, we've looked at map visualizations where the main subjects are geographic regions—countries in Europe or counties in Georgia. In those cases, choropleth maps were effective in showing the differences between regions. Not all map visualizations have the same focus, however. In some cases, we want to include a map more as context or background for the visualization data.

When we want to include a map as a visualization background, we're likely to find that traditional mapping libraries will serve us better than custom choropleth maps. The most well-known mapping library is probably Google Maps (*http://maps.google.com/*), and you've almost certainly seen many examples of embedded Google maps on web pages. There are, however, several free and open source alternatives to Google Maps. For this example, we'll use the Modest Maps library (*https://github.com/modestmaps/modestmaps-js/*) from Stamen Design. To show off this library, we'll visualize the major UFO sightings in the United States (*http://en.wikipedia.org/wiki/UFO_sightings_in_the_United_States*), or at least those important enough to merit a Wikipedia entry.

Step 1: Set Up the Web Page

For our visualization, we'll rely on a couple of components from the Modest Maps library: the core library itself and the spotlight extension that can be found in the library's examples folder. In production you would likely combine these and minify the result to optimize performance, but for our example, we'll include them separately.

```
<!DOCTYPE html>
<html lang="en">
  <head>
    <meta charset="utf-8">
    <title></title>
  </head>
  <body>
❶   <div id="map"></div>
    <script src="js/modestmaps.js"></script>
    <script src="js/spotlight.js"></script>
  </body>
</html>
```

We've also set aside a `<div>` at ❶ to hold the map. Not surprisingly, it has the id of `"map"`.

Step 2: Prepare the Data

The Wikipedia data can be formatted as an array of JavaScript objects. We can include whatever information we wish in the objects, but we'll definitely need the latitude and longitude of the sighting in order to place it on the map. Here's how you might structure the data.

```
var ufos = [
{
    "date": "April, 1941",
    "city": "Cape Girardeau",
    "state": "Missouri",
    "location": [37.309167, -89.546389],
    "url": "http://en.wikipedia.org/wiki/Cape_Girardeau_UFO_crash"
},{
    "date": "February 24, 1942",
    "city": "Los Angeles",
    "state": "California",
    "location": [34.05, -118.25],
    "url": "http://en.wikipedia.org/wiki/Battle_of_Los_Angeles"
},{
// Data set continues...
```

The `location` property holds the latitude and longitude (where negative values indicate west) as a two-element array.

Step 3: Choose a Map Style

As with most mapping libraries, Modest Maps builds its maps using layers. The layering process works much like it does in a graphics application such as Photoshop or Sketch. Subsequent layers add further visual information to the map. In most cases, the base layer for a map consists of image tiles. Additional layers such as markers or routes can be included on top of the image tiles.

When we tell Modest Maps to create a map, it calculates which tiles (both size and location) are needed and then it requests those tiles asynchronously over the Internet. The tiles define the visual style of the map. Stamen Design has published several tile sets itself; you can see them on *http://maps.stamen.com/*.

To use the Stamen tiles, we'll add one more, small JavaScript library to our page. That library is available directly from Stamen Design (*http://maps.stamen.com/js/tile.stamen.js*). It should be included *after* the Modest Maps library.

```
<!DOCTYPE html>
<html lang="en">
  <head>
    <meta charset="utf-8">
    <title></title>
  </head>
  <body>
    <div id="map"></div>
    <script src="js/modestmaps.js"></script>
    <script src="js/spotlight.js"></script>
    <script src="http://maps.stamen.com/js/tile.stamen.js"></script>
  </body>
</html>
```

For our example, the "toner" style is a good match, so we'll use those tiles. To use those tiles, we create a *tile layer* for the map.

```
var tiles = new MM.StamenTileLayer("toner");
```

When you consider a source for image tiles, be aware of any copyright restrictions. Some image tiles must be licensed, and even those that are freely available often require that any user identify the provider as the source.

Step 4: Draw the Map

Now we're ready to draw the map itself. That takes two JavaScript statements:

```
var map = new MM.Map("map", tiles);
map.setCenterZoom(new MM.Location(38.840278, -96.611389), 4);
```

First we create a new `MM.Map` object, giving it the `id` of the element containing the map and the tiles we just initialized. Then we provide the latitude and longitude for the map's center as well as an initial zoom level. For your own maps, you may need to experiment a bit to get the right values, but for this example, we'll center and zoom the map so that it comfortably shows the continental United States.

The resulting map, shown in Figure 6-9, forms a base for showing the sightings.

Map tiles by Stamen Design, under CC BY 3.0. Data by OpenStreetMap, under CC BY SA.

FIGURE 6-9: *Map libraries can show maps based on geographic coordinates.*

Notice that both Stamen Design and OpenStreetMap are credited. That attribution is required by the terms of the Stamen Design license.

Step 5: Add the Sightings

With our map in place, it's time to add the individual UFO sightings. We're using the spotlight extension to highlight these locations, so we first create a spotlight layer for the map. We'll also want to set the radius of the spotlight effect. As with the center and zoom parameters, a bit of trial and error helps here.

```
var layer = new SpotlightLayer();
layer.spotlight.radius = 15;
map.addLayer(layer);
```

Now we can iterate through the array of sightings that make up our data. For each sighting, we extract the latitude and longitude of the location and add that location to the spotlight layer.

```
ufos.forEach(function(ufo) {
    layer.addLocation(new MM.Location(ufo.location[0], ufo.location[1]));
});
```

At this point our visualization is complete. Figure 6-10 shows where UFOs have allegedly appeared over the United States in a suitably mysterious context.

Major UFO Sightings in the Continental United States

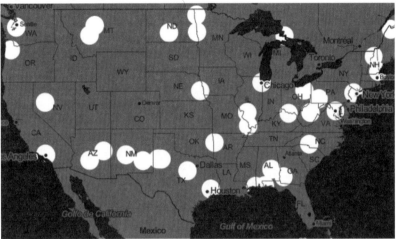

Map tiles by Stamen Design, under CC BY 3.0. Data by OpenStreetMap, under CC BY SA.

FIGURE 6-10: Adding layers in a map library can emphasize regions of a map.

Integrating a Full-Featured Mapping Library

The Modest Maps library of the previous example is a fine library for simple map visualizations, but it doesn't have all of the features and support of a full-featured service such as Google Maps. There is, however, an open source library that does provide those features: Leaflet (*http://leafletjs.com/*). In this example, we'll build a more complex visualization that features a Leaflet-based map.

In the 1940s, two private railroads were in competition for passenger traffic in the southeastern United States. Two routes that competed most directly were the Silver Comet (run by Seaboard Air Lines) and the Southerner (operated by Southern Railways). Both served passengers traveling between New York and Birmingham, Alabama. One factor cited in the Southerner's ultimate success was the shorter distance of its route. Trips on the Southerner were quicker, giving Southern Railways a competitive advantage. Let's create a visualization to demonstrate that advantage.

Step 1: Prepare the Data

The data for our visualization is readily available as timetables for the two routes. A more precise comparison might consider timetables from the same year, but for this example, we'll use the Southerner's timetable from 1941 (*http://www .streamlinerschedules.com/concourse/track1/southerner194112.html*) and the Silver Comet's timetable from 1947 (*http://www.streamlinerschedules.com/concourse/ track1/silvercomet194706.html*), as they are readily available on the Internet. The timetables only include station names, so we will have to look up latitude and longitude values (using, for example, Google Maps) for all of the stations in order to place them on a map. We can also calculate the time difference between stops, in minutes. Those calculations result in two arrays, one for each train.

```javascript
var seaboard = [
    { "stop": "Washington",
      "latitude": 38.895111, "longitude": -77.036667,
      "duration": 77 },
    { "stop": "Fredericksburg",
      "latitude": 38.301806, "longitude": -77.470833,
      "duration": 89 },
    { "stop": "Richmond",
      "latitude": 37.533333, "longitude": -77.466667,
      "duration": 29 },
    // Data set continues...
];
var southern = [
    { "stop": "Washington",
      "latitude": 38.895111, "longitude": -77.036667,
      "duration": 14 },
    { "stop": "Alexandria",
      "latitude": 38.804722, "longitude": -77.047222,
      "duration": 116 },
    { "stop": "Charlottesville",
      "latitude": 38.0299, "longitude": -78.479,
      "duration": 77 },
    // Data set continues...
];
```

Step 2: Set Up the Web Page and Libraries

To add Leaflet maps to our web page, we'll need to include the library and its companion style sheet. Both are available from a content distribution network, so there's no need to host them on our own servers.

```html
<!DOCTYPE html>
<html lang="en">
  <head>
    <meta charset="utf-8">
    <title></title>
    <link rel="stylesheet"
     href="http://cdn.leafletjs.com/leaflet-0.7.2/leaflet.css" />
  </head>
  <body>
    <div id="map"></div>
```

❶

```
    <script
      src="http://cdn.leafletjs.com/leaflet-0.7.2/leaflet.js">
    </script>
  </body>
</html>
```

When we create our page, we also define a `<div>` container for the map at ❶.

Step 3: Draw the Base Map

The Silver Comet and the Southerner traveled between New York and Birmingham (and, in the case of the Southerner, all the way to New Orleans). But the region that's relevant for our visualization lies between Washington, DC, and Atlanta, Georgia, because that's the only region where the train routes differed; for the rest of their journeys, the routes were essentially the same. Our map, therefore, will extend from Atlanta in the southwest to Washington, DC, in the northeast. Using a bit of trial and error, we can determine the best center point and zoom level for the map. The center point defines the latitude and longitude for the map's center, and the zoom level determines the area covered by the map on its initial display. When we create the map object, we give it the `id` of the containing element as well as those parameters.

```
var map = L.map("map",{
    center: [36.3, -80.2],
    zoom: 6
});
```

For this particular visualization, there is little point in zooming or panning the map, so we can include additional options to disable those interactions.

```
var map = L.map("map",{
    center: [36.3, -80.2],
❶  maxBounds: [ [33.32134852669881, -85.20996093749999],
❷               [39.16414104768742, -75.9814453125] ],
    zoom: 6,
❸  minZoom: 6,
❹  maxZoom: 6,
❺  dragging: false,
❻  zoomControl: false,
❼  touchZoom: false,
    scrollWheelZoom: false,
    doubleClickZoom: false,
❽  boxZoom: false,
❾  keyboard: false
});
```

Setting both the minimum zoom level ❸ and the maximum zoom level ❹ to be equal to the initial zoom level disables zooming. We also disable the onscreen map controls for zooming at ❻. The other zoom controls are likewise disabled (❼ through ❽). For panning, we disable dragging the map at ❺ and keyboard arrow keys at ❾. We also specify the latitude/longitude bounds for the map (❶ and ❷).

Because we've disabled the user's ability to pan or zoom the map, we should also make sure the mouse cursor doesn't mislead the user when it's hovering over the map. The *leaflet.css* style sheet expects zooming and panning to be enabled, so it sets the cursor to a "grabbing" hand icon. We can override that value with a style rule of our own. We have to define this rule *after* including the *leaflet.css* file.

```css
.leaflet-container {
    cursor: default;
}
```

As with the Modest Maps example, we base our map on a set of tiles. There are many tile providers that support Leaflet; some are open source, while others are commercial. Leaflet has a demo page (*http://leaflet-extras.github.io/leaflet-providers/preview/*) you can use to compare some of the open source tile providers. For our example, we want to avoid tiles with roads, as the highway network looked very different in the 1940s. Esri has a neutral WorldGrayCanvas set that works well for our visualization. It does include current county boundaries, and some counties may have changed their borders since the 1940s. For our example, we won't worry about that detail, though you might consider it in any production visualization. Leaflet's API lets us create the tile layer and add it to the map in a single statement. The Leaflet includes a built-in option to handle attribution so we can be sure to credit the tile source appropriately.

```
L.tileLayer("http://server.arcgisonline.com/ArcGIS/rest/services/"+
        "Canvas/World_Light_Gray_Base/MapServer/tile/{z}/{y}/{x}", {
        attribution: "Tiles &copy; Esri &mdash; Esri, DeLorme, NAVTEQ",
❶       maxZoom: 16
}).addTo(map);
```

Note that the maxZoom option at ❶ indicates the maximum zoom layer available for that particular tile set. That value is independent of the zoom level we're permitting for our map.

With a map and a base tile layer, we have a good starting point for our visualization in (see Figure 6-11).

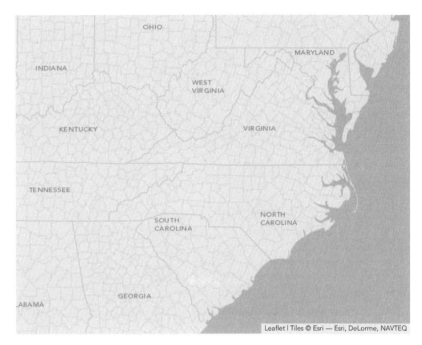

Leaflet | Tiles © Esri — Esri, DeLorme, NAVTEQ

FIGURE 6-11: *A base layer map provides the canvas for a visualization.*

Step 4: Add the Routes to the Map

For the next step in our visualization, we want to show the two routes on our map. First, we'll simply draw each route on the map. Then, we'll add an animation that traces both routes at the same time to show which one is faster.

The Leaflet library includes a function that does exactly what we need to draw each route: `polyline()` connects a series of lines defined by the latitude and longitude of their endpoints and prepares them for a map. Our data set includes the geographic coordinates of each route's stops, so we can use the JavaScript `map()` method to format those values for Leaflet. For the Silver Comet example, the following statement extracts its stops.

```
seaboard.map(function(stop) {
    return [stop.latitude, stop.longitude]
})
```

This statement returns an array of latitude/longitude pairs:

```
[
  [38.895111,-77.036667],
  [38.301806,-77.470833],
```

```
    [37.533333,-77.466667],
    [37.21295,-77.400417],
    /* Data set continues... */
]
```

That result is the perfect input to the `polyline()` function. We'll use it for each of the routes. The options let us specify a color for the lines, which we'll match with the associated railroad's official color from the era. We also indicate that the lines have no function when clicked by setting the `clickable` option to `false`.

```
L.polyline(
    seaboard.map(function(stop) {return [stop.latitude, stop.longitude]}),
    {color: "#88020B", weight: 1, clickable: false}
).addTo(map);

L.polyline(
    southern.map(function(stop) {return [stop.latitude, stop.longitude]}),
    {color: "#106634", weight: 1, clickable: false}
).addTo(map);
```

With this addition, the visualization shown in Figure 6-12 is starting to convey the relative distances of the two routes.

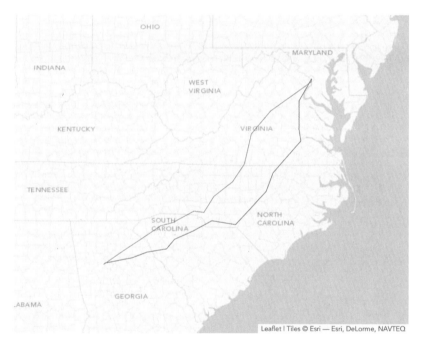

FIGURE 6-12: *Additional map layers add data to the canvas.*

Step 5: Add an Animation Control

Next, we'll animate the two routes. Not only will this emphasize the competitive advantage of the shorter route, but it will also make the visualization more interesting and engaging. We'll definitely want to let our users start and stop the animation, so our map will need a control button. The Leaflet library doesn't have its own animation control, but the library does have a lot of support for customizations. Part of that support is a generic `Control` object. We can create an animation control by starting with that object and extending it.

```
L.Control.Animate = L.Control.extend({
    // Custom code goes here
});
```

Next we define the options for our custom control. Those options include its position on the map, the text and tool tip (title) for its states, and functions to call when the animation starts or stops. We define these within an **options** object as follows, which lets Leaflet integrate them within its normal functionality.

```
L.Control.Animate = L.Control.extend({
    options: {
        position: "topleft",
        animateStartText: "▶",
        animateStartTitle: "Start Animation",
        animatePauseText: "■",
        animatePauseTitle: "Pause Animation",
        animateResumeText: "▶",
        animateResumeTitle: "Resume Animation",
        animateStartFn: null,
        animateStopFn: null
    },
```

For our example, we're using UTF-8 characters for the play and pause control. In a production visualization, you might consider using icon fonts or images to have maximum control over the appearance.

Our animation control also needs an `onAdd()` method for Leaflet to call when it adds a control to a map. This method constructs the HTML markup for the control and returns that to the caller.

```
    onAdd: function () {
❶      var animateName = "leaflet-control-animate",
            container = L.DomUtil.create(
                "div", animateName + " leaflet-bar"),
            options = this.options;

❷      this._button  = this._createButton(
            this.options.animateStartText,
            this.options.animateStartTitle,
            animateName,
            container,
```

```
        this._clicked);

        return container;
    },
```

Our implementation of onAdd() constructs the markup in two stages. First, starting at ❶, it creates a <div> element and gives that element two classes: leaflet-control-animate and leaflet-bar. The first class is unique to our animation control, and we can use it to apply CSS rules uniquely to our control. The second class is a general Leaflet class for all toolbars. By adding it to the animation control, we're making that control consistent with other Leaflet controls. Note that Leaflet includes the L.DomUtil.create() method at ❶ to handle the details of creating the element.

The second part of onAdd() creates a button element within this <div> container. Most of the work takes place in the _createButton() function at ❷, which we'll examine shortly. The parameters to the function include the following:

▶ The text for the button

▶ The tool tip (title) to display when the mouse hovers over the button

▶ The CSS class to apply to the button

▶ The container in which to insert the button

▶ A function to call when the button is clicked

If you're wondering why the name of this function begins with an underscore (_), that's the convention that Leaflet uses for private methods (and attributes). There's no requirement to follow it, but doing so will make it easier for someone familiar with Leaflet to understand our code.

The _createButton() method itself relies on Leaflet utility functions.

```
    _createButton: function (html, title, className, container, callback) {
❶      var link = L.DomUtil.create("a", className, container);
        link.innerHTML = html;
        link.href = "#";
❷      link.title = title;

        L.DomEvent
❸          .on(link, "mousedown dblclick", L.DomEvent.stopPropagation)
❹          .on(link, "click", L.DomEvent.stop)
❺          .on(link, "click", callback, this);

        return link;
    },
```

First it creates the button as an <a> element with the specified text, title, and class, and it creates that element within the appropriate container (❶ through ❷). It then binds several events to this <a> element. First it ignores initial mousedown and double-click events at ❸. It also prevents single-click events from propagating up the document tree and from implementing their default behavior at ❹. Finally, it executes the callback function on **click** events at ❺.

The callback function itself is our next task.

❶
```
    _running: false,

    _clicked: function() {
        if (this._running) {
            if (this.options.animateStopFn) {
                this.options.animateStopFn();
            }
            this._button.innerHTML = this.options.animateResumeText;
            this._button.title = this.options.animateResumeTitle;
        } else {
            if (this.options.animateStartFn) {
                this.options.animateStartFn();
            }
            this._button.innerHTML = this.options.animatePauseText;
            this._button.title = this.options.animatePauseTitle;
        }
        this._running = !this._running;
    },
```
❷ appears at the `if (this._running) {` line.

Before we get into the function, we add a single state variable (_running) to keep track of whether the animation is currently running. It starts out stopped at ❶. Then our callback function starts by checking this variable at ❷. If _running is true, that means the animation was running and has just been paused by the current click, so it changes the control to indicate that clicking will now resume the animation. If the animation isn't running, the callback function does the opposite: it changes the control to indicate that a subsequent click will pause it. In both cases, the callback function executes the appropriate control function if one exists. Finally, it sets the state of _running to its complement.

The last part of our custom control adds a **reset()** method to clear the animation. This function sets the control back to its initial state.

```
    reset: function() {
        this._running = false;
        this._button.innerHTML = this.options.animateStartText;
        this._button.title = this.options.animateStartTitle;
    }
});
```

To completely integrate our custom control into the Leaflet architecture, we add a function to the **L.control** object. Following the Leaflet convention, this function's name begins with a lowercase letter but is otherwise identical to the name of our control.

```
L.control.animate = function (options) {
    return new L.Control.Animate(options);
};
```

Defining this last function lets us create the control using a common Leaflet syntax.

```
L.control.animate().addTo(map);
```

This is the same syntax we've seen before with layers and polylines.

Step 6: Prepare the Animation

With a convenient user control in place, we can now begin work on the animation itself. Although this particular animation isn't especially taxing, we can still follow best practices and compute as much as possible in advance. Since we're animating two routes, we'll define a function that will build an animation for any input route. A second parameter will specify polyline options. This function will return an array of polyline paths, indexed by minutes. You can see the basic structure of this function next.

```
var buildAnimation = function(route, options) {
    var animation = [];

    // Code to build the polylines

    return animation;
}
```

The first element in the array will be the polyline for the first minute of the route. We'll build the entire array in the animation variable.

To build the paths, we iterate through the stops on the route.

❶
```
    for (var stopIdx=0, prevStops=[];
            stopIdx < route.length-1; stopIdx++) {
        // Code to calculate steps between current stop and next stop
    }
```

We want to keep track of all the stops we've already passed, so we define the prevStops array and initialize it as empty at ❶. Each iteration calculates the animation steps for the current stop up to the next stop. There's no need to go beyond the final stop on the route, so we terminate the loop at the next-to-last stop (stopIdx < route.length-1;).

As we start to calculate the paths beginning at the current stop, we'll store that stop and the next one in local variables, and we'll add the current stop to the prevStops array that's keeping track of previous stops.

```
var stop = route[stopIdx];
var nextStop = route[stopIdx+1]
prevStops.push([stop.latitude, stop.longitude]);
```

For each stop in our data sets, the **duration** property stores the number of minutes until the next stop. We'll use an inner loop, shown next, to count from 1 up to that value.

```
for (var minutes = 1; minutes <= stop.duration; minutes++) {
    var position = [
        stop.latitude +
          (nextStop.latitude - stop.latitude) *
          (minutes/stop.duration),
        stop.longitude +
          (nextStop.longitude - stop.longitude) *
          (minutes/stop.duration)
    ];
    animation.push(
        L.polyline(prevStops.concat([position]), options)
    );
}
```

Within the loop, we use a simple linear interpolation to calculate the position at the corresponding time. That position, when appended to the **prevStops** array, is the polyline path for that time. This code creates a polyline based on the path and adds it to the animation array.

When we use the array **concat()** method, we embed the position array within another array object. That keeps **concat()** from flattening the position array before appending it. You can see the difference in the following examples. It's the latter outcome that we want.

```
[[1,2], [3,4]].concat([5,6]);   // => [[1,2], [3,4], 5, 6]
[[1,2], [3,4]].concat([[5,6]]); // => [[1,2], [3,4], [5,6]]
```

Step 7: Animate the Routes

Now it's finally time to execute the animation. To initialize it, we create an array to hold the two routes.

```
var routeAnimations = [
    buildAnimation(seaboard,
      {clickable: false, color: "#88020B", weight: 8, opacity: 1.0}
    ),
    buildAnimation(southern,
      {clickable: false, color: "#106634", weight: 8, opacity: 1.0}
    )
];
```

Next we calculate the maximum number of animation steps. That's the minimum of the length of the two animation arrays.

```
var maxSteps = Math.min.apply(null,
    routeAnimations.map(function(animation) {
        return animation.length
    })
);
```

That statement might seem overly complex for finding the minimum length, but it works with an arbitrary number of routes. If, in the future, we decided to animate a third route on our map, we wouldn't have to change the code. The best way to understand the statement is to start in the middle and work outward. The following fragment converts the array of route animations into an array of lengths, specifically [870,775]:

```
routeAnimations.map(function(animation) {return animation.length})
```

To find the minimum value in an array, we can use the `Math.min()` function, except that function expects its parameters as a comma-separated list of arguments rather than an array. The `apply()` method (which is available for any JavaScript function) converts an array into a comma-separated list. Its first parameter is a context for the function, which in our case is irrelevant, so we pass `null` for that parameter.

The animation keeps track of its current state with the **step** variable, which we initialize to 0.

```
var step = 0;
```

The `animateStep()` function processes each step in the animation. There are four parts to this function.

```
var animateStep = function() {
    // Draw the next step in the animation
}
```

First we check to see whether this is the very first step in the animation.

```
    if (step > 0) {
        routeAnimations.forEach(function(animation) {
❶           map.removeLayer(animation[step-1]);
        });
    }
```

If it isn't, **step** will be greater than zero and we can remove the previous step's polylines from the map at ❶.

Next we check to see if we're already at the end of the animation. If so, then we restart the animation back at step 0.

```
if (step === maxSteps) {
    step = 0;
}
```

For the third part, we add the current step's polylines to the map.

```
routeAnimations.forEach(function(animation) {
    map.addLayer(animation[step]);
});
```

Finally, we return true if we've reached the end of the animation.

```
return ++step === maxSteps;
```

We'll execute this step function repeatedly in a JavaScript interval, shown next.

```
  var interval = null;
  var animate = function() {
      interval = window.setInterval(function() {
❶         if (animateStep()) {
              window.clearInterval(interval);
              control.reset();
          }
      }, 30);
  }
❷ var pause = function() {
      window.clearInterval(interval);
  }
```

We use a variable to keep a reference to that interval and add functions to start and stop it. In the **animate()** function, we check the return value from animateStep() at ❶. When it returns **true**, the animation is complete, so we clear the interval and reset our control. (We'll see where that control is defined shortly.) The pause() function at ❷ stops the interval.

Now all we need to do is define the animation control using the object we created in Step 5.

```
var control = L.control.animate({
    animateStartFn: animate,
    animateStopFn:  pause
});
control.addTo(map);
```

Once we add it to the map, the user will be able to activate the animation.

Step 8: Create Labels for the Stops

Before we wrap up the animation, we'll add some labels for each train stop. To emphasize the passage of time, we'll reveal each label as the animation reaches the corresponding stop. To do that, we'll create the labels using a special object; then we'll create a method to add labels to the map; and, to finish the label object, we'll add methods that get or set a label's status.

Since Leaflet doesn't have a predefined object for labels, we can once again create our own custom object. We start with the basic Leaflet `Class`.

```
L.Label = L.Class.extend({
    // Implement the Label object
});
```

Our `Label` object accepts parameters for its position on the map, its label text, and any options. Next, we extend the `initialize()` method of the Leaflet `Class` to handle those parameters.

```
      initialize: function(latLng, label, options) {
          this._latlng = latLng;
          this._label = label;
❶         L.Util.setOptions(this, options);
❷         this._status = "hidden";
      },
```

For position and text, we simply save their values for later use. For the options, we use a Leaflet utility at ❶ to easily support default values. The object includes one variable to keep track of its status. Initially all labels are hidden, so `this._status` is initialized appropriately at ❷.

Next we define the default option values with the `options` attribute.

```
      options: {
          offset: new L.Point(0, 0)
      },
});
```

The only option we need for our label is an offset for the standard position. By default, that offset will be 0 in both the x- and y-coordinates.

This `options` attribute, combined with the call to `L.Util.setOptions` in the `initialize` method, establishes a default value (0,0) for the offset that can be easily overridden when a `Label` object is created.

Next we write the method that adds a label to a map.

```
      onAdd: function(map) {
❶         this._container = L.DomUtil.create("div", "leaflet-label");
❷         this._container.style.lineHeight = "0";
❸         this._container.style.opacity = "0";
❹         map.getPanes().markerPane.appendChild(this._container);
❺         this._container.innerHTML = this._label;
```

```
❻        var position = map.latLngToLayerPoint(this._latlng);
❼        position = new L.Point(
             position.x + this.options.offset.x,
             position.y + this.options.offset.y
❽        );
❾        L.DomUtil.setPosition(this._container, position);
    },
```

This method does the following:

1. Creates a new `<div>` element with the CSS class `leaflet-label` at ❶
2. Sets the `line-height` of that element to 0 to work around a quirk in the way Leaflet calculates position at ❷
3. Sets the `opacity` of the element to 0 to match its initial `hidden` status at ❸
4. Adds the new element to the `markerPane` layer in the map at ❹
5. Sets the contents of the element to the label text at ❺
6. Calculates a position for the label using its defined latitude/longitude at ❻ and then adjusts for any offset (❼ through ❽)
7. Positions the element on the map at ❾

✳ NOTE: Step 2—setting the `line-height` to 0—addresses a problem in the method Leaflet uses to position elements on the map. In particular, Leaflet does not account for other elements in the same parent container. By setting all elements to have no line height, we nullify this effect so that the calculated position is correct.

Finally, we add methods to get and set the label's status. As the following code indicates, our labels can have three different status values, and those values determine the opacity of the label.

```
getStatus: function() {
    return this._status;
},
setStatus: function(status) {
    switch (status) {
        case "hidden":
            this._status = "hidden";
            this._container.style.opacity = "0";
            break;
        case "shown":
            this._status = "shown";
            this._container.style.opacity = "1";
            break;
        case "dimmed":
            this._status = "dimmed";
            this._container.style.opacity = "0.5";
            break;
    }
}
```

We included the option to adjust the label's position because not all labels will look good positioned exactly on the latitude and longitude of the station. Most will benefit from slight shifts to avoid interference with the route polylines, text on the base map tiles, or other labels. For a custom visualization such as this example, there's no substitute for trial-and-error adjustments. We'll capture those adjustments for each label by adding another **offset** field to our data set. The augmented data set might begin like this:

```
var seaboard = [
{ "stop": "Washington",     "offset": [-30,-10], /* Data continues... */ },
{ "stop": "Fredericksburg", "offset": [ 6,  4], /* Data continues... */ },
{ "stop": "Richmond",       "offset": [ 6,  4], /* Data continues... */ },
// Data set continues...
```

Step 9: Build the Label Animation

To create the label animation, we can once again iterate through the trains' routes. Because we have more than one route, a general-purpose function will let us avoid duplicating code. As you can see from the following code, we're not using a fixed number of arguments to our function. Instead, we let the caller pass in as many individual routes as desired. All of those input parameters will be stored in the **arguments** object.

The **arguments** object looks a lot like a JavaScript array. It has a **length** property, and we can access individual elements using, for example, **arguments[0]**. Unfortunately, the object isn't a true array, so we can't use the convenient array methods (such as **forEach**) on it. As a workaround, the very first statement in our **buildLabelAnimation()** function, shown next, relies on a simple trick to convert the **arguments** object into the true **args** array.

```
var buildLabelAnimation = function() {
❶     var args = Array.prototype.slice.call(arguments),
          labels = [];

      // Calculate label animation values

      return labels;
}
```

It's a bit long winded, but the statement at ❶ effectively executes the **slice()** method on **arguments**. That operation clones **arguments** into a true array.

❋ **NOTE: This same trick works for nearly all of JavaScript's "array-like" objects. You can often use it to convert them into true arrays.**

With the routes converted into an array, we can use **forEach** to iterate through all of them, regardless of their number.

```
args.forEach(function(route) {
    var minutes = 0;
    route.forEach(function(stop,idx) {
        // Process each stop on the route
    });
});
```

As we begin processing each route, we set the minutes value to 0. Then we can use forEach again to iterate through all the stops on the route.

```
    route.forEach(function(stop,idx) {
        if (idx !== 0 && idx < route.length-1) {
❶          var label = new L.Label(
                [stop.latitude, stop.longitude],
                stop.stop,
                {offset: new L.Point(stop.offset[0], stop.offset[1])}
            );
            map.addLayer(label);
❷          labels.push(
                {minutes: minutes, label: label, status: "shown"}
            );
❸          labels.push(
                {minutes: minutes+50, label: label, status: "dimmed"}
            );
        }
        minutes += stop.duration;
    });
```

For each stop in the route, we first check to see whether that stop is the first or last one. If so, we don't want to animate a label for that stop. Otherwise, we create a new Label object at ❶ and add it to the map. Then we append that Label object to the labels array that's accumulating the label animation data. Notice that we add each label to this array twice. The first time we add it (❷) is at the time the animation reaches the stop; in this case, we add it with a status of shown. We also add the label to the array 50 minutes later (❸), this time with a status of dimmed. When we execute the animation, it will show the label when the route first reaches the station and then dim it a bit later.

Once we've iterated through all the routes, our labels array will indicate when each label should change status. At this point, though, the labels aren't listed in the order of their animation state changes. To fix that, we sort the array in order of increasing time.

```
labels.sort(function(a,b) {return a.minutes - b.minutes;})
```

To use our new function, we call and pass in all the routes to animate.

```
var labels = buildLabelAnimation(seaboard, southern);
```

Because we're not animating the start (Washington, DC) or end (Atlanta) of any routes, we can go ahead and display those on the map from the start. We can get the coordinates from any route; the following example uses the **seaboard** data set.

```
var start = seaboard[0];
var label = new L.Label(
    [start.latitude, start.longitude],
    start.stop,
    {offset: new L.Point(start.offset[0], start.offset[1])}
);
map.addLayer(label);
label.setStatus("shown");

var finish = seaboard[seaboard.length-1];
label = new L.Label(
    [finish.latitude, finish.longitude],
    finish.stop,
    {offset: new L.Point(finish.offset[0], finish.offset[1])}
);
map.addLayer(label);
label.setStatus("shown");
```

Step 10: Incorporate Label Animation in the Animation Step

Now that the label animation data is available, we can make some adjustments to our animation function to incorporate the labels as well as the polyline paths. The first change is deciding when to conclude the animation. Because we're dimming the labels some time after the route passes their stops, we can't simply stop when all the paths are drawn. That might leave some labels undimmed. We'll need separate variables to store the number of steps for each animation, and the total number of animation steps will be whichever is greater.

```
var maxPathSteps = Math.min.apply(null,
    routeAnimations.map(function(animation) {
        return animation.length
    })
);
var maxLabelSteps = labels[labels.length-1].minutes;
var maxSteps = Math.max(maxPathSteps, maxLabelSteps);
```

We also need a copy of the label animation data that we can destroy during the animation, while keeping the original data intact. We don't want to destroy the original so that users can replay the animation if they wish. The easiest way to copy a JavaScript array is by calling its `slice(0)` method.

＊ *NOTE:* **We can't simply copy the array using an assignment statement (var labelAnimation = labels). In JavaScript this statement would simply set labelAnimation to reference the same actual array as labels. Any changes made to the first would also affect the latter.**

```
var labelAnimation = labels.slice(0);
```

The animation step function itself needs some additional code to handle labels. It will now have five major parts; we'll walk through each of them in the code that follows. Our first adjustment is to make sure the code removes previous poly-line paths only as long as we're still adding paths to the map. That's true only when step is less than maxPathSteps.

```
if (step > 0 && step < maxPathSteps) {
    routeAnimations.forEach(function(animation) {
        map.removeLayer(animation[step-1]);
    });
}
```

The next block handles the case in which the user replays the animation.

```
if (step === maxSteps) {
❶      routeAnimations.forEach(function(animation) {
            map.removeLayer(animation[maxPathSteps-1]);
❷      });
❸      labelAnimation = labels.slice(0);
❹      labelAnimation.forEach(function(label) {
            label.label.setStatus("hidden");
❺      });
❻      step = 0;
}
```

When the animation replays, the step value will still be set to maxSteps from the prior animation. To reset the animation, we remove the last polyline paths for each route (❶ through ❷), make a new copy of the label animation data (❸), and hide all the labels (❹ through ❺). We also reset the step variable to 0 (❻).

The third block is a completely new block that animates the labels.

```
while (labelAnimation.length && step === labelAnimation[0].minutes) {
    var label = labelAnimation[0].label;
    if (step < maxPathSteps || label.getStatus() === "shown") {
        label.setStatus(labelAnimation[0].status);
    }
    labelAnimation.shift();
}
```

This block looks at the first element in the labelAnimation array, if one exists. If the time value for that element (its minutes property) is the same as the animation step, we check to see if we need to process it. We always process label animations when we're still adding the paths. If the paths are complete, though, we process animations only for labels that are already shown. Once we're finished with the first element in labelAnimation, we remove it from the array (using the shift() method) and check again. We must keep checking in case multiple label animation actions are scheduled at the same time.

The preceding code explains a couple of things about our label animation preparation. First, because we sorted the label animation, we only need to look at the first element in that array. That's much more efficient than searching through the entire array. Secondly, because we're working with a copy of the label animation array instead of the original, it's safe to remove elements once we finish processing them.

Now that we've handled all the label animations, we can return to the polyline paths. As long as there are still paths to animate, we add them to the map as before.

```
if (step < maxPathSteps) {
    routeAnimations.forEach(function(animation) {
        map.addLayer(animation[step]);
    });
}
```

The final code block in our animation step function is the same as before. We return an indication of whether the animation is complete.

```
return ++step === maxSteps;
```

There's one more improvement we can make to the animation, in this case with a judicious bit of CSS. Because we use the **opacity** property to change the status of the labels, we can define a CSS transition for that property that will make any changes less abrupt.

```
.leaflet-label {
    -webkit-transition: opacity .5s ease-in-out;
       -moz-transition: opacity .5s ease-in-out;
        -ms-transition: opacity .5s ease-in-out;
         -o-transition: opacity .5s ease-in-out;
            transition: opacity .5s ease-in-out;
}
```

To accommodate all popular browsers, we use appropriate vendor prefixes, but the effect of the rule is consistent. Whenever the browser changes the opacity of elements within a `leaflet-label` class, it will ease the transition in and out over a 500-millisecond period. This transition prevents the label animations from distracting users too much from the path animation that is the visualization's main effect.

Step 11: Add a Title

To complete the visualization, all we need is a title and a bit of explanation. We can build the title as a Leaflet control, much as we did for the animation control. The code to do this is quite straightforward.

```
L.Control.Title = L.Control.extend({
    options: {
❶        position: "topleft"
    },

❷    initialize: function (title, options) {
        L.setOptions(this, options);
        this._title = title;
    },

    onAdd: function (map) {
        var container = L.DomUtil.create("div", "leaflet-control-title");
❸        container.innerHTML = this._title;
        return container;
    }
});

L.control.title = function(title, options) {
    return new L.Control.Title(title, options);
};
```

We provide a default position in the top left of the map (❶) and accept a title string as an initialization parameter (❷). At ❸, we make it so that title string becomes the innerHTML of the control when we add it to the map.

Now we can use the following code to create a title object with our desired content and immediately add it to the map. Here's a simple implementation; Figure 6-13 includes some extra information.

```
L.control.title("Geography as a Competitive Advantage").addTo(map);
```

To set the title's appearance, we can define CSS rules for children of the leaflet-control-title class.

At this point, we have the interactive visualization of the two train routes in Figure 6-13. Users can clearly see that the Southerner has a quicker route from Washington to Atlanta.

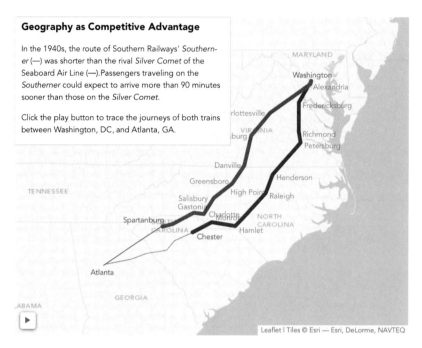

Geography as Competitive Advantage

In the 1940s, the route of Southern Railways' *Southern-er* (—) was shorter than the rival *Silver Comet* of the Seaboard Air Line (—). Passengers traveling on the *Southerner* could expect to arrive more than 90 minutes sooner than those on the *Silver Comet*.

Click the play button to trace the journeys of both trains between Washington, DC, and Atlanta, GA.

FIGURE 6-13: *Maps built in the browser with a map library can use interactivity to build interest.*

Summing Up

In this chapter, we've looked at several visualizations based on maps. In the first two examples, geographic regions were the main subjects of the visualization, and we built choropleth maps to compare and contrast those regions. Map fonts are quick and convenient, but only if they're available for the regions the visualization needs. Although it usually takes more effort, we have far more control over the map regions if we use SVGs to create our own custom maps. Unlike other image formats, SVG can be easily manipulated in a web page with just CSS and JavaScript. This chapter also looked at examples based on traditional mapping libraries. Mapping libraries are especially convenient when your data sets include latitude and longitude values, as the libraries take care of the complicated mathematics required to position those points on a two-dimensional projection. As we saw, some libraries are relatively simple yet perfectly capable of mapping a data set. Full-featured libraries such as Leaflet offer much more power and customization, and we relied on that extensibility for a custom, animated map.

7

Custom Visualizations
with D3.js

In this book we've looked at many JavaScript libraries that were designed for specific types of visualizations. If you need a certain type of visualization for your web page and there's a library that can create it, using that library is often the quickest and easiest way to create your visualization. There are drawbacks to such libraries, however. They all make assumptions about how the visualization should look and act, and despite the configuration options they provide, you don't have complete control over the results. Sometimes that's not an acceptable trade-off.

In this chapter, we'll look at an entirely different approach to JavaScript visualizations, one that allows us to be creative and to retain complete control over the results. As you might expect, that approach isn't always as easy as, for example, adding a charting library and feeding it data. Fortunately, there is a very powerful JavaScript library that can help: D3.js (*http://d3js.org/*). D3.js doesn't provide predefined visualizations such as charts, graphs, or maps. Instead, it's a toolbox for data visualization, and it gives you the tools to create *your own* charts, graphs, maps, and more.

To see some of the powerful features of D3.js, we'll take a whirlwind tour. This chapter's examples include the following:

▸   Adapting a traditional chart type for particular data

▸   Building a force-directed graph that responds to user interactions

▸   Displaying map-based data using high-quality SVGs

▸   Creating a fully customized visualization

Adapting a Traditional Chart Type

The most significant difference between D3.js and other JavaScript libraries is its philosophy. D3.js is not a tool for creating predefined types of charts and visualizations. Instead, it's a library to help you create any visualization, including custom and unique presentations. It takes more effort to create a standard chart with D3.js, but by using it we're not limited to standard charts. To get a sense of how D3.js works, we can create a custom chart that wouldn't be possible with a typical charting library.

For this example, we'll visualize one of the most important findings in modern physics—Hubble's law. According to that law, the universe is expanding, and as a result, the speed at which we perceive distant galaxies to be moving varies according to their distance from us. More precisely, Hubble's law proposes that the variation, or shift, in this speed is a linear function of distance. To visualize the law, we can chart the speed variation (known as *red shift velocity*) versus distance for several galaxies. If Hubble is right, the chart should look like a line. For our data, we'll use galaxies and clusters from Hubble's original 1929 paper (*http://www.pnas .org/content/15/3/168.full*) but updated with current values for distance and red shift velocities.

So far this task seems like a good match for a scatter chart. Distance could serve as the x-axis and velocity the y-axis. There's a twist, though: physicists don't actually know the distances or velocities that we want to chart, at least not exactly. The best they can do is estimate those values, and there is potential for error in both. But that's no reason to abandon the effort. In fact, potential errors in the values might be an important aspect for us to highlight in our visualization. To do that, we won't draw each value as a point. Rather, we'll show it as a box, and the box dimensions will correspond to the potential errors in the value. This approach isn't common for scatter plots, but D3.js can accommodate it with ease.

Step 1: Prepare the Data

Here is the data for our chart according to recent estimates.

Table 7-1: Distance and Red Shift Velocity for Nebulae and Clusters

Nebulae/cluster	Distance (Mpc)	Red shift velocity (km/s)
NGC 6822	0.500±0.010	57±2
NGC 221	0.763±0.024	200±6
NGC 598	0.835±0.105	179±3
NGC 4736	4.900±0.400	308±1
NGC 5457	6.400±0.500	241±2
NGC 4258	7.000±0.500	448±3
NGC 5194	7.100±1.200	463±3
NGC 4826	7.400±0.610	408±4
NGC 3627	11.000±1.500	727±3
NGC 7331	12.200±1.000	816±1
NGC 4486	16.400±0.500	1307±7
NGC 4649	16.800±1.200	1117±6
NGC 4472	17.100±1.200	729±2

We can represent that in JavaScript using the following array.

```
hubble_data = [
    { nebulae: "NGC 6822", distance:  0.500, distance_error: 0.010,
      velocity:   57, velocity_error: 2, },
    { nebulae: "NGC 221", distance:  0.763, distance_error: 0.024,
      velocity:  200, velocity_error: 6, },
    { nebulae: "NGC 598", distance:  0.835, distance_error: 0.105,
      velocity:  179, velocity_error: 3, },
    // Data set continues...
```

Step 2: Set Up the Web Page

D3.js doesn't depend on any other libraries, and it's available on most CDNs. All we need to do is include it in the page.

```
<!DOCTYPE html>
<html lang="en">
  <head>
    <meta charset="utf-8">
    <title></title>
  </head>
  <body>
❶   <div id="container"></div>
❷   <script
      src="//cdnjs.cloudflare.com/ajax/libs/d3/3.4.6/d3.min.js">
    </script>
  </body>
</html>
```

We include D3.js at ❷, and we set up a `<div>` with the `id` "container" at ❶ to contain our visualization.

Step 3: Create a Stage for the Visualization

Unlike higher-level libraries, D3.js doesn't draw the visualization on the page. We'll have to do that ourselves. In exchange for the additional effort, though, we get the freedom to pick our own drawing technology. We could follow the same approach as most libraries in this book and use HTML5's `<canvas>` element, or we could simply use native HTML. Now that we've seen it in action in Chapter 6, however, it seems using SVG is the best approach for our chart. The root of our graph, therefore, will be an `<svg>` element, and we need to add that to the page. We can define its dimensions at the same time using attributes.

If we were using jQuery, we might do something like the following:

```
var svg = $("<svg>").attr("height", height).attr("width", width);
$("#container").append(svg);
```

With D3.js our code is very similar:

```
var svg = d3.select("#container").append("svg")
    .attr("height", height)
    .attr("width", width);
```

With this statement, we're selecting the container, appending an `<svg>` element to it, and setting the attributes of that `<svg>` element. This statement highlights one important difference between D3.js and jQuery that often trips up developers starting out with D3.js. In jQuery the `append()` method returns the original selection so that you can continue operating on that selection. More specifically, `$("#container").append(svg)` returns `$("#container")`.

With D3.js, on the other hand, `append()` returns a different selection, the newly appended element(s). So `d3.select("#container").append("svg")` doesn't return the container selection, but rather a selection of the new `<svg>` element. The `attr()` calls that follow, therefore, apply to the `<svg>` element and not the "#container".

Step 4: Control the Chart's Dimensions

So far we haven't specified the actual values for the chart's height and width; we've only used `height` and `width` variables. Having the dimensions in variables will come in handy, and it will make it easy to incorporate margins into the visualization. The following code sets up those dimensions; its form is a common convention in D3.js visualizations.

```
var margin = {top: 20, right: 20, bottom: 30, left: 40},
    width = 640 - margin.left - margin.right,
    height = 400 - margin.top - margin.bottom;
```

We'll have to adjust the code that creates the main `<svg>` container to account for these margins.

```
var svg = d3.select("#chart1").append("svg")
    .attr("height", height + margin.left + margin.right)
    .attr("width", width + margin.top + margin.bottom);
```

To make sure our chart honors the defined margins, we'll construct it entirely within a child SVG group (`<g>`) element. The `<g>` element is just an arbitrary containing element in SVG, much like the `<div>` element for HTML. We can use D3.js to create the element and position it appropriately within the main `<svg>` element.

```
var chart = svg.append("g")
    .attr("transform",
        "translate(" + margin.left + "," + margin.top + ")"
    );
```

Visualizations must often rescale the source data. In our case, we'll need to rescale the data to fit within the chart dimensions. Instead of ranging from 0.5 to 17 Mpc, for example, galactic distance should be scaled between 0 and 920 pixels. Since this type of requirement is common for visualizations, D3.js has tools to help. Not surprisingly, they're **scale** objects. We'll create scales for both the x- and y-dimensions.

As the following code indicates, both of our scales are linear. Linear transformations are pretty simple (and we really don't need D3.js to manage them); however, D3.js supports other types of scales that can be quite complex. With D3.js, using more sophisticated scaling is just as easy as using linear scales.

```
var xScale = d3.scale.linear()
    .range([0,width]);
var yScale = d3.scale.linear()
    .range([height,0]);
```

We define both ranges as the desired limits for each scale. The x-scale ranges from 0 to the chart's width, and the y-scale ranges from 0 to the chart's height. Note, though, that we've reversed the normal order for the y-scale. That's because SVG dimensions (just like HTML dimensions) place 0 at the top of the area. That convention is the opposite of the normal chart convention, which places 0 at the bottom. To account for the reversal, we swap the values when defining the range.

At this point, we've set the ranges for each scale, and those ranges define the desired output. We also have to specify the possible inputs to each scale, which D3.js calls the *domain*. Those inputs are the minimum and maximum values for the distance and velocity. We can use D3.js to extract the values directly from the data. Here's how to get the minimum distance:

```
var minDist = d3.min(hubble_data, function(nebulae) {
    return nebulae.distance - nebulae.distance_error;
});
```

We can't simply find the minimum value in the data, because we have to account for the distance error. As we can see in the preceding snippet, D3.js accepts a function as a parameter to `d3.min()`, and that function can make the necessary adjustment. We can use the same approach for maximum values as well. Here's the complete code for defining the domains of both scales:

```
xScale.domain([
        d3.min(hubble_data, function(nebulae) {
            return nebulae.distance - nebulae.distance_error;
        }),
        d3.max(hubble_data, function(nebulae) {
            return nebulae.distance + nebulae.distance_error;
        })
    ])
    .nice();
yScale.domain([
        d3.min(hubble_data, function(nebulae) {
            return nebulae.velocity - nebulae.velocity_error;
        }),
        d3.max(hubble_data, function(nebulae) {
            return nebulae.velocity + nebulae.velocity_error;
        })
    ])
    .nice();
```

Step 5: Draw the Chart Framework

Axes are another common feature in visualizations, and D3.js has tools for those as well. To create the axes for our chart, we specify the appropriate scales and an orientation. As you can see from the following code, D3.js supports axes as part of its SVG utilities.

```
var xAxis = d3.svg.axis()
    .scale(xScale)
    .orient("bottom");
```

```
var yAxis = d3.svg.axis()
    .scale(yScale)
    .orient("left");
```

After defining the axes, we can use D3.js to add the appropriate SVG elements to the page. We'll contain each axis within its own `<g>` group. For the x-axis, we need to shift that group to the bottom of the chart.

```
var xAxisGroup = chart.append("g")
    .attr("transform", "translate(0," + height + ")");
```

To create the SVG elements that make up the axis, we could call the xAxis object and pass it the containing group as a parameter.

```
xAxis(xAxisGroup);
```

With D3.js, though, there's a more concise expression that avoids creating unnecessary local variables and preserves method chaining.

```
chart.append("g")
    .attr("transform", "translate(0," + height + ")")
    .call(xAxis);
```

And as long as we're preserving method chaining, we can take advantage of it to add yet another element to our chart: this time, it's the label for the axis.

```
chart.append("g")
    .attr("transform", "translate(0," + height + ")")
    .call(xAxis)
  .append("text")
    .attr("x", width)
    .attr("y", -6)
    .style("text-anchor", "end")
    .text("Distance (Mpc)");
```

If you look under the hood, you'll find that D3.js has done quite a bit of work for us in creating the axis, its tick marks, and its labels. Here's a taste of the SVG it builds:

```
<g class="x axis" transform="translate(0,450)">
    <g class="tick" transform="translate(0,0)" style="opacity: 1;">
        <line y2="6" x2="0"></line>
        <text y="9" x="0" dy=".71em" style="text-anchor: middle;">0</text>
    </g>
    <g class="tick" transform="translate(77.77,0)" style="opacity: 1;">
        <line y2="6" x2="0"></line>
        <text y="9" x="0" dy=".71em" style="text-anchor: middle;">2</text>
    </g>
    <!-- Additional tick marks... -->
```

```
<path class="domain" d="M0,6V0H700V6"></path>
<text x="700" y="-6" style="text-anchor: end;">Distance (Mpc)</text>
</g>
```

When we add the code for the y-axis, we've completed the framework for the chart.

```
chart.append("g")
    .attr("transform", "translate(0," + height + ")")
    .call(xAxis)
  .append("text")
    .attr("x", width)
    .attr("y", -6)
    .style("text-anchor", "end")
    .text("Distance (Mpc)");

chart.append("g")
    .call(yAxis)
  .append("text")
    .attr("transform", "rotate(-90)")
    .attr("y", 6)
    .attr("dy", ".71em")
    .style("text-anchor", "end")
    .text("Red Shift Velocity (km/s)")
```

The result of Figure 7-1 isn't very exciting without any data, but it does give us a framework for the chart.

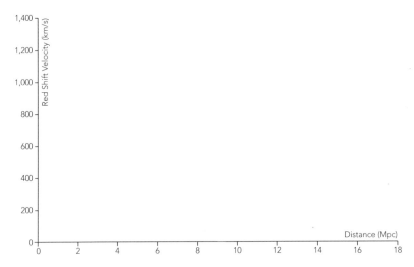

FIGURE 7-1: *D3.js provides tools to create the framework for a chart.*

As you can tell, we've had to write quite a bit of code just to get a couple of axes on the page. That's the nature of D3.js. It's not a library to which you can simply pass a data set and get a chart as an output. Instead, think of it as a collection of very useful utilities that you can use to help create your own charts.

Step 6: Add the Data to the Chart

Now that our chart's framework is ready, we can add the actual data. Because we want to show both the distance and velocity errors in the data, we can draw each point as a rectangle. For a simple, static chart, we can add SVG <rect> elements just as we've created the rest of the chart. We can take advantage of our x- and y-scales to calculate the dimensions of the rectangles.

```
hubble_data.forEach(function(nebulae) {
    chart2.append("rect")
        .attr("x", xScale(nebulae.distance - nebulae.distance_error))
        .attr("width", xScale(2 * nebulae.distance_error))
        .attr("y", yScale(nebulae.velocity - nebulae.velocity_error))
        .attr("height", height - yScale(2 * nebulae.velocity_error));
});
```

The preceding approach works fine for this example and results in the chart in Figure 7-2. Typically, however, D3.js visualizations combine their data sets directly with markup elements and rely on D3's **enter**, **update**, and **exit** selections to add the data to the page. We'll defer further discussion of this alternative approach until the next example.

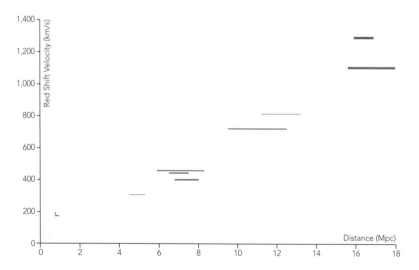

FIGURE 7-2: D3.js can render the data elements using any valid markup, including SVG <rect> elements with defined dimensions.

Step 7: Answer Users' Questions

Whenever you create a visualization, it's a good idea to anticipate questions that users might ask when they view it. In our example so far, we've presented a data set that leads to Hubble's law. But we haven't (yet) shown how well the data fits that law. Since that is such an obvious question, let's answer it right on the chart itself.

The current estimate for the Hubble constant (H_0) is about 70 km/s/Mpc. To show how that matches the data on our chart, we can create a line graph with that slope beginning at the point (0,0). A single SVG `<line>` is all that's required. Once again we rely on the D3.js scales to define the line's coordinates.

```
chart.append("line")
    .attr("x1",xScale(0))
    .attr("y1",yScale(0))
    .attr("x2",xScale(20))
    .attr("y2",yScale(1400));
```

In Figure 7-3 we can see that Hubble's law remains a good approximation.

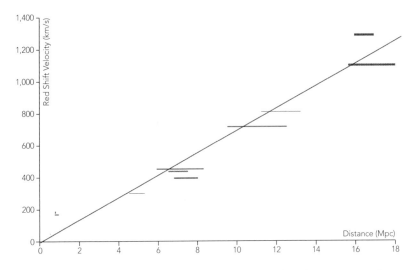

FIGURE 7-3: *The complete custom chart shows the data set exactly as we wish.*

Creating a Force-Directed Network Graph

Unlike the JavaScript plotting libraries we considered in the early chapters, D3.js is not limited to standard charts. In fact, it excels at specialized and custom graph types. To see its power, we'll create another version of the network graph from Chapter 4. In the earlier implementation we used the Sigma library, and most of our work was structuring the data into the format that library requires. We didn't have to decide how to draw the nodes and edges, how to connect them, or, once we enabled layouts, how to position them on the page. As we'll see next, D3.js doesn't make those decisions for us. For this example, we'll have to draw the nodes and edges, connect them to each other appropriately, and position them on the page. That may sound like a lot of work, but, as we'll also see, D3.js gives us a lot of tools to help.

Step 1: Prepare the Data

Since we're replicating the network graph from Chapter 4, we start with the same data set.

```
var albums = [
  {
    album: "Miles Davis - Kind of Blue",
    musicians: [
      "Cannonball Adderley",
      "Paul Chambers",
      "Jimmy Cobb",
      "John Coltrane",
      "Miles Davis",
      "Bill Evans"
    ]
  },{
    album: "John Coltrane - A Love Supreme",
    musicians: [
      "John Coltrane",
      "Jimmy Garrison",
      "Elvin Jones",
      "McCoy Tyner"
    ]
  // Data set continues...
```

For the visualization, it will be helpful to have two separate arrays, one for the graph's nodes and one for the graph's edges. Extracting those arrays from the original data is straightforward, so we won't bother looking at it in this chapter. You can, however, see the full implementation in the book's source code. The result looks like the following:

```
var nodes = [
  {
    "name": "Miles Davis - Kind of Blue",
    "links": [
      "Cannonball Adderley",
      "Paul Chambers",
      "Jimmy Cobb",
      "John Coltrane",
      "Miles Davis",
      "Bill Evans"
    ],
    "x": 270,
    "y": 200
```

```
    },
    {
      "name": "John Coltrane - A Love Supreme",
      "links": [
        "John Coltrane",
        "Jimmy Garrison",
        "Elvin Jones",
        "McCoy Tyner"
      ],
      "x": 307.303483,
      "y": 195.287474
    },
    // Data set continues...
];
```

For the nodes, we've added x and y properties to define a position on the graph. Initially the code arbitrarily sets these values so that the nodes are positioned in a circle.

```
var edges = [
    {
      "source": 0,
      "target": 16,
      "links": [
        "Cannonball Adderley",
        "Miles Davis"
      ]
    },
    {
      "source": 0,
      "target": 6,
      "links": [
        "Paul Chambers",
        "John Coltrane"
      ]
    },
    // Data set continues...
];
```

The edges indicate the two nodes that they connect as indices in the nodes array, and they include an array of the individual musicians that are common between the albums.

Step 2: Set Up the Page

As noted in the previous example, D3.js doesn't depend on any other libraries, and it's available on most content distribution networks. All we need to do is include it in the page.

```
<!DOCTYPE html>
<html lang="en">
  <head>
    <meta charset="utf-8">
    <title></title>
  </head>
  <body>
    <div id="container"></div>
    <script
      src="//cdnjs.cloudflare.com/ajax/libs/d3/3.4.6/d3.min.js">
    </script>
  </body>
</html>
```

Just as in the previous example, we set up a container for the visualization by including a `<div>` with the `id` "container".

Step 3: Create a Stage for the Visualization

This step is also the same as in the previous example.

```
var svg = d3.select("#container").append("svg")
    .attr("height", 500)
    .attr("width", 960);
```

We ask D3.js to select the container element and then insert an `<svg>` element within it. We also define `<svg>` element's size by setting the `height` and `width` attributes.

Step 4: Draw the Graph's Nodes

We'll draw each node as a circle by appending `<circle>` elements inside the `<svg>` stage. Based on the previous step, you might think that would be as simple as executing `svg.append("circle")` for each element in the `nodes` array.

```
nodes.forEach(function(node) {
    svg.append("circle");
});
```

That code will indeed add 25 circles to the visualization. What it *won't* do, though, is create any links between the data (nodes in the array) and the document (circle elements on the page). D3.js has another way to add the circles to the page that does create that linkage. In fact, not only will D3.js create the links, it will even manage them for us. This support becomes especially valuable as visualizations grow more complex.

＊ *NOTE:* **This feature is really the core of D3.js and, in fact, is the source for the name *D3*, which is shorthand for *data-driven documents*.**

Here's how we can use D3.js more effectively to add the `<circle>` elements to the graph:

```
var selection = svg.selectAll("circle")
    .data(nodes);

selection.enter().append("circle");
```

If you haven't seen D3.js code before, that fragment surely looks very strange. What are we trying to do by selecting `<circle>` elements before we've even created any? Won't the result just be empty? And if so, what's the point of the `data()` function that follows? To answer those questions, we have to understand how D3.js differs from traditional JavaScript libraries like jQuery. In those libraries a selection represents elements of HTML markup. With jQuery, `$("circle")` is nothing more than the `<circle>` elements in the page. With D3.js, however, selections are more than just markup elements. D3.js selections can contain both markup *and* data.

D3.js puts markup elements and data objects together with the `data()` function. The object on which it operates (`svg.selectAll("circle")` in the preceding code) supplies the elements, and its parameter (`nodes`, in this case) provides the data. The first statement in the fragment, therefore, tells D3.js that we want to match `<circle>` elements with nodes in our graph. We are, in effect, saying that we want one `<circle>` to represent each value in the `nodes` array.

The result is easiest to understand when there are exactly as many elements as there are data values. Figure 7-4 shows four `<circle>` elements and four albums. D3.js dutifully combines the two sets, giving us a selection of four objects. Each object has both a `<circle>` and an album.

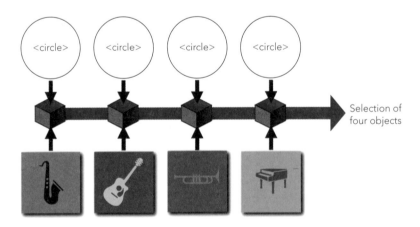

FIGURE 7-4: *D3.js selections can associate page content such as `<circle>` elements with data items such as albums.*

In general, though, we can't guarantee that there will be exactly as many elements as data values. Suppose, for example, only two <circle> elements existed for our four albums. As Figure 7-5 shows, D3.js still creates a selection of four objects, even though there aren't enough circles for all of them. Two of the objects will have a data value but no element.

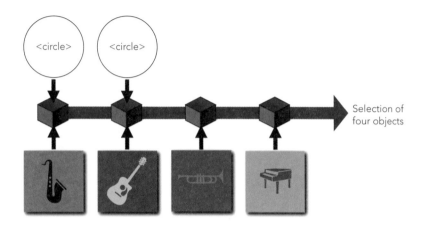

FIGURE 7-5: *D3.js selections keep track of page content that doesn't exist (yet).*

Our code fragment is an even more extreme example. When it executes, there are absolutely no circles on the page. There are, however, values in the nodes array that we're telling D3.js to use as data. D3.js, therefore, creates an object for each of those data values. It just won't have a <circle> element to go with them.

(Take a breath because magic is about to happen.)

Now we can look at the second statement in our code fragment. It starts with **selection.enter()**. The **enter()** function is a special D3.js function. It tells D3.js to search through the selection and find all of the objects that have a data value *but no markup element*. We then complete the statement by taking that subset of the selection and calling **append("circle")**. And with that function call, D3.js will take any object in the selection without a markup element and create a circle for it. That's how we add <circle> elements to the graph.

To be a little more concise, we can combine our two statements into a single one.

```
var nodeSelection = svg.selectAll("circle")
    .data(nodes)
    .enter().append("circle");
```

The effect for our visualization is to create a <circle> within the <svg> container for every node in the graph.

Step 5: Draw the Graph's Edges

You won't be surprised to find that adding the edges to the graph works just like adding nodes. We simply append `<line>` elements instead of circles.

```
var edgeSelection = svg.selectAll("line")
    .data(edges)
    .enter().append("line");
```

Even though we won't need to use them for this example, D3.js has other functions that complement the `enter()` function. To find objects that have a markup element but no data value, you can use the function `exit()`. And to find objects that have a markup element with a data value that has changed, you can use the function `update()`. The names *enter* and *exit* derive from a theater metaphor that D3.js associates with a visualization. The `enter()` subset represents those elements that are entering the stage, while the `exit()` subset represents elements exiting the stage.

Because we're using SVG elements for both the nodes and the edges, we can use CSS rules to style them. That's especially important for the edges because, by default, SVG lines have a stroke width of 0.

```
circle {
    fill: #ccc;
    stroke: #fff;
    stroke-width: 1px;
}

line {
    stroke: #777;
    stroke-width: 1px;
}
```

Step 6: Position the Elements

At this point, we've added the necessary markup elements to our visualization, but we haven't given them any dimensions or positions. As noted before, D3.js doesn't do any drawing, so we'll have to write the code to do it. And as noted in Step 2, we did assign somewhat arbitrary positions to the nodes by arranging them in a circle. For now, we can use that to position them.

To position an SVG circle, we set its `cx` and `cy` attributes to correspond to the circle's center. We also specify the circle's radius with the `r` attribute. Let's start with the radius; we'll set it to a fixed value for all nodes. We've already created a D3.js selection for all of those nodes. Setting their `r` attributes is a simple statement:

```
nodeSelection.attr("r", 10);
```

The cx and cy values are a little trickier because they're not the same for all of the nodes. Those values depend on properties of the data associated with the nodes. More specifically, each element in the nodes array has x and y properties. D3.js, however, makes it very easy to access those properties.

```
nodeSelection
    .attr("r", 10)
    .attr("cx", function(dataValue) { return dataValue.x; })
    .attr("cy", function(dataValue) { return dataValue.y; });
```

Instead of providing constant values for the attributes, we provide functions. D3.js will then call those functions and pass the data values as parameters. Our functions will return the appropriate value for the attribute.

Positioning the edges relies on a similar strategy. We want to set the endpoints of the lines to the centers of the corresponding nodes. Those endpoints are the x1,y1 and x2,y2 attributes of the <line> elements. Here's the code to set those attributes.

```
edgeSelection
    .attr("x1", function(d) { return nodes[d.source].x; })
    .attr("y1", function(d) { return nodes[d.source].y; })
    .attr("x2", function(d) { return nodes[d.target].x; })
    .attr("y2", function(d) { return nodes[d.target].y; });
```

As is conventional with D3.js, the parameter d is the data value.

With the elements finally drawn and positioned, we have the first version of our visualization with Figure 7-6.

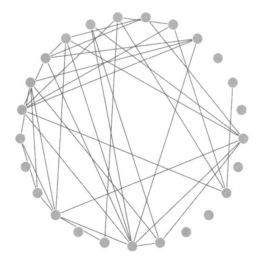

FIGURE 7-6: *D3.js provides tools to help draw the circles and lines for a network graph.*

Step 7: Add Force Direction to the Graph

The graph has all the essential components, but its layout doesn't make identifying the connections as easy as we'd like. In Chapter 4 the Sigma library could automate the layout with only a couple of lines of JavaScript. To perform that automation, Sigma uses a force-direction algorithm. Force direction treats nodes as physical objects and simulates the effect of forces such as gravity and electromagnetism.

With D3.js we cannot rely on the library to fully automate the layout. As we've seen, D3.js does not draw any of the graph elements, so it cannot, by itself, set positions and dimensions. D3.js does, however, provide a lot of tools to help us create our own graph layouts. One of those tools is the *force layout tool*. As you might expect, the force layout tool helps us draw our own force-directed graph. It handles all of the messy and complex calculations that underlie force direction and gives us results we can use directly in code that draws the graph.

To get started with the layout, we define a new **force** object. That object accepts many configuration parameters, but only five are essential for our visualization:

▶ The dimensions of the graph

▶ The nodes in the graph

▶ The edges in the graph

▶ The distance we'd like to see between connected nodes

▶ How strongly nodes repel each other, a parameter D3.js calls *charge*

The last parameter can take a bit of trial and error to optimize for any particular visualization. In our case, we'll want to increase it substantially above its default (**-30**) because we have a lot of nodes in a small space. (Negative charge values indicate repulsion.) Here's the code to set all of those values:

```
var force = d3.layout.charge()
    .size([width, height])
    .nodes(nodes)
    .links(edges)
    .linkDistance(40)
    .charge(-500);
```

When we tell D3.js to start its force-direction calculations, it will generate events at intermediate steps and when the calculations complete. Force direction often takes several seconds to execute fully, and if we wait until the calculations are complete before we draw the graph, users may think the browser has frozen. It's usually better to update the graph at each iteration so users see some indication of progress. To do that, we can add a function to respond to the intermediate force-direction calculations. That happens on a D3.js **tick** event.

```
force.on("tick", function() {
    // Update graph with intermediate results
});
```

Each time D3.js calls our event handler function, it will have updated the x and y properties of the nodes array. The new values will reflect how the force direction has nudged the nodes on the graph's stage. We can update our graph accordingly by changing the SVG attributes of the circles and lines. Before we do that, however, we can take advantage of the fact that D3.js is giving us an opportunity to tweak the force-direction algorithm as it executes. One problem that we may encounter, especially with the large charge force we defined, is that nodes may repel each other so strongly that some tend to drift off the stage entirely. We can prevent that by ensuring that the node positions remain within the dimensions of the graph.

```
force.on("tick", function() {
    nodeSelection.each(function(node) {
        node.x = Math.max(node.x, 5);
        node.y = Math.max(node.y, 5);
        node.x = Math.min(node.x, width-5);
        node.y = Math.min(node.y, height-5);
    });
    // Update graph with intermediate results
});
```

We've added or subtracted 5 in the preceding fragment to account for the radius of the nodes' circles.

Once we've adjusted the nodes' properties to keep them on the stage, we can update their positions. The code is exactly the same as the code we used to position them initially.

```
nodeSelection
    .attr("cx", function(d) { return d.x; })
    .attr("cy", function(d) { return d.y; });
```

We'll also want to adjust the endpoints of our edge lines. For these objects, however, there's a small twist. When we initialized the edges array, we set the source and target properties to the indices of the respective nodes in the nodes array. When the D3.js force layout tool begins execution, it replaces those indices with direct references to the nodes themselves. That makes it a little easier for us to find the appropriate coordinates for the lines.

```
edgeSelection
    .attr("x1", function(d) { return d.source.x; })
    .attr("y1", function(d) { return d.source.y; })
    .attr("x2", function(d) { return d.target.x; })
    .attr("y2", function(d) { return d.target.y; });
```

With our function ready to handle updates from the force-direction calculations, we can tell D3.js to start its work. That's a simple method of the force object.

```
force.start();
```

With that statement, the graph begins an animated transition to its final, force-directed state, as Figure 7-7 shows.

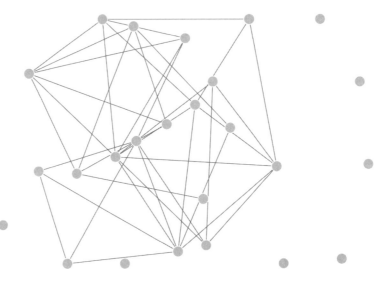

FIGURE 7-7: *The D3.js force layout tool provides the information to reposition network graph elements.*

Step 8: Add Interactivity

Since D3.js is a JavaScript library, you would expect it to support interactions with the user. It does, and to demonstrate, we can add a simple interaction to the graph. When a user clicks on one of the nodes in the graph, we can emphasize that node and its neighbors.

Event handlers in D3.js closely resemble those in other JavaScript libraries such as jQuery. We define an event handler using the on( ) method of a selection, as in the following code.

```
nodeSelection.on("click", function(d) {
    // Handle the click event
});
```

The first parameter to on( ) is the event type, and the second parameter is a function that D3.js will call when the event occurs. The parameter to this function is the data object that corresponds to the selection element, and by convention it's named d. Because we're adding the event to the selection of nodes (nodeSelection), d will be one of the graph nodes.

For our visualization, we'll emphasize the clicked node by adding a CSS-accessible class to the corresponding <circle> and by increasing the circle's size. The class makes it possible to style the circle uniquely, but a circle's size cannot be specified with CSS rules. Ultimately, therefore, we have to do two things to the circle: add the selected class and increase the radius using the r attribute. Of course, in order to do either, we have to select the <circle> element. When D3.js calls an event handler, it sets this equal to the target of the event; we can turn that target into a selection with d3.select(this). The following code, therefore, is all it takes to change the clicked node's circle.

```
d3.select(this)
    .classed("selected", true)
    .attr("r", 1.5*nodeRadius);
```

We can do something similar by adding a selected class to all the edges that connect to the clicked node. To find those edges we can iterate through the full edge selection. D3.js provides the each() function to do just that.

```
edgeSelection.each(function(edge) {
    if ((edge.source === d) || (edge.target === d)) {
❶       d3.select(this).classed("selected",true);
    }
});
```

As we look at each edge, we check the source and target properties to see if either matches our clicked node. When we find a match, we add the selected class to the edge. Note that at ❶ we're once again using d3.select(this). In this example the code is inside the each() function, so this will equal the particular element of the current iteration. In our case that's the <line> for the edge.

The preceding code handles setting the selected class, but we still need to remove it when appropriate. We can remove it from all the other circles (and make sure their radii are restored to their default values) by operating on the node selection.

```
nodeSelection
❶   .filter(function(node) { return node !== d; })
    .classed("selected", false)
    .attr("r", nodeRadius);
```

The code looks the same as we've seen before, except that at ❶ we use the D3.js filter() function to limit the selection to the nodes other than the one that was clicked.

A similar process resets the **selected** class on all the edges. We can remove the class from all edges first, before we add to the appropriate edges in the previous code fragment. Here's the code that removes it; with D3.js it takes only a single line:

```
edgeSelection.classed("selected", false);
```

And finally, if the user clicks on a node that's already selected, we can restore it to its default state like so:

```
d3.select(this)
    .classed("selected", true)
    .attr("r", 1.5*nodeRadius);
```

When you put all of the preceding code fragments together, you have the complete event handler shown here:

```
nodeSelection.on("click", function(d) {

    nodeSelection
        .filter(function(node) { return node !== d; })
        .classed("selected", false)
        .attr("r", nodeRadius);

    edgeSelection.classed("selected", false);

    if (d3.select(this).classed("selected")) {
        d3.select(this)
            .classed("selected", false)
            .attr("r", nodeRadius)

    } else {
        d3.select(this)
            .classed("selected", true)
            .attr("r", 1.5*nodeRadius);

        edgeSelection.each(function(edge) {
            if ((edge.source === d) || (edge.target === d)) {
                d3.select(this).classed("selected",true);
            }
        });
    }
});
```

Along with a bit of CSS styling to emphasize the selected circles and lines, this code results in the interactive visualization of Figure 7-8.

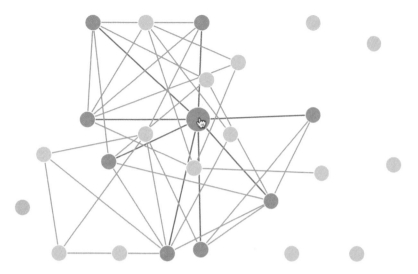

FIGURE 7-8: D3.js includes functions to make visualizations interactive.

Step 9: Experiment with Other Enhancements

Our example has explored many of the features that D3.js provides for custom visualizations. The code so far, however, has only scratched the surface of D3's capabilities. We haven't added labels to our graph or animated the transitions in the graph's state. In fact, it's a pretty safe bet that if there is anything we want to add to the visualization, D3.js has tools to help. And although we don't have the time or space to consider other enhancements here, the source code for the book does include a more full-featured implementation that takes advantage of other D3.js capabilities.

Creating a Scalable Map

The first two examples touched on some of the capabilities of D3.js, but the library includes many others. From the examples in Chapter 6, we know some of the best visualizations rely on maps, and D3.js—as a general-purpose visualization library— has extensive support for mapping. To illustrate that support, we'll create a map that shows tornado sightings in the continental United States.

Step 1: Prepare the Data

The US National Oceanic and Atmospheric Administration (*http://www.noaa.gov/*) publishes an extensive set of weather and climate data on its Climate Data Online site (*http://www.ncdc.noaa.gov/cdo-web/*). That data includes all storm events reported in the United States and its territories. We can download the data set for the year 2013 as a comma-separated value (CSV) file. Because the file is extremely large and contains many events that aren't tornadoes, we can edit it to remove the extraneous information using a spreadsheet application such as Microsoft

Excel or Numbers for Mac. For this visualization, we need only records that have an event_type equal to "Tornado", and we want only the columns for the tornado's latitude, longitude, and Enhanced Fujita Scale classification (a measure of tornado strength). Once we've pruned the CSV file appropriately, it will look something like the following data.

```
f_scale,latitude,longitude
EF1,33.87,-88.23
EF1,33.73,-87.9
EF0,33.93,-87.5
EF1,34.06,-87.37
EF1,34.21,-87.18
EF1,34.23,-87.11
EF1,31.54,-88.16
EF1,31.59,-88.06
EF1,31.62,-87.85
--snip--
```

Since we're going to access this data using JavaScript, you might be tempted to convert the file from CSV to JSON format. It's better, however, to keep the data in a CSV file. D3.js has full support for CSV, so we don't really gain anything by converting to JSON. More importantly, the JSON file would be more than four times larger than the CSV version, and that extra size would slow down the loading of our web page.

Step 2: Set Up the Page

Our skeletal web page is no different from the other D3.js examples. We set aside a container for the map and include the D3.js library.

```
<!DOCTYPE html>
<html lang="en">
  <head>
    <meta charset="utf-8">
    <title></title>
  </head>
  <body>
    <div id="map"></div>
    <script
      src="//cdnjs.cloudflare.com/ajax/libs/d3/3.4.6/d3.min.js">
    </script>
  </body>
</html>
```

Step 3: Create a Map Projection

If you can't quite recall your geography lessons about map projections, don't worry; D3.js can handle all of the heavy lifting. Not only does it have extensive support for common projections, but it also supports extensions for custom projections tailored specifically for visualizations. For example, there's a modified Albers projection that's optimized for choropleth maps of the United States. It repositions (and resizes) Alaska and Hawaii to provide a convenient map of all 50 states. In our case, since there were no tornado sightings in Alaska or Hawaii in 2013, we can use a standard Albers projection.

We set up the projection in the following code.

```
❶ var width = 640,
❷     height = 400;

❸ var projection = d3.geo.albers()
❹     .scale(888)
❺     .translate([width / 2, height / 2]);

❻ var path = d3.geo.path()
❼     .projection(projection);
```

First, at ❶ and ❷, we define the size of our map in pixels. Then, at ❸, we create the Albers projection. D3.js supports many adjustments to position the projection appropriately on the page, but the default values are fine in our case. We need only to scale the map at ❹ and center it at ❺.

To draw the map on the page, we're going to use SVG <path> elements, but our map data takes the form of latitude and longitude values. D3.js has a **path** object to translate geographic coordinates to SVG paths based on a particular map projection. At ❻ and ❼, we create our **path** object.

Step 4: Initialize the SVG Container

We can create an SVG container to hold the map, just as we did in the previous D3.js example.

```
var svg = d3.select("#map").append("svg")
    .attr("width", width)
    .attr("height", height);

❶ var g = svg.append("g");
```

As we'll see in later steps, it will be helpful have an inner group in which to place the map. This inner group (defined by a <g> element) acts much like an arbitrary <div> element in HTML. We create that inner group at ❶.

Step 5: Retrieve the Map Data

For our visualization, the map data is nothing but a map of the United States with individual states. D3.js uses GeoJSON (*http://geojson.org/*) for its map data. Unlike most of the image tiles that we used in Chapter 6, GeoJSON data is vector based, so it can be used at any scale. GeoJSON data is also in JSON format, which makes it especially compatible with JavaScript.

Since our data is in a JSON format, we can use the `d3.json()` function to retrieve it. This function is almost identical to the jQuery `$.getJSON()` function.

```
d3.json("data/us-states.json", function(map) {
    // Process the JSON map data
});
```

Step 6: Draw the Map

Once we have our data, we can draw the map on the page. The code in this step is very similar to that in the previous example. Each state will be a `<path>` element within the `<g>` container.

```
❶ g.selectAll("path")
❷     .data(map.features)
❸   .enter().append("path")
❹     .attr("d", path);
```

Using D3.js conventions, we create a selection of `<path>` elements at ❶ and bind those elements to our data at ❷. When there is no element, we create one ❸ and we set its **d** attribute to be the path associated with the data, given our projection. Note that **path** at ❹ is the object we created in Step 4. It is a function that translates the latitude and longitude information into appropriate SVG coordinates.

As we can see from Figure 7-9, D3.js gives us the paths required to create a nice SVG map.

FIGURE 7-9: *D3.js helps create vector maps from geographic JSON data.*

Step 7: Retrieve the Weather Data

Now our map is ready for some data. We can retrieve the CSV file using another D3.js utility. Note, though, that all of the properties of a CSV file are considered text strings. We'll want to convert those strings to numbers. We also want to filter out the few tornado sightings that don't include latitude and longitude information.

```
   d3.csv("tornadoes.csv", function(data) {
❶      data = data.filter(function(d, i) {
❷          if (d.latitude && d.longitude) {
❸              d.latitude = +d.latitude;
❹              d.longitude = +d.longitude;
❺              d.f_scale = +d.f_scale[2];
❻              d.position = projection([
❼                  d.longitude, d.latitude
                ]);
❽              return true;
            }
        });
        // Continue creating the visualization...
   });
```

Once the browser has retrieved the CSV file from the server, we can begin processing it at ❶. Here we're using the .filter() method of arrays to iterate through the data values. The .filter() method eliminates the data points without latitude and longitude values. It only returns true at ❽ if both values are present ❷. While we're checking the data points for latitude and longitude, we convert the string values into numbers at ❸ and ❹, extract the number from the Enhanced Fujita Scale classification at ❺, and calculate the position of the sighting in SVG coordinates at ❻ and ❼ using the projection function we created in Step 3.

Step 8: Plot the Data

With the data retrieved, cleaned, and converted, it's a simple matter to plot the points on the map. Once again we'll use the traditional D3.js approach.

```
   g.selectAll("circle")
       .data(data)
     .enter().append("circle")
       .attr("cx", function(d) { return d.position[0]; })
       .attr("cy", function(d) { return d.position[1]; })
❶     .attr("r",  function(d)  { return 4 + 2*d.f_scale; });
```

Each data point is an SVG <circle> element, so we select those elements, bind the data to the selection, and use the .enter() function to create new <circle> elements to match the data.

As you can see, we set the position of the circles using the `position` property we created in the previous step. Also, to indicate the relative strength of each tornado, we make the size of the circle proportional to the Enhanced Fujita Scale classification at **❶**. The result in Figure 7-10 is a nice map of 2013 tornado sightings in the continental United States.

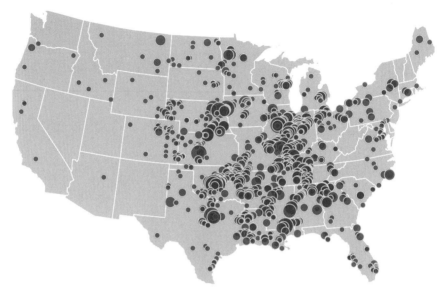

FIGURE 7-10: *Adding points to a map is easy with D3.js projections.*

Step 9: Add Interactivity

Maps naturally invite users to zoom in and pan around, and D3.js makes it easy to support those standard map interactions. In fact, D3.js gives us complete control, so we're not limited to standard map interaction conventions. Let's do something a little different with our map. We can make it so that a user can click any state to zoom in on it. Clicking a state that's already zoomed in on will then zoom the map back out to its default. As you'll see, this behavior is easy to implement with D3.js.

The first bit of code we'll add is a variable that keeps track of the particular state into which the map is zoomed. Initially, the user won't have zoomed anywhere, so that variable is empty.

```
var active = d3.select(null)
```

Next we add an event handler to all of the state `<path>` elements. We can do that when we create the elements (which we did earlier in Step 6).

```
g.selectAll("path")
    .data(map.features)
  .enter().append("path")
    .attr("d", path)
❶    .on("click", clicked);
```

The extra statement is at ❶. Like jQuery, D3.js gives us an easy way to add event handlers to HTML and SVG elements. Now we have to write that event handler.

The handler needs to identify the state that the user clicked, calculate the position of that state (in SVG coordinates), and transition the map to zoom to those coordinates. Before we look at the implementation in detail, it's worth noting that D3.js event handlers are optimized to work with data visualizations (which shouldn't be surprising). In particular, the parameter passed to the handler is the data item associated with the target element (conventionally named d). The JavaScript context (this) is set to the specific element that received the event. If the handler needs access to the other properties of the JavaScript event, they're available in the d3.event global variable. Here's how those conventions work in a real event handler:

```
var clicked = function(d) {
❶    active.attr("fill", "#cccccc");
    active = d3.select(this)
        .attr("fill", "#F77B15");

❷    var bounds = path.bounds(d),
        dx = bounds[1][0] - bounds[0][0],
        dy = bounds[1][1] - bounds[0][1],
        x = (bounds[0][0] + bounds[1][0]) / 2,
        y = (bounds[0][1] + bounds[1][1]) / 2,
❸        scale = .9 / Math.max(dx / width, dy / height),
❹        translate = [
            width / 2 - scale * x,
            height / 2 - scale * y];

❺    g.transition()
        .duration(750)
        .attr("transform", "translate(" +
            translate + ")scale(" +
            scale + ")");
};
```

In the first code block (starting at ❶), we manipulate the map colors. The previously zoomed state is reset to a muted gray, and the clicked state is filled with a vibrant orange. Notice that this same code resets the active variable so that it accurately tracks the zoomed state. Next, starting at ❷, we calculate the bounds of the zoomed state. Or rather, we let D3.js do the calculation. All the work happens in the **bounds()** function we call at ❷. The other lines are mostly just extracting the individual parts of that calculation. At ❸, we calculate how to scale the map so that the zoomed state fills 90 percent of the map. Then, starting at ❹, we calculate how to shift the map to center that state. The final block of code, starting at ❺, adjusts the map by scaling and translating the SVG. As you can see, we're using a D3.js transition to animate the change in view.

The code we've seen so far still needs a few minor additions to deal with some loose ends, but I'll leave those to the book's source code (*http://jsDataV.is/source/*). The result in Figure 7-11 is a nice interactive map of our data.

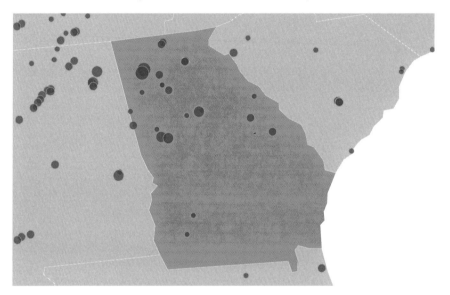

FIGURE 7-11: *D3.js makes it easy to add custom interactions to maps.*

Creating a Unique Visualization

If you've followed the first three examples in this chapter, you're probably beginning to appreciate the level of flexibility D3.js offers compared to traditional JavaScript libraries. Instead of creating visualizations for you, it provides many tools and utilities that you can use however you wish. We've used that flexibility to add unconventional error bars to a chart, to refine the behavior of a network graph, and to customize user interactions with a map. With D3.js, however, we aren't limited to minor adjustments to existing visualization types. Instead, we can use the library to create unique visualizations that are nothing like those found in traditional libraries.

In this example, we'll use the same data from the previous visualization—tornado sightings in 2013 from the US National Oceanic and Atmospheric Administration's Climate Data Online site (*http://www.noaa.gov/cdo-web/*). Rather than placing the sightings on a map, however, we'll create an interactive, hierarchical visualization that lets users understand the number of sightings by region, state, or even counties within a state. A circular hierarchy can be especially effective for this subject matter, so we'll create a sunburst visualization with rotational animations. The code that follows is based on an example (*http://bl.ocks.org/ mbostock/4348373/*) developed by Mike Bostock, the lead D3.js developer.

✳ *NOTE:* **It is also possible to create sunburst visualizations using some charting libraries, generally by customizing a variation of the pie chart. Those libraries, however, are much more focused on off-the-shelf use. Creating custom visualizations is generally much easier with a library like D3.js, which is designed especially for customization.**

Step 1: Prepare the Data

As before, we'll clean and prune the 2013 tornado sightings data set. Instead of longitude, latitude, and Enhanced Fujita Scale classification, however, we'll keep the state and county. We'll also add a region name as a way to group subsets of states. The resulting CSV file begins as follows.

```
state,region,county
Connecticut,New England,Fairfield County
Connecticut,New England,Hartford County
Connecticut,New England,Hartford County
Connecticut,New England,Tolland County
Maine,New England,Somerset County
Maine,New England,Washington County
Maine,New England,Piscataquis County
--snip--
```

Step 2: Set Up the Page

Our skeletal web page is no different from the other D3.js examples. We set aside a container for the visualization and include the D3.js library.

```
<!DOCTYPE html>
<html lang="en">
  <head>
    <meta charset="utf-8">
    <title></title>
  </head>
  <body>
    <div id="chart"></div>
    <script
      src="//cdnjs.cloudflare.com/ajax/libs/d3/3.4.6/d3.min.js">
    </script>
  </body>
</html>
```

Step 3: Create a Stage for the Visualization

As with our other D3.js examples, we start by creating an `<svg>` container for the visualization. Within that container, we'll also add a group (`<g>`) element.

```
var width = 640,
    height = 400,
❶    maxRadius = Math.min(width, height) / 2;

var svg = d3.select("#chart").append("svg")
    .attr("width", width)
    .attr("height", height);

var g = svg.append("g");
❷    .attr("transform", "translate(" +
        (width  / 2) + "," +
        (height / 2) + ")");
```

This code contains a couple of new wrinkles. First, at ❶, we calculate the maximum radius for the visualization. This value—which is half of the height or the width, whichever is smaller—will come in handy in the code that follows. More interestingly, starting at ❷, we translate the inner `<g>` container so that its coordinate system places the point (0,0) right in the center of the visualization. This translation makes it easy to center the sunburst and calculate sunburst parameters.

Step 4: Create Scales

When it's complete, our visualization will consist of areas corresponding to regions in the United States; larger areas will represent regions with more tornadoes. Because we're dealing with areas, we'll need two dimensions for each region. But we're not going to draw our areas as simple rectangles; instead we're going to use arcs. That will require a bit of trigonometry, but fortunately, D3.js provides a lot of help. We'll start by defining some **scale** objects. We first saw scales in Step 4 of "Adapting a Traditional Chart Type" on page 227, where we used them to translate data values to SVG coordinates. The scales in the following code do much the same, except they're using polar coordinates.

```
var theta = d3.scale.linear()
    .range([0, 2 * Math.PI]);
var radius= d3.scale.sqrt()
    .range([0, maxRadius]);
```

As you can see, the angular scale is a linear scale that ranges from 0 to 2π (or 360°). The radial scale ranges from 0 to the maximum radius, but it's not linear. Instead, this scale is a square root scale; D3.js takes the square root of the input before computing the output. The area of an arc varies as the square of its radius, and the square root scale compensates for this effect.

The scales we've defined come in handy in the next bit of code, where we define a function that calculates the SVG path for a single arc. Most of the work takes place in the D3.js function **d3.svg.arc()**, which computes an arc's path. That function, though, needs four parameters: the starting and ending angles and the starting and ending radii for the arc. The values for those parameters come from our scales.

When we use our **arc()** function later in the code, we're going to call it with a D3.js selection. That selection will have a data value associated with it, and the data value will include four properties:

.x the starting x–position for the data

.dx the data's length along the x–axis (Δx)

.y the starting y–position for the data

.dx the data's length along the y–axis (Δy)

Given those properties, here's the code that generates the arc path.

```
var arc = d3.svg.arc()
    .startAngle(function(d) {
        return Math.max(0, Math.min(2 * Math.PI, theta(d.x)));
    })
    .endAngle(function(d) {
        return Math.max(0, Math.min(2 * Math.PI, theta(d.x + d.dx)));
    })
    .innerRadius(function(d) {
        return Math.max(0, radius(d.y));
    })
    .outerRadius(function(d) {
        return Math.max(0, radius(d.y + d.dy));
    });
```

The code itself is pretty straightforward, but a picture helps explain why we're using the code this way. Assume that the data associated with a selection has an (x,y) position of (12.5,10), a width of 25, and a height of 30. The data properties would then be:

▶ .x = 12.5

▶ .dx = 25

▶ .y = 10

▶ .dy = 30

With Cartesian coordinates, we could draw the selection as on the left side of Figure 7-12. Our scales and arc function will transform the rectangle to the arc shown on the right side of the figure.

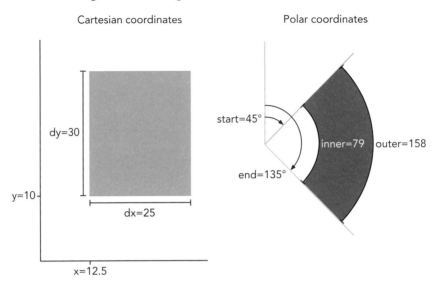

FIGURE 7-12: *D3.js helps transform a rectangular area into an arc.*

We haven't specified the ranges of the x- and y-scales, but assume for now that each ranges from 0 to 100. The starting x-value of 12.5, therefore, is 12.5 percent of the full range. When we convert that value to polar coordinates, the result will be 12.5 percent of the full 360°. That's 45°, or π/4. The x-value extends another 25 percent, so the final x-value adds another 90°, or π/2, to the starting value. For the y-values, our scales take the square root and map the results to the domain from 0 to 250 (`maxRadius`). The initial value of 10, therefore, is divided by 100 (for the range) and transformed to $\sqrt{0.1} \times 250$, or 79. The final value of 10 + 30 results in a radius of $\sqrt{0.4} \times 250$, or 158. That's the process that creates an SVG for each data value.

Step 5: Retrieve the Data

With the initial preparation complete, we're now ready to process the data. As in the previous example, we'll use **d3.csv()** to retrieve the CSV file from the server.

```
d3.csv("tornadoes.csv", function(data) {
    // Continue processing the data...
});
```

When D3.js retrieves the file, it creates a data structure that begins like the following fragment.

```
[ {
    "state":"Connecticut",
    "region":"New England",
    "county":"Fairfield County"
  },{
    "state":"Connecticut",
    "region":"New England",
    "county":"Hartford County"
  },{
    "state":"Connecticut",
    "region":"New England",
    "county":"Hartford County"
  },
// Data set continues...
```

That data structure reflects the data, but it doesn't include the `.x`, `.dx`, `.y`, and `.dy` properties that we need to draw the arcs. There's additional work to be done to calculate those values. If you recall the second example in this chapter, we've seen this situation before. We have a set of raw data, but we need to augment that raw data with additional properties for the visualization. In the earlier example, we used the D3.js force layout to calculate the extra properties. In this case, we can use the partition layout.

Before we can use the partition layout, however, we have to restructure our data. The partition layout works with hierarchical data, and right now all we have is a single dimensional array. We must structure the data to reflect the natural hierarchy of region, state, and county. Here again, however, D3.js can help us. The `d3.nest()` operator analyzes an array of data and extracts the hierarchy from it. If you're familiar with database commands, it's the D3.js equivalent of the GROUP BY operation. We can use the operator to create a new version of the data.

```
❶ var hierarchy = {
       key: "United States",
       values: d3.nest()
❷          .key(function(d) { return d.region; })
           .key(function(d) { return d.state; })
           .key(function(d) { return d.county; })
❸          .rollup(function(leaves) {
❹              return leaves.length;
           })
❺          .entries(data)
   };
```

First, at ❶, we define the variable that will hold our restructured data. It's an object with two properties. The `.key` property is set to `"United States"`, and the `.values` property is the result of the `d3.nest()` operation. Starting at ❷, we tell the operator to group the data, first by `.region`, then by `.state`, and finally by `.county`. Then, at ❸ and ❹, we tell the operator to set the final value to be the count of entries for the final grouping. Finally, at ❺, we pass the original data set to the operator. When this statement finishes, the `hierarchy` variable contains a structured version of our data that begins like the following fragment:

```
{
    "key": "United States",
    "values": [
        {
            "key": "New England",
            "values": [
                {
                    "key": "Connecticut",
                    "values": [
                        {
                            "key": "Fairfield County",
                            "values": 1
                        },{
                            "key": "Hartford County",
                            "values": 2
                        },{
// Data set continues...
```

This structure matches what the partition layout needs, but there's still one more step we need to take. The **d3.nest()** operator places both child arrays and leaf data in the `.values` property. By default, however, the partition layout expects the data to use different property names for each type of property. More specifically, it expects child nodes to be stored in the `.children` property and data values in the `.value` property. Since the **d3.nest()** operator doesn't create exactly that structure, we have to extend the default partition layout. Here's the code to do that:

```
var partition = d3.layout.partition()
❶      .children(function(d) {
❷          return Array.isArray(d.values) ? d.values : null;
        })
❸      .value(function(d) {
❹          return d.values;
        });
```

At ❶ and ❷, we provide a custom function to return a node's children. If the node's `.values` property is an array, then that property contains the children. Otherwise, the node has no children and we return `null`. Then at ❸ and ❹, we provide a custom function to return a node's value. Since this function is used only when no children exist, the `.values` property has to contain the node value.

Step 6: Draw the Visualization

It's taken a bit of work to get to this point, but now we're ready to draw the visualization. Here's where we see the payoff for all the work. It takes only a few lines of code to create the visualization.

```
❶ var path = g.selectAll("path")
      .data(partition.nodes(hierarchy))
❷   .enter().append("path")
❸     .attr("d", arc);
```

This code follows the same structure we've used for all of our D3.js examples. At ❶, we create a selection of the SVG elements that represent our data; in this case we're using <path> elements. We then bind the selection to the hierarchical data using the custom partition layout. At ❷, we identify the data values that don't (yet) have an associated SVG element, and at ❸ we create new elements for those values. That final step relies on the .arc() function that we created in Step 4. We haven't yet added any colors or labels, but we can see from Figure 7-13 that we're on the right track.

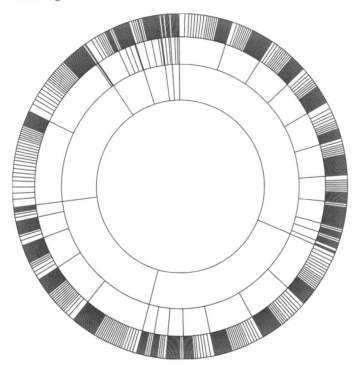

FIGURE 7-13: *D3.js handles the math required to create a sunburst diagram.*

Step 7: Color the Areas

Now we can turn our attention to coloring the visualization. We want to give each region a unique, dominant color and then shade that color for states and counties within the region. A good starting point for us is a different type of D3.js scale, a categorical scale for colors. All of the scales we've seen so far are cardinal scales; they map numerical values to properties for the visualization. Categorical scales work with data values that are not numerical; rather, the values simply represent different categories of some quantity. In our case, the regions represent categorical data. After all, there isn't anything intrinsically numerical about New England or the Southwest.

As the name suggests, a categorical *color* scale maps different category values to different colors. D3.js includes several of these predefined color scales. Since we have fewer than 10 regions in our data, the d3.scale.category10() scale works fine for this example. Figure 7-14 shows the colors in this scale.

FIGURE 7-14: *D3.js includes color scales for categorical data.*

Our next task is assigning colors from this scale to the arcs in our visualization. To do that, we'll define our own **color()** function. That function will accept a data node from the partition layout as input.

```
❶ var color = function(d) {
       var colors;
       if (!d.parent) {
❷          colors = d3.scale.category10();
❸          d.color = "#fff";
       }

       // More code needed...
```

First, at ❶, we create a local variable that we'll use to store colors. We then check to see if the input node is the root of the hierarchy. If it is, we then create a color scale at ❷ for the node's children and assign the node its own color at ❸. The root node in our visualization, which represents the entire United States, will be white. That assigned color will eventually be returned by the function.

After we create a color scale for the child nodes, we want to distribute the individual colors to those nodes. There's a slight catch, though. The nodes in the d.children array aren't necessarily distributed in the clockwise order we want for our visualization. To make sure the colors from our scale are distributed in order, we'll have to sort the d.children array first. Here's the complete code for this step.

```
   if (d.children) {
❶      d.children.map(function(child, i) {
           return {value: child.value, idx: i};
❷      }).sort(function(a,b) {
           return b.value - a.value
❸      }).forEach(function(child, i) {
           d.children[child.idx].color = colors(i);
       });
   }
```

In the first line, we make sure that there is a children array. If there is, we create a copy of the children array that contains just the node values and their original array index at ❶. Then, at ❷, we sort that copy based on the node values. Finally, at ❸, we iterate through the sorted array and assign colors to the child nodes.

So far we've created a categorical color scale and assigned its colors to the first-level children. That takes care of colors for the regions, but there are also states and counties that need colors. For those, we can create a different scale based on the parent color. Let's go back to our function definition and add an `else` clause for non-root nodes. In this clause, we also create a color scale for the children. These child nodes, however, are not regions; they are states or counties. For states of a region and counties of a state, we don't want unique, distinct colors like those from a categorical scale. Instead, we want colors related to the color of the parent. That calls for a linear gradient.

```
var color = function(d) {
    var colors;
    if (!d.parent) {
        // Handle root node as above...
    } else if (d.children) {

❶      var startColor = d3.hcl(d.color)
                            .darker(),
            endColor  = d3.hcl(d.color)
                            .brighter();

❷      colors = d3.scale.linear()
❸              .interpolate(d3.interpolateHcl)
❹              .range([
                    startColor.toString(),
                    endColor.toString()
                ])
❺              .domain([0,d.children.length+1]);

    }

    // Code continues...
```

Starting at ❶, we define the starting and ending colors for our gradient. To create those colors, we start with the parent node's color (`d.color`) and darken or brighten it. In both cases we use hue, chroma, and luminance (HCL) as the basis for the color manipulations. The HCL color space is based on human visual perception, unlike the purely mathematical basis for the more familiar RGB color space. Using HCL generally results in a more visually pleasing gradient.

The code block starting at ❷ actually creates the gradient. We're using a D3.js linear scale and a built-in interpolation algorithm for HCL colors ❸. Our gradient ranges between the start and end colors ❹, and its domain is the indices of the node's children ❺.

Now all we need to do is assign the appropriate color when we create each data value's <path> element. That requires a one-line addition, .attr("fill", color), to the code that creates those paths.

```
var path = g.selectAll("path")
    .data(partition.nodes(hierarchy))
  .enter().append("path")
    .attr("d", arc)
    .attr("fill", color);
```

As Figure 7-15 shows, our visualization now includes appropriate colors.

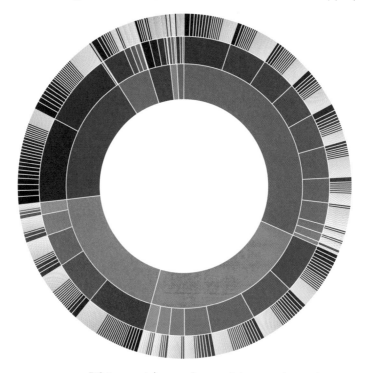

FIGURE 7-15: D3.js provides tools to add attractive colors to visualizations such as our sunburst.

Step 8: Make the Visualization Interactive

To conclude this example, we will add some interactivity. When a user clicks an area in the chart, the chart will zoom in to show more detail for that area. To emphasize the subject matter, we'll create a custom rotating animation effect for this zoom. The easiest part of this step is adding the function to handle click events. We can do that when we add the <path> elements to the page.

```
var path = g.selectAll("path")
    .data(partition.nodes(hierarchy))
```

```
    .enter().append("path")
      .attr("d", arc)
      .attr("fill", color)
❶       .on("click", handleClick);
```

The `handleClick` function at ❶ is the event handler that we'll have to write. Conceptually, the function is pretty straightforward. When the user clicks an area, we want to modify all the paths to make that area the focal point of the visualization. The complete function is shown in the following code.

```
function handleClick(datum) {
    path.transition().duration(750)
        .attrTween("d", arcTween(datum));
};
```

The function's single parameter is the data value corresponding to the clicked element. Conventionally, D3.js uses d for that value; in this case, however, we're using **datum** to avoid confusion with the SVG **"d"** attribute. The first line in the function references all of the paths in the visualization and sets up an animated transition for those paths. The next line tells D3.js what values we're going to transition. In this case, we're changing an attribute of the <path> elements (so we use the function **attrTween**), and the specific attribute we're changing is the **"d"** attribute (the first parameter to that function). The second parameter, arcTween(datum), is a function that returns a function.

Here's the complete implementation of `arcTween()`.

```
function arcTween(datum) {
    var thetaDomain  = d3.interpolate(theta.domain(),
                            [datum.x, datum.x + datum.dx]),
        radiusDomain = d3.interpolate(radius.domain(),
                            [datum.y, 1]),
        radiusRange  = d3.interpolate(radius.range(),
                            [datum.y ? 20 : 0, maxRadius]);

    return function calculateNewPath(d, i) {
        return i ?
            function interpolatePathForRoot(t) {
                return arc(d);
            } :
            function interpolatePathForNonRoot(t) {
                theta.domain(thetaDomain(t));
                radius.domain(radiusDomain(t)).range(radiusRange(t));
                return arc(d);
            };
    };
};
```

You can see that this code block defines several different functions. First, there's **arcTween()**. It returns another function **calculateNewPath()**, and *that* function returns either `interpolatePathForRoot()` or `interpolatePathForNonRoot()`. Before we look at the details of the implementation, let me go over the distinctions between these functions.

▸ `arcTween()` is called once (for a single click) in the click event handler. Its input parameter is the data value corresponding to the clicked element.

▸ `calculateNewPath()` is then called once for every path element, a total of 702 times for each click. Its input parameters are the data value and index of the path element.

▸ `interpolatePathForRoot()` or `interpolatePathForNonRoot()` are called multiple times for each path element. Every call provides the input parameter **t** (for time) that represents the amount of progress in the current animation transition. The time parameter ranges from 0 when the animation starts to 1 when the animation ends. If, for example, D3.js requires 100 individual animation steps for the transition, then these functions will be called 70,200 times for each click.

Now that we know when each of these functions is called, we can start to look at what they actually do. A concrete example definitely helps, so let's consider what happens when the user clicks the state of Kentucky. As Figure 7-16 shows, it's on the second row in the upper-right section of the visualization.

FIGURE 7-16: *The tornado sightings sunburst graph with Kentucky highlighted*

The data value associated with this SVG `<path>` will have properties calculated by the partition layout, specifically:

- an **x** value of 0.051330798479087454
- a **y** value of 0.5
- a **dx** value of 0.04182509505703422
- a **dy** value of 0.25

In terms of our visualization, the area begins at an angular position of 18.479° (**x**) and continues for another 15.057° (**dx**). Its innermost radius begins 177 pixels (**y**) from the center. When the user clicks Kentucky, we want the visualization to zoom in on Kentucky and its counties. That's the region that Figure 7-17 highlights. The angle begins at 18.479° and continues for another 15.057°; the radius begins at 177 pixels and continues to the `maxRadius` value, a total length of 73 pixels.

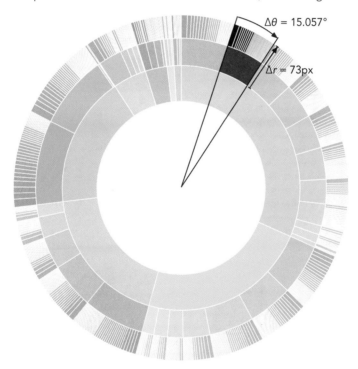

FIGURE 7-17: *When the user clicks Kentucky, we want the visualization to focus on that small area.*

The concrete example helps explain the `arcTween()` implementation. The function first creates three `d3.interpolate` objects. These objects provide a convenient way to handle the mathematical calculations for interpolations. The first object interpolates from the starting **theta** domain (initially 0 to 1) to our desired subset (0.051 to 0.093 for Kentucky). The second object does the same for the radius, interpolating from the starting radius domain (initially 0 to 1) to our desired subset (0.5 to 1 for Kentucky and its counties). The final object provides a new, interpolated range for the radius. If the clicked element has a non-zero y value, the new range will start at 20 instead of 0. If the clicked element was the `<path>` representing the entire United States, then the range reverts to the initial starting value of 0.

arcTween() returns the calculateNewPath function after creating the d3.interpolate objects. D3.js calls this function once for each `<path>` element. When it executes, calculateNewPath() checks to see if the associated `<path>` element is the root (representing the entire United States). If so, calculateNewPath() returns the interpolatePathForRoot function. For the root, no interpolation is necessary, so the desired path is just the regular path that our arc() function (from Step 4) creates. For all other elements, however, we use the d3.interpolate objects to redefine the theta and radius scales. Instead of the full 0 to 2π and 0 to maxRadius, we set these scales to be the desired area of focus. Furthermore, we use the amount of progress in the transition from the parameter t to interpolate how close we are to those desired values. With the scales redefined, calling the arc() function returns a path appropriate for the new scales. As the transition progresses, the paths reshape themselves to fit the desired outcome. You can see the intermediate steps in Figure 7-18.

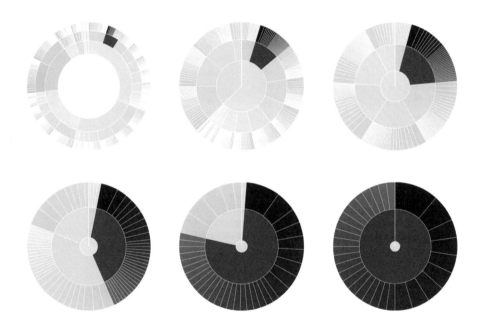

FIGURE 7-18: *The transition smoothly animates the visualization to zoom in on the area of focus.*

With this final bit of code, our visualization is complete. Figure 7-19 shows the result. It includes some additional hover effects in lieu of a true legend; you can find the complete implementation in the book's source code (*http://jsDataV.is/source/*).

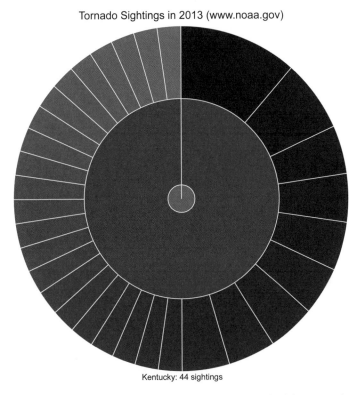

Tornado Sightings in 2013 (www.noaa.gov)

Kentucky: 44 sightings

FIGURE 7-19: *D3.js provides all the tools needed for complex custom interactive visualizations like this animated zoomable sunburst.*

Summing Up

As we've seen in these examples, D3.js is a very powerful library for building JavaScript visualizations. Using it effectively requires a deeper understanding of JavaScript techniques than most of the other libraries we've seen in this book. If you make the investment to learn D3.js, though, you'll have more control and flexibility over the results.

8

Managing Data in the Browser

So far in the book, we've looked at a lot of visualization tools and techniques, but we haven't spent much time considering the data part of data visualization. The emphasis on visualization is appropriate in many cases. Especially if the data is static, we can take all the time we need to clean and organize it before it's even represented in JavaScript. But what if the data is dynamic and we have no choice but to import the raw source directly into our JavaScript application? We have much less control over data from third-party REST APIs, Google Docs spreadsheets, or automatically generated CSV files. With those types of data sources, we often need to validate, reformat, recalculate, or otherwise manipulate the data in the browser.

This chapter considers a JavaScript library that is particularly helpful for managing large data sets in the web browser: Underscore.js (*http://underscorejs.org/*). We'll cover the following aspects of Underscore.js:

▶ Functional programming, the programming style that Underscore.js encourages

▶ Working with simple arrays using Underscore.js utilities

▶ Enhancing JavaScript objects

▶ Manipulating collections of objects

The format of this chapter differs from the other chapters in the book. Instead of covering a few examples of moderate complexity, we'll look at a lot of simple, short examples. Each section collects several related examples together, but each of the short examples is independent. The first section differs even further. It's a brief introduction to functional programming cast as a step-by-step migration from the more common imperative programming style. Understanding functional programming is very helpful, as its philosophy underlies almost all of the Underscore.js utilities.

This chapter serves as a tour of the Underscore.js library with a special focus on managing data. (As a concession to the book's overall focus on data visualization, it also includes several illustrations.) We'll see many of the Underscore.js utilities covered here at work in a larger web application project in the subsequent chapters.

Using Functional Programming

When we're working with data that's part of a visualization, we often have to iterate through the data one item at a time to transform, extract, or otherwise manipulate it to fit our application. Using only the core JavaScript language, our code may rely on a **for** loop like the following:

```
for (var i=0, len=data.length; i<len; i++) {
    // Code continues...
}
```

Although this style, known as *imperative programming*, is a common JavaScript idiom, it can present a few problems in large, complex applications. In particular, it might result in code that's harder than necessary to debug, test, and maintain. This section introduces a different programming style—*functional programming*—that eliminates many of those problems. As you'll see, functional programming can result in code that's much more concise and readable, and therefore often much less error prone.

To compare these two programming styles, let's consider a simple programming problem: writing a function to calculate the Fibonacci numbers. The first two Fibonacci numbers are 0 and 1, and subsequent numbers are the sum of the two preceding values. The sequence starts like this:

0, 1, 1, 2, 3, 5, 8, 13, 21, 34, 55, 89, . . .

Step 1: Start with an Imperative Version

To begin, let's consider a traditional, imperative approach to the problem. Here's a first attempt:

```
var fib = function(n) {
    // If 0th or 1st, just return n itself
    if (n < 2) return n;

    // Otherwise, initialize variable to compute result
    var f0=0, f1=1, f=1;

    // Iterate until we reach n
    for (i=2; i<=n; i++) {

        // At each iteration, slide the intermediate
        // values down a step
        f0 = f1 = f;

        // And calculate sum for the next pass
        f = f0 + f1;
    }

    // After all the iterations, return the result
    return f;
}
```

This `fib()` function takes as its input a parameter n and returns as its output the nth Fibonacci number. (By convention, the 0th and 1st Fibonacci numbers are 0 and 1.)

Step 2: Debug the Imperative Code

If you aren't checking closely, you might be surprised to find that the preceding trivial example contains three bugs. Of course, it's a contrived example and the bugs are deliberate, but can you find all of them without reading any further? More to the point, if even a trivial example can hide so many bugs, can you imagine what might be lurking in a complex web application?

To understand why imperative programming can introduce these bugs, let's fix them one at a time.

One bug is in the for loop:

```
for (i=2; i<=n; i++) {
```

The conditional that determines the loop termination checks for a less-than-or-equal (<=) value; instead, it should check for a less-than (<) value.

A second bug occurs in this line:

```
f0 = f1 = f;
```

Although we think and read left to right (at least in English), JavaScript executes multiple assignments from right to left. Instead of shifting the values in our variables, this statement simply assigns the value of f to all three. We need to break the single statement into two:

```
f0 = f1;
f1 = f;
```

The final bug is the most subtle, and it's also in the for loop. We're using the local variable i, but we haven't declared it. As a result, JavaScript will treat it as a global variable. That won't cause our function to return incorrect results, but it could well introduce a conflict—and a hard-to-find bug—elsewhere in our application. The correct code declares the variable as local:

```
for (var i=2; i<n; i++) {
```

Step 3: Understand the Problems Imperative Programming May Introduce

The bugs in this short and straightforward piece of code are meant to demonstrate some problematic features of imperative programming in general. In particular, conditional logic and state variables, by their very nature, tend to invite certain errors.

Consider the first bug. Its error was using an incorrect test (<= instead of <) for the conditional that terminates the loop. Precise conditional logic is critical for computer programs, but such precision doesn't always come naturally to most people, including programmers. Conditional logic has to be perfect, and sometimes making it perfect is tricky.

The other two errors both relate to state variables, f0 and f1 in the first case and i in the second. Here again there's a difference between how programmers think and how programs operate. When programmers write the code to iterate through the numbers, they're probably concentrating on the specific problem at hand. It may be easy to neglect the potential effect on other areas of the application. More technically, state variables can introduce side effects into a program, and side effects may result in bugs.

Step 4: Rewrite Using Functional Programming Style

Proponents of functional programming claim that by eliminating conditionals and state variables, a functional programming style can produce code that's more concise, more maintainable, and less prone to errors than imperative programming.

The "functional" in "functional programming" does not refer to functions in programming languages but rather to mathematical functions such as $y=f(x)$. Functional programming attempts to emulate mathematical functions in the context of computer programming. Instead of iterating over values by using a `for` loop, functional programming often uses recursion, where a function calls itself multiple times to make a calculation or manipulate values.

Here's how we can implement the Fibonacci algorithm with functional programming:

```
var fib = function(n) { return n < 2 ? n : fib(n-1) + fib(n-2); }
```

Notice that this version has no state variables and, except for the edge case to handle 0 or 1, no conditional statements. It's much more concise, and notice how the code mirrors almost word-for-word the statement of the original problem: "The first two Fibonacci numbers are 0 and 1" corresponds to `n < 2 ? n`, and "subsequent numbers are the sum of the two preceding values" corresponds to `fib(n-1) + fib(n-2)`.

Functional programming implementations often express the desired outcome directly. They can therefore minimize the chance of misinterpretations or errors in an intermediate algorithm.

Step 5: Evaluate Performance

From what we've seen so far, it may seem that we should always adopt a functional programming style. Certainly functional programming has its advantages, but it can have some significant disadvantages as well. The Fibonacci code is a perfect example. Since functional programming eschews the notion of loops, our example relies instead on recursion.

In our specific case the `fib()` function calls itself twice at every level until the recursion reaches 0 or 1. Since each intermediate call itself results in more intermediate calls, the number of calls to `fib()` increases exponentially. Finding the 28th Fibonacci number by executing `fib(28)` results in over one million calls to the `fib()` function.

As you might imagine, the resulting performance is simply unacceptable. Table 8-1 shows the execution times for both the functional and the imperative versions of `fib()`.

Table 8-1: Execution Times for fib()

Version	Parameter	Execution time (ms)
Imperative	28	0.231
Functional	28	296.9

As you can see, the functional programming version is over a thousand times slower. In the real world, such performance is rarely acceptable.

Step 6: Fix the Performance Problem

Fortunately, we can reap the benefits of functional programming without suffering the performance penalty. We simply turn to the tiny but powerful Underscore.js library. As the library's web page explains,

> Underscore is a utility-belt library for JavaScript that provides . . . functional programming support.

Of course, we need to include that library in our web pages. If you're including libraries individually, Underscore.js is available on many content distribution networks, such as CloudFlare.

```
<!DOCTYPE html>
<html lang="en">
  <head>
    <meta charset="utf-8">
    <title></title>
  </head>
  <body>
    <!-- Content goes here -->
    <script
      src="//cdnjs.cloudflare.com/ajax/libs/underscore.js/1.4.4/"+
          "underscore-min.js">
    </script>
  </body>
</html>
```

With Underscore.js in place, we can now optimize the performance of our Fibonacci implementation.

The problem with the recursive implementation is that it results in many unnecessary calls to `fib()`. For example, executing `fib(28)` requires more than 100,000 calls to `fib(3)`. And each time `fib(3)` is called, the return value is recalculated from scratch. It would be better if the implementation called `fib(3)` only once, and every subsequent time it needed to know the value of `fib(3)` it reused the previous result instead of recalculating it from scratch. In effect, we'd like to implement a cache in front of the `fib()` function. The cache could eliminate the repetitive calculations.

This approach is known as *memoizing*, and the Underscore.js library has a simple method to automatically and transparently memoize JavaScript functions. Not surprisingly, that method is called `memoize()`. To use it, we first wrap the function we want to memoize within the Underscore object. Just as jQuery uses the dollar sign ($) for wrapping, Underscore.js uses the underscore character (_).

After wrapping our function, we simply call the `memoize()` method. Here's the complete code:

```
var fib = _( function(n) {
        return n < 2 ? n : fib(n-1) + fib(n-2);
    } ).memoize()
```

As you can see, we haven't really lost any of the readability or conciseness of functional programming. And it would still be a challenge to introduce a bug in this implementation. The only real change is performance, and it's substantially better, as shown in Table 8-2.

Table 8-2: Execution Times for fib(), Continued

Version	Parameter	Execution time (ms)
Imperative fib()	28	0.231
Functional fib()	28	296.9
Memoized fib()	28	0.352

Just by including the Underscore.js library and using one of its methods, our functional implementation has nearly the same performance as the imperative version.

For the rest of this chapter, we'll look at many of the other improvements and utilities that Underscore.js provides. With its support for functional programming, Underscore.js makes it significantly easier to work with data in the browser.

Working with Arrays

If your visualization relies on a significant amount of data, that data is most likely contained in arrays. Unfortunately, it's very tempting to resort to imperative programming when you are working with arrays. Arrays suggest the use of programming loops, and, as we saw earlier, programming loops are an imperative construct that often causes errors. If we can avoid loops and rely on functional programming instead, we can improve the quality of our JavaScript. The core JavaScript language includes a few utilities and methods to help applications cope with arrays in a functional style, but Underscore.js adds many others. This section describes many of the Underscore.js array utilities that are most helpful for data visualizations.

Extracting Elements by Position

If you need only a subset of an array for your visualization, Underscore.js has many utilities that make it easy to extract the right one. For the following examples, we'll consider a simple array (shown in Figure 8-1).

```
var arr = [1,2,3,4,5,6,7,8,9];
```

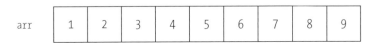

FIGURE 8-1: *Underscore.js has many utilities to make working with arrays easy.*

Underscore.js's `first()` method provides a simple way to extract the first element of an array, or the first *n* elements (see Figure 8-2):

```
> _(arr).first()
  1
> _(arr).first(3)
  [1, 2, 3]
```

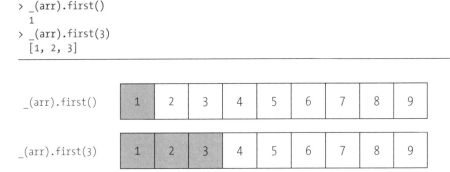

FIGURE 8-2: *The `first()` function returns the first element or the first*
n *elements in an array.*

Notice that `first()` (without any parameter) returns a simple element, while `first(n)` returns an array of elements. That means, for example, that `first()` and `first(1)` have different return values (1 versus [1] in the example).

As you might expect, Underscore.js also has a `last()` method to extract elements from the end of an array (see Figure 8-3).

```
> _(arr).last()
  9
> _(arr).last(3)
  [7, 8, 9]
```

FIGURE 8-3: *The `last()` function returns the last element or the last*
n *elements in an array.*

Without any parameters, `last()` returns the last element in the array. With a parameter n, it returns a new array with the last *n* elements from the original.

The more general versions of both of these functions (.first(3) and .last(3)) would require some potentially tricky (and error-prone) code to implement in an imperative style. In the functional style that Underscore.js supports, however, our code is clean and simple.

What if you want to extract from the beginning of the array, but instead of knowing how many elements you want to include in the result, you know only how many elements you want to omit? In other words, you need "all but the last *n*" elements. The initial() method performs this extraction (see Figure 8-4). As with all of these methods, if you omit the optional parameter, Underscore.js assumes a value of 1.

```
> _(arr).initial()
  [1, 2, 3, 4, 5, 6, 7, 8]
> _(arr).initial(3)
  [1, 2, 3, 4, 5, 6]
```

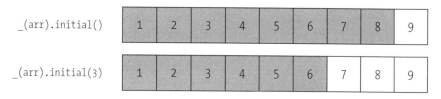

FIGURE 8-4: The *initial()* function returns all but the last element or all but the last n elements in an array.

Finally, you may need the opposite of initial(). The rest() method skips past a defined number of elements in the beginning of the array and returns whatever remains (see Figure 8-5).

```
> _(arr).rest()
  [2, 3, 4, 5, 6, 7, 8, 9]
> _(arr).rest(3)
  [4, 5, 6, 7, 8, 9]
```

FIGURE 8-5: The *rest()* function returns all but the first element or all but the first n elements in an array.

Again, these functions would be tricky to implement using traditional, imperative programming, but they are a breeze with Underscore.js.

Combining Arrays

Underscore.js includes another set of utilities for combining two or more arrays. These include functions that mimic standard mathematical *set* operations, as well as more-sophisticated combinations. For the next few examples, we'll use two arrays, one containing the first few Fibonacci numbers and the other containing the first five even integers (see Figure 8-6).

```
var fibs = [0, 1, 1, 2, 3, 5, 8];
var even = [0, 2, 4, 6, 8];
```

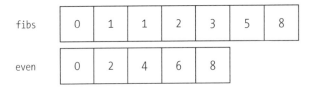

FIGURE 8-6: *Underscore.js also has many utilities to work with multiple arrays.*

The union() method is a straightforward combination of multiple arrays. It returns an array containing all elements that are in any of the inputs, and it removes any duplicates (Figure 8-7).

```
> _(fibs).union(even)
  [0, 1, 2, 3, 5, 8, 4, 6]
```

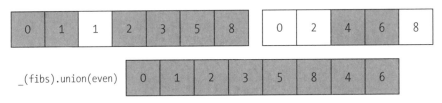

FIGURE 8-7: *The union() function creates the union of multiple arrays, removing any duplicates.*

Notice that union() removes duplicates whether they appear in separate inputs (0, 2, and 8) or in the same array (1).

✳ NOTE: Although this chapter considers combinations of just two arrays, most Underscore.js methods can accept an unlimited number of parameters. For example, _.union(a,b,c,d,e) returns the union of five different arrays. You can even find the union of an array of arrays with the JavaScript apply() function with something like _.union.prototype.apply(this, arrOfArrs).

The `intersection()` method acts just as you would expect, returning only those elements that appear in all of the input arrays (Figure 8-8).

```
> _(fibs).intersection(even)
  [0, 2, 8]
```

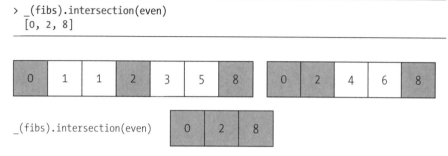

FIGURE 8-8: *The `intersection()` function returns elements in common among multiple arrays.*

The `difference()` method is the opposite of `intersection()`. It returns those elements in the first input array that are *not* present in the other inputs (Figure 8-9).

```
> _(fibs).difference(even)
  [1, 1, 3, 5]
```

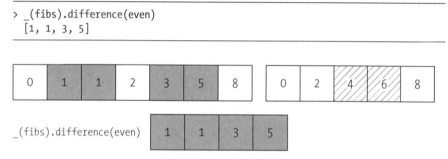

FIGURE 8-9: *The `difference()` function returns elements that are present only in the first of multiple arrays.*

If you need to eliminate duplicate elements but have only one array—making `union()` inappropriate—then you can use the `uniq()` method (Figure 8-10).

```
> _(fibs).uniq()
  [0, 1, 2, 3, 5, 8]
```

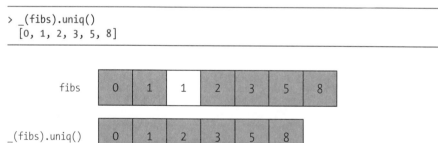

FIGURE 8-10: *The `uniq()` function removes duplicate elements from an array.*

Finally, Underscore.js has a `zip()` method. Its name doesn't come from the popular compression algorithm but rather because it acts a bit like a zipper. It takes multiple input arrays and combines them, element by element, into an output array. That output is an array of arrays, where the inner arrays are the combined elements.

```
> var naturals = [1, 2, 3, 4, 5];
> var primes = [2, 3, 5, 7, 11];
> _.zip(naturals, primes)
  [ [1,2], [2,3], [3,5], [4,7], [5,11] ]
```

The operation is perhaps most clearly understood through a picture; see Figure 8-11.

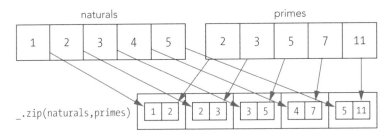

FIGURE 8-11: *The zip() function pairs elements from multiple arrays together into a single array.*

This example demonstrates an alternative style for Underscore.js. Instead of wrapping an array within the _ object as we've done so far, we call the `zip()` method on the _ object itself. The alternative style seems a better fit for the underlying functionality in this case, but if you prefer `_(naturals).zip(prime)`, you'll get the exact same result.

Removing Invalid Data Values

One of the banes of visualization applications is invalid data values. Although we'd like to think that our data sources ensure that all the data they provide is scrupulously correct, that is, unfortunately, rarely the case. More seriously, if JavaScript encounters an invalid value, the most common result is an *unhandled exception*, which halts all further JavaScript execution on the page.

To avoid such an unpleasant error, we should validate all data sets and remove invalid values before we pass the data to graphing or charting libraries. Underscore.js has several utilities to help.

The simplest of these Underscore.js methods is `compact()`. This function removes any data values that JavaScript treats as `false` from the input arrays. Eliminated values include the Boolean value `false`, the numeric value `0`, an empty string, and the special values `NaN` (not a number; for example, `1/0`), `undefined`, and `null`.

```
> var raw = [0, 1, false, 2,  "", 3, NaN, 4, , 5, null];
> _(raw).compact()
  [1, 2, 3, 4, 5]
```

It is worth emphasizing that `compact()` removes elements with a value of 0. If you use `compact()` to clean a data array, be sure that 0 isn't a valid data value in your data set.

Another common problem with raw data is excessively nested arrays. If you want to eliminate extra nesting levels from a data set, the `flatten()` method is available to help.

```
> var raw = [1, 2, 3, [[4]], 5];
> _(raw).flatten()
  [1, 2, 3, 4, 5]
```

By default, `flatten()` removes all nesting, even multiple levels of nesting, from arrays. If you set the `shallow` parameter to `true`, however, it removes only a single level of nesting.

```
> var raw = [1, 2, 3, [[4]], 5];
> _(raw).flatten(true)
  [1, 2, 3, [4], 5]
```

Finally, if you have specific values that you want to eliminate from an array, you can use the `without()` method. Its parameters provide a list of values that the function should remove from the input array.

```
> var raw = [1, 2, 3, 4];
> _(raw).without(2, 3)
  [1, 4]
```

Finding Elements in an Array

JavaScript has always defined the `indexOf()` method for strings. It returns the position of a given substring within a larger string. Recent versions of JavaScript have added this method to array objects, so you can easily find the first occurrence of a given value in an array. Unfortunately, older browsers (specifically IE8 and earlier) don't support this method.

Underscore.js provides its own `indexOf()` method to fill the gap those older browsers create. If Underscore.js finds itself running in an environment with native support for array `indexOf`, then it defers to the native method to avoid any performance penalty.

```
> var primes = [2, 3, 5, 7, 11];
> _(primes).indexOf(5)
  2
```

To begin your search somewhere in the middle of the array, you can specify that starting position as the second argument to indexOf().

```
> var arr = [2, 3, 5, 7, 11, 7, 5, 3, 2];
> _(arr).indexOf(5, 4)
  6
```

You can also search backward from the end of an array using the lastIndexOf() method.

```
> var arr = [2, 3, 5, 7, 11, 7, 5, 3, 2];
> _(arr).lastIndexOf(5)
  6
```

If you don't want to start at the very end of the array, you can pass in the starting index as an optional parameter.

Underscore.js provides a few helpful optimizations for sorted arrays. Both the uniq() and the indexOf() methods accept an optional Boolean parameter. If that parameter is **true**, then the functions assume that the array is sorted. The performance improvements this assumption allows can be especially significant for large data sets.

The library also includes the special sortedIndex() function. This function also assumes that the input array is sorted. It finds the position at which a specific value *should* be inserted to maintain the array's sort order.

```
> var arr = [2, 3, 5, 7, 11];
> _(arr).sortedIndex(6)
  3
```

If you have a custom sorting function, you can pass that to sortedIndex() as well.

Generating Arrays

The final array utility I'll mention is a convenient method to generate arrays. The range() method tells Underscore.js to create an array with the specified number of elements. You may also specify a starting value (the default is 0) and the increment between adjacent values (the default is 1).

```
> _.range(10)
  [0, 1, 2, 3, 4, 5, 6, 7, 8, 9]
> _.range(20,10)
  [20, 21, 22, 23, 24, 25, 26, 27, 28, 29]
> _.range(0, 10, 100)
  [0, 100, 200, 300, 400, 500, 600, 700, 800, 900]
```

The range() function can be quite useful if you need to generate x-axis values to match an array of y-axis values.

```
> var yvalues = [0.1277, 1.2803, 1.7697, 3.1882]
> _.zip(_.range(yvalues.length),yvalues)
  [ [0, 0.1277], [1, 1.2803], [2, 1.7697], [3, 3.1882] ]
```

Here we use range() to generate the matching x-axis values, and use zip() to combine them with the y-values.

Enhancing Objects

Although the previous section's examples show numeric arrays, often our visualization data consists of JavaScript objects instead of simple numbers. That's especially likely if we get the data via a REST interface, because such interfaces almost always deliver data in JavaScript Object Notation (JSON). If we need to enhance or transform objects without resorting to imperative constructs, Underscore.js has another set of utilities that can help. For the following examples, we can use a simple pizza object (see Figure 8-12).

```
var pizza = {
    size: 10,
    crust: "thin",
    cheese: true,
    toppings: [ "pepperoni","sausage"]
};
```

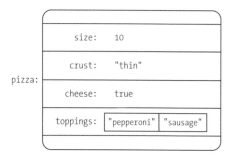

FIGURE 8-12: *Underscore.js has many utilities for working with arbitrary JavaScript objects.*

Working with Keys and Values

Underscore.js includes several methods to work with the keys and values that make up objects. For example, the keys() function creates an array consisting solely of an object's keys (see Figure 8-13).

```
> _(pizza).keys()
  [ "size", "crust", "cheese", "toppings"]
```

_(pizza).keys() | "size" | "crust" | "cheese" | "toppings" |

FIGURE 8-13: *The keys() function returns the keys of an object as an array.*

Similarly, the `values()` function creates an array consisting solely of an object's values (Figure 8-14).

```
> _(pizza).values()
  [10,  "thin", true, [ "pepperoni","sausage"]]
```

_(pizza).values() | 10 | "thin" | true | "pepperoni" | "sausage" |

FIGURE 8-14: *The values() function returns just the values of an object as an array.*

The `pairs()` function creates a two-dimensional array. Each element of the outer array is itself an array that contains an object's key and its corresponding value (Figure 8-15).

```
> _(pizza).pairs()
[
  [ "size",10],
  [ "crust","thin"],
 ·[ "cheese",true],
  [ "toppings",[ "pepperoni","sausage"]]
]
```

FIGURE 8-15: *The pairs() function converts an object into an array of array pairs.*

To reverse this transformation and convert an array into an object, we can use the `object()` function.

```
> var arr = [ [ "size",10], [ "crust","thin"], [ "cheese",true],
            [ "toppings",[ "pepperoni","sausage"]] ]
> _(arr).object()
  { size: 10, crust:  "thin", cheese: true, toppings: [ "pepperoni","sausage"]}
```

Finally, we can swap the roles of keys and values in an object with the `invert()` function (Figure 8-16).

```
> _(pizza).invert()
 {10:  "size", thin:  "crust", true:  "cheese",  "pepperoni,sausage":
"toppings"}
```

```
                        "10":  "size"

                        "thin":  "crust"
_(pizza).invert()
                        "true":  "cheese"

            "pepperoni,sausage":  "toppings"
```

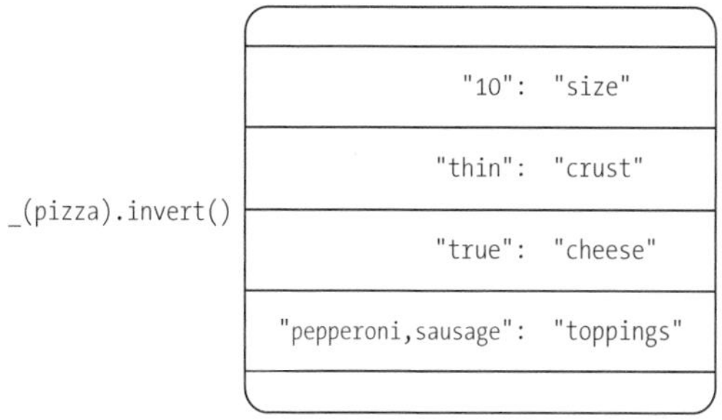

FIGURE 8-16: *The invert() function swaps keys and values in an object.*

As the preceding example shows, Underscore.js can even invert an object if the value isn't a simple type. In this case it takes an array, `["pepperoni","sausage"]`, and converts it to a value by joining the individual array elements with commas, creating the key `"pepperoni,sausage"`.

Note also that JavaScript requires that all of an object's keys are unique. That's not necessarily the case for values. If you have an object in which multiple keys have the same value, then `invert()` keeps only the last of those keys in the inverted object. For example, `_({key1: value, key2: value}).invert()` returns `{value: key2}`.

Cleaning Up Object Subsets

When you want to clean up an object by eliminating unnecessary attributes, you can use Underscore.js's `pick()` function. Simply pass it a list of attributes that you want to retain (Figure 8-17).

```
> _(pizza).pick( "size","crust")
 {size: 10, crust:  "thin"}
```

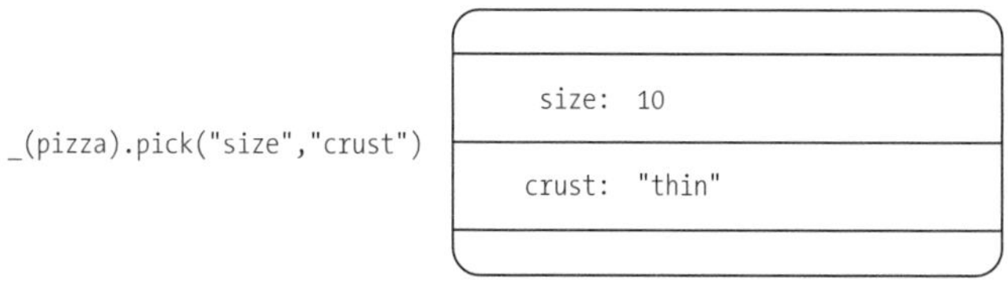

```
                        size:  10
_(pizza).pick("size","crust")
                        crust:  "thin"
```

FIGURE 8-17: *The pick() function selects specific properties from an object.*

We can also do the opposite of `pick()` by using `omit()` and listing the attributes that we want to delete (Figure 8-18). Underscore.js keeps all the other attributes in the object.

```
> _(pizza).omit( "size","crust")
{cheese: true, toppings: [ "pepperoni","sausage"]}
```

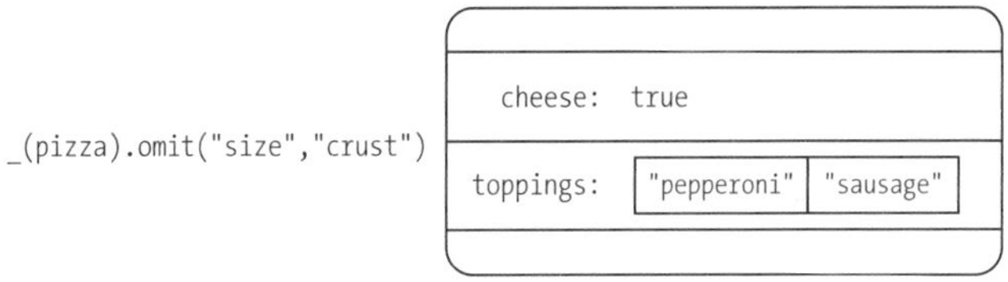

FIGURE 8-18: *The `omit()` function removes properties from an object.*

Updating Attributes

When you are updating objects, a common requirement is to make sure that an object includes certain attributes and that those attributes have appropriate default values. Underscore.js includes two utilities for this purpose.

The two utilities, `extend()` and `defaults()`, both start with one object and adjust its properties based on those of other objects. If the secondary objects include attributes that the original object lacks, these utilities add those properties to the original. The utilities differ in how they handle properties that are already present in the original. The `extend()` function overrides the original properties with new values (see Figure 8-19):

```
> var standard = { size: 12, crust: "regular", cheese: true }
> var order = { size: 10, crust: "thin",
  toppings: [ "pepperoni","sausage"] };
> _.extend(standard, order)
  { size: 10, crust: "thin", cheese: true,
  toppings: [ "pepperoni","sausage"] };
```

Meanwhile, `defaults()` leaves the original properties unchanged (Figure 8-20):

```
> var order = { size: 10, crust: "thin",
  toppings: [ "pepperoni","sausage"] };
> var standard = { size: 12, crust: "regular", cheese: true }
> _.defaults(order, standard)
  { size: 10, crust: "thin",
  toppings [ "pepperoni","sausage"], cheese: true };
```

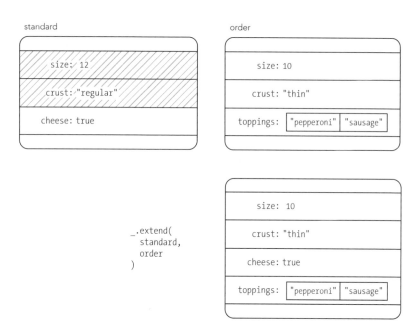

FIGURE 8-19: *The extend() function updates and adds missing properties to an object.*

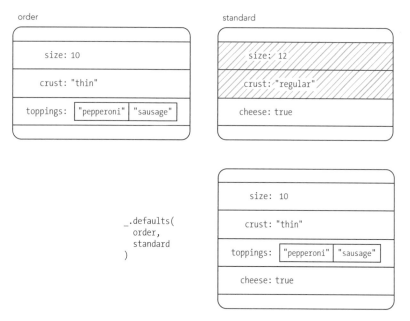

FIGURE 8-20: *The defaults() function adds missing properties to an object.*

Note that both extend() and defaults() modify the original object directly; they do not make a copy of that object and return the copy. Consider, for example, the following:

```
> var order = { size: 10, crust:  "thin",
  toppings: [ "pepperoni","sausage"] };
> var standard = { size: 12, crust: "regular", cheese: true }
> var pizza = _.extend(standard, order)
  { size: 10, crust:  "thin", cheese: true,
  toppings: [ "pepperoni","sausage"] };
```

This code sets the pizza variable as you would expect, but it also sets the standard variable to that same object. More specifically, the code modifies standard with the properties from order, and then it sets a new variable pizza equal to standard. The modification of standard is probably not intended. If you need to use either extend() or defaults() in a way that does not modify input parameters, start with an empty object.

```
> var order = { size: 10, crust:  "thin",
  toppings: [ "pepperoni","sausage"] };
> var standard = { size: 12, crust:  "regular", cheese: true }
> var pizza = _.extend({}, standard, order)
  { size: 10, crust:  "thin", cheese: true,
  toppings: [ "pepperoni","sausage"] };
```

This version gets us the desired pizza object without modifying standard.

Manipulating Collections

So far we've seen various Underscore.js tools that are suited specifically for either arrays or objects. Next, we'll see some tools for manipulating collections in general. In Underscore.js both arrays and objects are *collections*, so the tools in this section can be applied to pure arrays, pure objects, or data structures that combine both. In this section, we'll try out these utilities on an array of objects, since that's the data structure we most often deal with in the context of data visualization.

Here's a small data set we can use for the examples that follow. It contains a few statistics from the 2012 Major League Baseball season.

```
var national_league = [
    { name: "Arizona Diamondbacks",  wins: 81, losses:  81,
      division: "west" },
    { name: "Atlanta Braves",        wins: 94, losses:  68,
      division: "east" },
    { name: "Chicago Cubs",          wins: 61, losses: 101,
      division: "central" },
    { name: "Cincinnati Reds",       wins: 97, losses:  65,
      division: "central" },
    { name: "Colorado Rockies",      wins: 64, losses:  98,
      division: "west" },
```

```
 { name: "Houston Astros",        wins: 55, losses: 107,
   division: "central" },
 { name: "Los Angeles Dodgers",   wins: 86, losses:  76,
   division: "west" },
 { name: "Miami Marlins",         wins: 69, losses:  93,
   division: "east" },
 { name: "Milwaukee Brewers",     wins: 83, losses:  79,
   division: "central" },
 { name: "New York Mets",         wins: 74, losses:  88,
   division: "east" },
 { name: "Philadelphia Phillies", wins: 81, losses:  81,
   division: "east" },
 { name: "Pittsburgh Pirates",    wins: 79, losses:  83,
   division: "central" },
 { name: "San Diego Padres",      wins: 76, losses:  86,
   division: "west" },
 { name: "San Francisco Giants",  wins: 94, losses:  68,
   division: "west" },
 { name: "St. Louis Cardinals",   wins: 88, losses:  74,
   division: "central" },
 { name: "Washington Nationals",  wins: 98, losses:  64,
   division: "east" }
];
```

Working with Iteration Utilities

In the first section, we saw some of the pitfalls of traditional JavaScript iteration loops as well as the improvements that functional programming can provide. Our Fibonacci example eliminated iteration by using recursion, but many algorithms don't lend themselves to a recursive implementation. In those cases, we can still use a functional programming style, however, by taking advantage of the iteration utilities in Underscore.js.

The most basic Underscore utility is each(). It executes an arbitrary function on every element in a collection and often serves as a direct functional replacement for the traditional for (i=0; i<len; i++) loop.

```
> _(national_league).each(function(team) { console.log(team.name); })
  Arizona Diamondbacks
  Atlanta Braves
  // Console output continues...
  Washington Nationals
```

If you're familiar with the jQuery library, you may know that jQuery includes a similar $.each() utility. There are two important differences between the Underscore .js and jQuery versions, however. First, the parameters passed to the iterator function differ between the two. Underscore.js passes (element, index, list) for arrays and (value, key, list) for simple objects, while jQuery passes (index, value). Secondly, at least as of this writing, the Underscore.js implementation can execute much faster than the jQuery version, depending on the browser. (jQuery also includes a `$.map()` function that's similar to the Underscore.js method.)

The Underscore.js `map()` method iterates through a collection and transforms each element with an arbitrary function. It returns a new collection containing the transformed elements. Here, for example, is how to create an array of all the teams' winning percentages:

```
> _(national_league).map(function(team) {
      return Math.round(100*team.wins/(team.wins + team.losses);
  })
  [50, 58, 38, 60, 40, 34, 53, 43, 51, 46, 50, 49, 47, 58, 54, 60]
```

The `reduce()` method iterates through a collection and returns a single value. One parameter initializes this value, and the other parameter is an arbitrary function that updates the value for each element in the collection. We can use `reduce()`, for example, to calculate how many teams have a winning percentage over 500.

```
> _(national_league).reduce(
❶     function(count, team) {
❷         return count + (team.wins > team.losses);
      },
❸     0  // Starting point for reduced value
  )
  7
```

As the comment at ❶ indicates, we start our count at 0. That value is passed as the first parameter to the function at ❷, and the function returns an updated value at ❸.

✳ **NOTE:** If you've followed the development of "big data" implementations such as Hadoop or Google's search, you may know that the fundamental algorithm behind those technologies is MapReduce. Although the context differs, the same concepts underlie the `map()` and `reduce()` utilities in Underscore.js.

Finding Elements in a Collection

Underscore.js has several methods to help us find elements or sets of elements in a collection. We can, for example, use `find()` to get a team with more than 90 wins.

```
> _(national_league).find( function(team) { return team.wins > 90; })
  { name: "Atlanta Braves", wins: 94, losses: 68, division: "east" }
```

The `find()` function returns the first element in the array that meets the criterion. To find all elements that meet our criterion, use the `filter()` function.

```
> _(national_league).filter( function(team) { return team.wins > 90; })
  [ { name: "Atlanta Braves", wins: 94, losses: 68, division: "east" },
    { name: "Cincinnati Reds", wins: 97, losses: 65, division: "central" },
```

```
    { name: "San Francisco Giants", wins: 94, losses: 68, division: "west" },
    { name: "Washington Nationals", wins: 98, losses: 64, division: "east" }
]
```

The opposite of the `filter()` function is `reject()`. It returns an array of elements that don't meet the criterion.

```
> _(national_league).reject( function(team) { return team.wins > 90; })
  [ { name: "Arizona Diamondbacks", wins: 81, losses:  81, division: "west" },
    { name: "Chicago Cubs", wins: 61, losses: 101, division: "central" },
    // Console output continues...
    { name: "St. Louis Cardinals", wins: 88, losses: 74, division: "central" }
  ]
```

If your criterion can be described as a property value, you can use a simpler version of `filter()`: the `where()` function. Instead of an arbitrary function to check for a match, `where()` takes for its parameter a set of properties that must match. We can use it to extract all the teams in the Eastern Division.

```
> _(national_league).where({division: "east"})
  [ { name: "Atlanta Braves", wins: 94, losses: 68, division: "east" },
    { name: "Miami Marlins", wins: 69, losses: 93, division: "east" },
    { name: "New York Mets", wins: 74, losses: 88, division: "east" },
    { name: "Philadelphia Phillies", wins: 81, losses: 81, division: "east" },
    { name: "Washington Nationals", wins: 98, losses: 64, division: "east" }
  ]
```

The `findWhere()` method combines the functionality of `find()` with the simplicity of `where()`. It returns the first element in a collection with properties that match specific values.

```
> _(national_league).where({name: "Atlanta Braves"})
  {name: "Atlanta Braves", wins: 94, losses: 68, division: "east"}
```

Another Underscore.js utility that's especially handy is `pluck()`. This function creates an array by extracting only the specified property from a collection. We could use it to extract an array of nothing but team names, for example.

```
> _(national_league).pluck( "team")
  [
    "Arizona Diamondbacks",
    "Atlanta Braves",
    /* Data continues... */,
    "Washington Nationals"
  ]
```

Testing a Collection

Sometimes we don't necessarily need to transform a collection; we simply want to check some aspect of it. Underscore.js provides several utilities to help with these tests.

The `every()` function tells us whether all elements in a collection pass an arbitrary test. We could use it to check if every team in our data set had at least 70 wins.

```
> _(national_league).every(function(team) { return team.wins >= 70; })
  false
```

Perhaps we'd like to know if *any* team had at least 70 wins. In that case, the `any()` function provides an answer.

```
> _(national_league).any(function(team) { return team.wins >= 70; })
  true
```

Underscore.js also lets us use arbitrary functions to find the maximum and minimum elements in a collection. If our criteria is number of wins, we use `max()` to find the "maximum" team.

```
> _(national_league).max(function(team) { return team.wins; })
  { name: "Washington Nationals", wins: 98, losses: 64, division: "east" }
```

Not surprisingly, the `min()` function works the same way.

```
> _(national_league).min(function(team) { return team.wins; })
  { name: "Houston Astros", wins: 55, losses: 107, division: "central" }
```

Rearranging Collections

To sort a collection, we can use the `sortBy()` method and supply an arbitrary function to provide sortable values. Here's how to reorder our collection in order of increasing wins.

```
> _(national_league).sortBy(function(team) { return team.wins; })
  [ { name: "Houston Astros", wins: 55, losses: 107, division: "central" }
    { name: "Chicago Cubs", wins: 61, losses: 101, division: "central" },
    // Data continues...
    { name: "Washington Nationals", wins: 98, losses: 64, division: "east" }
```

We could also reorganize our collection by grouping its elements according to a property. The Underscore.js function that helps in this case is `groupBy()`. One possibility is reorganizing the teams according to their division.

```
> _(national_league).groupBy( "division")
{
    { west:
        { name: "Arizona Diamondbacks", wins: 81, losses: 81, division: "west" },
        { name: "Colorado Rockies", wins: 64, losses: 98, division: "west" },
        { name: "Los Angeles Dodgers", wins: 86, losses: 76, division: "west" },
        { name: "San Diego Padres", wins: 76, losses: 86, division: "west" },
        { name: "San Francisco Giants", wins: 94, losses: 68, division: "west" },
    },
    { east:
        { name: "Atlanta Braves", wins: 94, losses: 68, division: "east" },
        { name: "Miami Marlins", wins: 69, losses: 93, division: "east" },
        { name: "New York Mets", wins: 74, losses: 88, division: "east" },
        { name: "Philadelphia Phillies", wins: 81, losses: 81,
            division: "east" },
        { name: "Washington Nationals", wins: 98, losses: 64, division: "east" }
    },
    { central:
        { name: "Chicago Cubs", wins: 61, losses: 101, division: "central" },
        { name: "Cincinnati Reds", wins: 97, losses: 65, division: "central" },
        { name: "Houston Astros", wins: 55, losses: 107, division: "central" },
        { name: "Milwaukee Brewers", wins: 83, losses: 79, division: "central" },
        { name: "Pittsburgh Pirates", wins: 79, losses:  83,
            division: "central" },
        { name: "St. Louis Cardinals",  wins: 88, losses: 74,
            division: "central" },
    }
}
```

We can also use the countBy() function to simply count the number of elements in each group.

```
> _(national_league).countBy( "division")
{west: 5, east: 5, central: 6}
```

✳ **NOTE:** Although we've used a property value ("division") for groupBy() and countBy(), both methods also accept an arbitrary function if the criteria for grouping isn't a simple property.

As a final trick, Underscore.js lets us randomly reorder a collection using the shuffle() function.

```
_(national_league).shuffle()
```

Summing Up

Although this chapter takes a different approach than the rest of the book, its ultimate focus is still on data visualizations. As we've seen in earlier chapters (and as you'll certainly encounter in your own projects), the raw data for our visualizations isn't always perfect as delivered. Sometimes we need to clean the data by removing invalid values, and other times we need to rearrange or transform it so that it's appropriate for our visualization libraries.

The Underscore.js library contains a wealth of tools and utilities to help with those tasks. It lets us easily manage arrays, modify objects, and transform collections. Furthermore, Underscore.js supports an underlying philosophy based on functional programming, so our code that uses Underscore.js remains highly readable and resistant to bugs and defects.

9

Building Data-Driven Web Applications: Part 1

So far we've had a chance to see many of the tools and libraries for creating individual JavaScript visualizations, but we've considered them only in the context of a traditional web page. Today, of course, the Web is much more than traditional web pages. Especially on desktop computers, websites are effectively full-featured software applications. (Even on mobile devices many "apps" are really just websites enclosed in a thin wrapper.) When a web application is structured around data, there's a good chance it can benefit from data visualizations. That's exactly what we'll consider in this final project: how to integrate data visualization into a true web application.

The sections that follow will walk through the development of an example application driven by data. The source of the data will be Nike's Nike+ (*http://nikeplus.com/*) service for runners. Nike sells many products and applications that let runners track their activities and save the results for analysis and review. In this chapter and the next, we'll build a web application to retrieve that data from Nike and present it to a user. Nike, of course, has its own web app for viewing Nike+ data, and that app is far superior to the simple example here. We're certainly not trying to compete with Nike; rather, we're just using the Nike+ service to structure our example.

* *NOTE:* **This sample project is based on the version of the interface at the time of this writing. There may have been changes to the interface since then.**

Unlike most other chapters, this chapter won't include multiple independent examples. Instead, it will walk through the main stages in the development and testing of a single data-driven application. We'll see how to build up the basic structure and functionality of the web application. This includes the following:

► How to structure a web application using a framework or library

► How to organize an application into models and views

► How to incorporate visualizations in views

In Chapter 10, we'll focus on some of the finer details by dealing with several quirks of the Nike+ interface and adding some finishing touches to round out the single-page application.

* *NOTE:* **To use the Nike+ data in an actual product, you must register your application with Nike and get the necessary credentials and security keys. That process also grants you access to the full documentation for the service, which is not publicly available. Since we're not building a real application in this example, we won't cover that step. We will, however, base the application on the Nike+ API, which is documented publicly on Nike's developer website (*https://developer.nike.com/index.html*). Because the example doesn't include the credentials and security keys, it won't be able to access the real Nike+ service. The book's source code, however, does include actual Nike+ data that can be used to emulate the Nike+ service for testing and development.**

Frameworks and Libraries

If we're using JavaScript to add data visualizations to traditional web pages, we don't have to worry too much about organizing and structuring our JavaScript. After all, it's often a relatively small amount of code, especially compared to the HTML markup and CSS styles that are also part of the page. With web applications, however, the code can grow to be more extensive and more complex. To help keep our code organized and manageable, we'll take advantage of a JavaScript application library, also called a *framework*.

Step 1: Select an Application Library

Deciding to use an application library might be easier than deciding which one to use. The number of these libraries has exploded in the past few years; there are now over 30 high-quality libraries from which to choose. A good place to see all the alternatives is TodoMVC (*http://todomvc.com/*), which shows how to implement a simple to-do application in each library.

There is an important question to ask that can help you narrow down the choices: is an application library a *pure library* or an *application framework*? Those terms are often used interchangeably, but there is a significant distinction. A pure library functions like jQuery or other libraries we've used throughout this book. It provides a set of tools for our application, and we can use as many—or as few— of those tools as we like. An application framework, on the other hand, dictates exactly how the application should work. The code that we write must follow the strictures and conventions of the framework. Fundamentally, the difference is about control. With a pure library, our code is in control and the library is at our disposal. With a framework, the framework code is in control, and we simply add the code that makes our application unique.

The main advantage of a pure library is flexibility. Our code is in control of the application, and we have full latitude to structure the application to our own requirements. That's not always a good thing, however. The constraints of a framework can protect us from making poor design decisions. Some of the world's best JavaScript developers are responsible for the popular frameworks, and they've put a lot of thought into what makes a good web application. There's another benefit to frameworks: because the framework assumes more responsibility for the application, there's generally less code we're required to write.

It's worth noting this distinction between frameworks and pure libraries, but almost any web application can be built effectively with either. Both approaches provide the organization and structure necessary for a high-quality application. For our example, we'll use the Backbone.js (*http://backbonejs.org/*) library. It is by far the most popular of the pure (nonframework) libraries, and it's used by dozens of the largest sites on the Web. The general approach that we'll follow, however (including tools such as Yeoman), works well with almost any popular application library.

Step 2: Install Development Tools

When you start building your first real web application, deciding how to begin can be a bit intimidating. One tool that can be a big help at this stage is Yeoman (*http://yeoman.io/*), which describes itself as "The Web's Scaffolding Tool for Modern Webapps." That's a pretty accurate description. Yeoman can define and initialize a project structure for a large number of different web application frameworks, including Backbone.js. As we'll see, it also sets up and configures most of the other tools we'll need during the application's development.

Before we can use Yeoman, we must first install Node.js (*http://nodejs.org/*). Node.js is a powerful application development platform all by itself, but we won't need to worry about the details here. It is, however, the application platform required by many modern web development tools like Yeoman. To install Node.js, follow the instructions on its website (*http://nodejs.org/*).

With Node.js installed, we can install the main Yeoman application as well as everything necessary to create a Backbone.js application (*https://github.com/yeoman/generator-backbone/*) with one command.

```
$ npm install -g generator-backbone
```

You can execute this command in the Terminal app (on Mac OS X) or from the Windows command prompt.

Step 3: Define a New Project

The development tools we just installed will make it easy to create a new web app project. First, with the following commands, we create a new folder (named *running*) for our application and then **cd** (change directory) into that folder.

```
$ mkdir running
$ cd running
```

From within that new folder, executing the command **yo backbone** will initialize the project structure.

```
$ yo backbone
```

As part of the initialization, Yeoman will ask for permission to send diagnostic information (mainly which frameworks and features our app uses) back to the Yeoman developers. It will then give us a choice to add a few more tools to the app. For our example, we'll skip any of the suggested options.

```
Out of the box I include HTML5 Boilerplate, jQuery, Backbone.js and Modernizr.
[?] What more would you like? (Press <space> to select)
>O Bootstrap for Sass
 O Use CoffeeScript
 O Use RequireJs
```

Yeoman will then do its magic, creating several subfolders, installing extra tools and applications, and setting up reasonable defaults. As you watch all the pages and pages of installation information scroll by in your window, you can be glad that Yeoman is doing all this work for you. When Yeoman finishes, you'll have a project structure like the one shown in Figure 9-1. It may not look exactly like the figure here, since web applications may have changed since this text was written, but rest assured that it will follow the best practices and conventions.

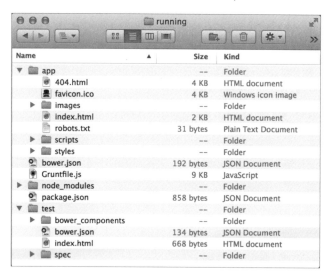

FIGURE 9-1: *Yeoman creates a default project structure for a web application.*

We'll spend more time with most of these files and folders in the sections that follow, but here's a quick overview of the project that Yeoman has set up for us.

app/ The folder that will contain all the code for our app

bower.json A file that keeps track of all the third-party libraries our app uses

Gruntfile.js A file that controls how to test and build our app

node_modules/ A folder that contains the tools used to build and test our app

package.json A file that identifies the tools used to build and test our app

test/ A folder that will contain the code we'll write to test our app

At this point Yeoman has set up a complete web app (albeit one that doesn't do anything). You can execute the command grunt serve from the command prompt to see it in a browser.

```
$ grunt serve
Running "serve" task

Running "clean:server" (clean) task

Running "createDefaultTemplate" task

Running "jst:compile" (jst) task
>> Destination not written because compiled files were empty.

Running "connect:livereload" (connect) task
Started connect web server on http://localhost:9000

Running "open:server" (open) task

Running "watch:livereload" (watch) task
Waiting...
```

The grunt command runs one of the tools that's part of the Yeoman package. When passed the serve option, it cleans up the application folder, starts a web server to host the application, launches a web browser, and navigates to the skeleton app. You'll see something like Figure 9-2 in your browser.

FIGURE 9-2: *The default Yeoman web application runs in the browser.*

Congratulations! Our web app, as basic as it is, is now running.

Step 4: Add Our Unique Dependencies

Yeoman sets up sensible defaults and tools for a new app, but our app needs a few JavaScript libraries that aren't part of those defaults, such as Leaflet for maps and Flot for charts. The Moment.js (*http://momentjs.com/*) library for dealing with dates and times will also come in handy, as will the Underscore.string (*http://epeli .github.io/underscore.string/*) library. We can add these libraries to our project with some simple commands. The --**save** option tells the bower tool (which is part of the Yeoman package) to remember that our project depends on these libraries.

```
$ bower install leaflet --save
$ bower install flot --save
$ bower install momentjs --save
$ bower install underscore.string --save
```

Perhaps you've already begun to appreciate how tools like Yeoman make development easier. The simple commands shown here save us from having to find the libraries on the Web, download the appropriate files, copy them to the right place in our project, and so on.

Even more importantly, Yeoman (technically, the bower tool) automatically takes care of any additional libraries on which these libraries depend. The Flot library, for example, requires jQuery. When Yeoman installs Flot, it will also check and make sure that jQuery is installed in the project. In our case, it is because Backbone.js depends on it, but if jQuery weren't already installed, Yeoman would automatically find it and install it as well.

For most libraries, bower can completely install all the necessary components and files. In the case of Leaflet, however, we need to perform a few extra steps. Change directory to the *leaflet* folder within *app/bower_components*. From there, run two commands to install the unique tools that Leaflet requires:

```
$ npm install
$ npm install jake -g
```

Executing the command **jake** will then run all of Leaflet's tests and, provided they pass, create a Leaflet.js library for our app.

```
$ jake
Checking for JS errors...
    Check passed.

Checking for specs JS errors...
    Check passed.

Running tests...

.........................................................................
.........................................................................
.........................................................................
..............................................
```

```
PhantomJS 1.9.7 (Mac OS X): Executed 280 of 280 SUCCESS (0.881 secs / 0.496 secs)
    Tests ran successfully.


Concatenating and compressing 75 files...
    Uncompressed: 217.22 KB (unchanged)
    Compressed: 122.27 KB (unchanged)
    Gzipped: 32.71 KB
```

All that's left to do is add the other libraries into our HTML files. That's easy enough. The main page for our app is *index.html* in the *app* folder. There's already a block of code that includes jQuery, Underscore.js, and Backbone.js:

```html
<!-- build:js scripts/vendor.js -->
<script src="bower_components/jquery/dist/jquery.js"></script>
<script src="bower_components/underscore/underscore.js"></script>
<script src="bower_components/backbone/backbone.js"></script>
<!-- endbuild -->
```

We can add our new libraries after Backbone.js.

```html
<!-- build:js scripts/vendor.js -->
<script src="bower_components/jquery/dist/jquery.js"></script>
<script src="bower_components/underscore/underscore.js"></script>
<script src="bower_components/backbone/backbone.js"></script>
<script src="bower_components/flot/jquery.flot.js"></script>
<script src="bower_components/leaflet/dist/leaflet-src.js"></script>
<script src="bower_components/momentjs/moment.js"></script>
<script
    src="bower_components/underscore.string/lib/underscore.string.js">
</script>
<!-- endbuild -->
```

Leaflet, as we saw in Chapter 6, also requires its own style sheet. We add that to the top of *index.html* just before *main.css*.

```html
<!-- build:css(.tmp) styles/main.css -->
<link rel="stylesheet" href="bower_components/leaflet/dist/leaflet.css">
<link rel="stylesheet" href="styles/main.css">
<!-- endbuild -->
```

Now that we've set up the structure of our app and installed the necessary libraries, it's time to start development.

Models and Views

There are many application libraries available for web apps, and each has its quirks, but most of the libraries agree on the key principles that should guide an app's architecture. Perhaps the most fundamental of those principles is separating *models* from *views*. The code that keeps track of the core data for the app (the models) should be separate from the code that presents that data to the user (the views). Enforcing this separation makes it easier to update and modify either. If you want to present your data in a table instead of a chart, you can do that without any changes to the models. And if you need to change your data source from a local file to a REST API, you can do that without any changes to the views. We've been employing this principle in an informal way throughout the book. In all of the examples, we've isolated the steps required to obtain and format our data from the steps we used to visualize it. Using an application library like Backbone.js gives us the tools to manage models and views more explicitly.

Step 1: Define the Application's Models

Our running app is designed to work with Nike+, which provides details about runs—training runs, interval workouts, trail runs, races, and so on. The data set we want consists of nothing but runs, so our app's core model is, naturally, a run.

The Yeoman tool makes it very easy to define a model for our app. A simple command defines a new model and creates the JavaScript files and scaffolding for that model.

```
$ yo backbone:model run
   create app/scripts/models/run.js
   invoke    backbone-mocha:model
   create    test/models/run.spec.js
```

That command creates two new files: *run.js* in the *app/scripts/models/* folder and *run.spec.js* in the *test/* folder. Let's take a look at the file Yeoman created for our model. It's quite short.

❶ `/*Global Running, Backbone*/`

❷ `Running.Models = Running.Models || {};`

```
(function () {
    "use strict";
    Running.Models.Run = Backbone.Model.extend({
        url: "",
        initialize: function() {
        },
        defaults: {
        },
        validate: function(attrs, options) {
        },
        parse: function(response, options)  {
            return response;
        }
    });
})();
```

At ❶ is a comment that lists the global variables our model requires. In this case there are only two: Running (that's our app) and Backbone. Next, at ❷, this file creates a .Models property of the Running object unless that property already exists.

When the browser encounters this line, it will check to see if Running.Models exists. If it does, then Running.Models won't be false, and the browser never has to consider the second clause of the logical or (||). The statement simply assigns Running.Models to itself, so it has no practical effect. If Running.Models does not exist, however, then it evaluates to false, and the browser will continue to the second clause, where it assigns an empty object ({}) to Running.Models. Ultimately, this statement makes sure that the object Running.Models exists.

The rest of the code in the file is enclosed within an *immediately invoked function expression*. If you haven't seen this pattern before, it may look a little strange.

```
(function () {
    /* Code goes here */
})();
```

If we rewrite the block as a single line, though, it might be easier to understand.

```
( function () { /* Code goes here */ } ) ();
```

The statement defines a JavaScript function with a function expression, function () { /* ... */ }, and then, with the concluding (), it calls (technically *invokes*) that newly created function. All we're really doing, therefore, is putting our code inside a function and calling that function. You'll see this pattern a lot in professional JavaScript because it protects a block of code from interfering with other code blocks in the application.

When you define a variable in JavaScript, it is a *global* variable, available everywhere in the code. As a consequence, if two different sections of code try to define the same global variable, those definitions will clash. This interaction can cause bugs that are very hard to find, as code in one section inadvertently interferes with code in a completely different section. To prevent this problem, we can avoid using global variables, and the easiest way to do that in JavaScript is to define our variables inside a function. That's the purpose of an immediately invoked function expression. It makes sure that any variables our code defines are *local* to the function rather than global, and it prevents our code blocks from interfering with one another.

Step 2: Implement the Model

Our application really only needs this one model, and it's already complete! That's right: the scaffolding that Yeoman has set up for us is a complete and functioning model for a run. In fact, if it weren't for some quirks in Nike's REST API, we wouldn't have to touch the model code at all. We'll address those quirks in Chapter 10.

Before we move on to the next step, though, let's look at what we can do with our newly created model. To do that we'll make a temporary addition to the model code. We won't use the following code in the final app; it's only meant to show off what our model can already do.

First, let's add the URL to retrieve details about a run (Nike+ uses the more general term *activity*). From the Nike+ documentation, we find that this URL is *https://api.nike.com/v1/me/sport/activities/<activityId>*.

```
Running.Models.Run = Backbone.Model.extend({
❶    url: "https://api.nike.com/v1/me/sport/activities/",
    initialize: function() {
    },
    defaults: {
    },
    validate: function(attrs, options) {
    },
    parse: function(response, options)  {
        return response;
    }
});
```

The final part of the URL depends on the specific activity, so here we add only the general part of the URL to our model (❶).

Now imagine that we want to get the details for a specific run from the Nike+ service. The run in question has a unique identifier of 2126456911. If the Nike+ API followed typical conventions, we could create a variable representing that run, *and get all its data*, with the hypothetical two statements that follow. (We'll consider the quirks of the actual Nike+ interface in Step 7 of "Connecting with the Nike+ Service" on page 318.)

```
var run = new Running.Models.Run({id: 2126456911});
run.fetch();
```

Since many APIs *do* follow typical conventions, it's worth spending some time understanding how that code works. The first statement creates a new instance of the Run model and specifies its identifier. The second statement tells Backbone to retrieve the model's data from the server. Backbone will take care of all the communication with Nike+, including error handling, time-outs, parsing the response, and so on. Once the fetch completes, detailed information from that run will be available from the model. If we provide a callback function, we could output some of the details. Here's an example:

```
var run = new Running.Models.Run({id: 2126456911});
run.fetch({success: function() {
    console.log("Run started at ", run.get("startTime"));
    console.log("    Duration: ", run.get("metricSummary").duration);
    console.log("    Distance: ", run.get("metricSummary").distance);
    console.log("    Calories: ", run.get("metricSummary").calories);
}});
```

The output in the browser's console would be the following:

```
Run started at 2013-04-09T10:54:33Z
    Duration: 0:22:39.000
    Distance: 3.7524
    Calories: 240
```

Not bad for a few simple lines of code! The code in this step, though, is really just a detour. Our application won't use individual models in this way. Instead, we'll use an even more powerful Backbone.js feature: collections.

Step 3: Define the Application's Collections

The model we created is designed to capture the data for a single run. Our users, however, aren't interested in just a single run. They'd like to see all of their runs—dozens, hundreds, possibly thousands of them. We can handle all of these runs with a *collection,* or group of models. The collection is one of the core concepts of Backbone.js, and it will be a big help for our app. Let's define a collection for all of the user's runs.

Yeoman makes it easy to define and set up scaffolding for our collection. We execute the single command yo `backbone:collection runs` from the command line. (Yes, we're being very original and calling our collection of runs, well, *runs.*)

```
$ yo backbone:collection runs
    create app/scripts/collections/runs.js
    invoke   backbone-mocha:collection
    create    test/collections/runs.spec.js
```

Yeoman does the same thing for collections as it did for models: it creates an implementation file (*runs.js* in the *app/scripts/collections/* folder) and a test file. For now, let's take a look at *runs.js.*

```
/*Global Running, Backbone*/

Running.Collections = Running.Collections || {};

(function () {
    "use strict";
    Running.Collections.Runs = Backbone.Collection.extend({
        model: Running.Models.Runs
    });
})();
```

This file is even simpler than our model; the default collection has only a single property to indicate what type of model the collection contains. Unfortunately, Yeoman isn't smart enough to handle plurals, so it assumes the name of the model is the same as the name of the collection. That's not true for our app, as our model is Run (singular) and the collection is Runs (plural). While we're removing that *s*, we can also add a property to specify the REST API for the collection. That's a URL from the Nike+ service.

```
Running.Collections.Runs = Backbone.Collection.extend({
    url: "https://api.nike.com/v1/me/sport/activities/",
    model: Running.Models.Run
});
```

With those two small changes, we're ready to take advantage of our new collection (aside from handling a few quirks with the Nike+ API; we'll ignore that complication for now and address it later). All we need to do is create a new instance of the Runs collection and then fetch its data.

```
var runs = new Running.Collections.Runs();
runs.fetch();
```

That's all it takes to build a collection containing the user's runs. Backbone.js creates a model for each and retrieves the model's data from the server. Even better, those run models are stored in a true Underscore.js collection, which gives us access to many powerful methods to manipulate and search through the collection. Suppose, for example, we want to find the total distance for all of a user's runs. That's tailor-made for the Underscore.js reduce() function.

```
var totalDistance = runs.reduce( function(sum, run) {
    return sum + run.get("metricSummary").distance;
}, 0);
```

That code could tell us, for example, that the user has logged a total of 3,358 kilometers with Nike+.

✳ **NOTE:** As you may have noticed, we're taking advantage of many utilities from Underscore.js in our Backbone.js application. That is not a coincidence. Jeremy Ashkenas is the lead developer for both projects.

Step 4: Define the Application's Main View

Now that we have all the running data for a user, it's time to present that data. We'll do that with Backbone.js *views*. To keep our example simple, we'll consider only two ways to show the running data. First we'll display a table listing summary information about each run. Then, if the user clicks on a table row, we'll show details about that specific run, including any visualizations. The main view of our application will be the summary table, so let's focus on that first.

A Backbone.js view is responsible for presenting data to the user, and that data may be maintained in a collection or a model. For the main page of our app, we want to show summary information for all of a user's runs. That view, therefore, is a view of the entire collection. We'll call the view *Summary*.

The bulk of the table for this Summary view will be a series of table rows, where each row presents summary data about an individual run. That means we can simply create a view of a single Run model presented as a table row, and design our main Summary view to be made up (mostly) of many SummaryRow views. We can once again rely on Yeoman to set up the scaffolding for both of those types of views.

```
$ yo backbone:view summary
   create app/scripts/templates/summary.ejs
   create app/scripts/views/summary.js
   invoke   backbone-mocha:view
   create      test/views/summary.spec.js
$ yo backbone:view summaryRow
   create app/scripts/templates/summaryRow.ejs
   create app/scripts/views/summaryRow.js
   invoke   backbone-mocha:view
   create      test/views/summaryRow.spec.js
```

The scaffolding that Yeoman sets up is pretty much the same for each view; only the name varies. Here's what a Summary view looks like.

```
/*Global Running, Backbone, JST*/

Running.Views = Running.Views || {};

(function () {
    "use strict";
    Running.Views.Summary = Backbone.View.extend({
        template: JST["app/scripts/templates/summary.ejs"],
        tagName: "div",
        id: "",
        className: "",
        events: {},
        initialize: function () {
            this.listenTo(this.model, "change", this.render);
        },
        render: function () {
            this.$el.html(this.template(this.model.toJSON()));
        }
    });
})();
```

The overall structure of the file is the same as our model and our collection, but there's a bit more going on in the view itself. Let's step through the view's properties one at a time. The first property is **template**. That's where we define the exact HTML markup for the view, and we'll look at this in more detail in the next step.

The **tagName** property defines the HTML tag that our view will use as its parent. Yeoman defaults it to a generic <div>, but we know that in our case, it will be a <table>. We'll change that in a moment.

The id and className properties specify HTML id attributes or class values to add to the main container (in our case, the <table>). We could, for example, base some CSS styles on these values. For our example, we're not considering styles, so we can leave both properties blank or delete them entirely.

Next is the events property. This property identifies user events (such as mouse clicks) that are relevant for the view. In the case of the Summary view, there are no events, so we can leave the object empty or simply delete it.

The last two properties, initialize() and render(), are both methods. Before we consider those, let's see the Summary view after we make the tweaks just mentioned. Now that we've omitted the properties we won't be using, we're down to just the template and tagName properties, plus the initialize() and render() methods:

```
Running.Views.Summary = Backbone.View.extend({
    template: JST["app/scripts/templates/summary.ejs"],
    tagName: "table",
    initialize: function () {
            this.listenTo(this.model, "change", this.render);
    },
    render: function () {
            this.$el.html(this.template(this.model.toJSON()));
    }
});
```

Now let's look inside the last two methods, starting with initialize(). That method has a single statement (other than the return statement that we just added). By calling listenTo(), it tells Backbone.js that the view wants to listen for events. The first parameter, this.collection, specifies the event target, so the statement says that the view wants to listen to events affecting the collection. The second parameter specifies the type of events. In this case, the view wants to know whenever the collection changes. The final parameter is the function Backbone.js should call when the event occurs. Every time the Runs collection changes, we want Backbone.js to call the view's render() method. That makes sense, because whenever the Runs collection changes, whatever we were displaying on the page is now out of date. To make it current, our view should refresh its contents.

Most of the real work of a view takes place in its render() method. After all, this is the code that actually creates the HTML markup for the web page. Yeoman has gotten us started with a template, but in the case of a collection view, that's not enough. The template takes care of the HTML for the collection as a whole, but it doesn't handle the models that are part of the collection. For the individual runs, we can use the each() function from Underscore.js to iterate through the collection and render each run.

As you can see from the following code, we've also added a return this; statement to each method. In a bit we'll take advantage of this addition to *chain* together calls to multiple methods in a single, concise statement.

```
Running.Views.Summary = Backbone.View.extend({
    template: JST["app/scripts/templates/summary.ejs"],
    tagName: "table",
    initialize: function () {
        this.listenTo(this.collection, "change", this.render);
        return this;
    },
     render: function () {
        this.$el.html(this.template());
        this.collection.each(this.renderRun, this);
        return this;
    }
});
```

Now we have to write the `renderRun()` method that handles each individual run. Here's what we want that function to do:

1. Create a new SummaryRow view for the run.
2. Render that SummaryRow view.
3. Append the resulting HTML to the `<tbody>` in the Summary view.

The code to implement those steps is straightforward, but it's helpful to take each step one at a time.

1. Create a new SummaryRow view: `new SummaryRow({model: run})`
2. Render that SummaryRow view: `.render()`
3. Append the result: `this.$("tbody").append();`

When we put the steps together, we have the `renderRun()` method.

```
renderRun: function (run) {
    this.$("tbody").append(new Running.Views.SummaryRow({
        model: run
    }).render().el);
}
```

Most of the changes we made to the Summary view are also appropriate for the SummaryRow view, although we don't need to add anything to the `render()` method. Here's our first implementation of the SummaryRow. Note that we've set the `tagName` property to `"tr"` because we want each run model presented as a table row.

```
Running.Views.SummaryRow = Backbone.View.extend({
    template: JST["app/scripts/templates/summaryRow.ejs"],
    tagName: "tr",
    events: {},
    initialize: function () {
        this.listenTo(this.model, "change", this.render);
        return this;
    },
```

```
    render: function () {
        this.$el.html(this.template(this.model.toJSON()));
        return this;
    }
});
```

Now we have all the JavaScript code we need to show the main summary view for our app.

Step 5: Define the Main View Templates

So far we've developed the JavaScript code to manipulate our Summary and SummaryRow views. That code doesn't generate the actual HTML markup, though. For that task we rely on *templates*. Templates are skeletal HTML markup with placeholders for individual values. Confining HTML markup to templates helps keep our JavaScript code clean, well structured, and easy to maintain.

Just as there are many popular JavaScript application libraries, there are also many template languages. Our application doesn't require any fancy template functionality, however, so we'll stick with the default template process that Yeoman has set up for us. That process relies on a JST tool (*https://github.com/gruntjs/grunt-contrib-jst/*) to process templates, and the tool uses the Underscore.js template language (*http://underscorejs.org/#template/*). It's easy to see how this works through an example, so let's dive in.

The first template we'll tackle is the template for a SummaryRow. In our view, we've already established that the SummaryRow is a `<tr>` element, so the template needs to supply only the content that lives within that `<tr>`. We'll get that content from the associated Run model, which, in turn, comes from the Nike+ service. Here's an example activity that Nike+ could return.

```
{
    "activityId": "2126456911",
    "activityType": "RUN",
    "startTime": "2013-04-09T10:54:33Z",
    "activityTimeZone": "GMT-04:00",
    "status": "COMPLETE",
    "deviceType": "IPOD",
    "metricSummary": {
        "calories": 240,
        "fuel": 790,
        "distance": 3.7524,
        "steps": 0,
        "duration": "0:22:39.000"
    },
    "tags": [/* Data continues... */],
    "metrics": [/* Data continues... */],
    "gps": {/* Data continues... */}
}
```

For a first implementation, let's show the time of the run, as well as its duration, distance, and calories. Our table row, therefore, will have four cells, with each cell holding one of these values. We can find the template, *summaryRow.ejs*, in the *app/scripts/templates* folder. By default, Yeoman sets it to a simple paragraph.

```
<p>Your content here.</p>
```

Let's replace that with four table cells.

```
<td></td>
<td></td>
<td></td>
<td></td>
```

As placeholders for the cells' content, we can use model attributes enclosed in special <%= and %> delimiters. The full SummaryRow template is as follows.

```
<td><%= startTime %></td>
<td><%= metricSummary.duration %></td>
<td><%= metricSummary.distance %></td>
<td><%= metricSummary.calories %></td>
```

The other template we need to supply is the Summary template. Since we've already set the view's main tag to be a `<table>`, this template should specify the content within that `<table>`: a table header row plus an empty `<tbody>` element (whose individual rows will come from the Run models).

```
<thead>
    <tr>
        <th>Time</th>
        <th>Duration</th>
        <th>Distance</th>
        <th>Calories</th>
    </tr>
</thead>
<tbody></tbody>
```

Now we're finally ready to construct the main view for our runs. The steps are quite straightforward:

1. Create a new Runs collection.
2. Fetch the data for that collection from the server.
3. Create a new Summary view for the collection.
4. Render the view.

Here's the JavaScript code for those four steps:

```javascript
var runs = new Running.Collection.Runs();
runs.fetch();
var summaryView = new Running.Views.Summary({collection: runs});
summaryView.render();
```

We can access the constructed `<table>` as the el (short for *element*) property of the view. It will look something like the following:

```html
<table>
  <thead>
    <tr>
        <th>Time</th>
        <th>Duration</th>
        <th>Distance</th>
        <th>Calories</th>
    </tr>
  </thead>
  <tbody>
    <tr>
        <td>2013-04-09T10:54:33Z</td>
        <td>0:22:39.000</td>
        <td>3.7524</td>
        <td>240</td>
    </tr>
    <tr>
        <td>2013-04-07T12:34:40Z</td>
        <td>0:44:59.000</td>
        <td>8.1724</td>
        <td>569</td>
    </tr>
    <tr>
        <td>2013-04-06T13:28:36Z</td>
        <td>1:28:59.000</td>
        <td>16.068001</td>
        <td>1200</td>
    </tr>
  </tbody>
</table>
```

When we insert that markup in the page, our users can see a simple summary table listing their runs, as shown in Figure 9-3.

Time	Duration	Distance	Calories
2013-04-09T10:54:33Z	0:22:39.000	3.7524	240
2013-04-07T12:34:40Z	0:44:59.000	8.1724	569
2013-04-06T13:28:36Z	1:28:59.000	16.068001	1,200
2013-04-04T11:57:16Z	0:58:44.000	9.623	736
2013-04-02T11:42:47Z	0:22:37.000	3.6368	293
2013-03-31T12:44:00Z	0:34:04.000	6.3987	445
2013-03-30T13:15:35Z	1:29:31.000	16.0548	1,203
2013-03-28T11:42:17Z	1:04:09.000	11.1741	852
2013-03-26T12:21:52Z	0:39:33.000	7.3032	514
2013-03-24T20:15:31Z	0:33:49.000	6.2886	455

FIGURE 9-3: *A simple table with a summary of run information*

Step 6: Refine the Main View

Now we're starting to get somewhere, though the table contents could use some tweaking. After all, does the last digit in a run of 16.068001 kilometers really matter? Since Nike+ determines the attributes of our Run model, it might seem like we have no control over the values passed to our template. Fortunately, that's not the case. If we look at the SummaryView's `render()` method, we can see how the template gets its values.

```
render: function () {
    this.$el.html(this.template(this.model.toJSON()));
    return this;
}
```

The template values come from a JavaScript object that we're creating directly from the model. Backbone.js provided the `toJSON()` method, which returns a JavaScript object corresponding to the model's attributes. We can actually pass any JavaScript object to the template, even one we create ourselves within the `render()` method. Let's rewrite that method to provide a more user-friendly Summary view. We'll take the model's attributes one at a time.

First is the date of the run. A date of "2013-04-09T10:54:33Z" isn't very readable for average users, and it's probably not even in their time zone. Working with dates and times is actually quite tricky, but the excellent Moment.js library (*http://momentjs.com/*) can handle all of the complexity. Since we added that library to our app in an earlier section, we can take advantage of it now.

```
render: function () {
    var run = {};
    run.date = moment(this.model.get("startTime")).calendar();
```

* *NOTE:* **In the interest of brevity, we're cheating a little with the preceding code because it converts the UTC timestamp to the local time zone of the browser. It would probably be more correct to convert it to the time zone for the run, which Nike+ provides in the data.**

Next up is the run's duration. It's doubtful that we need to show the fractions of seconds that Nike+ includes, so let's simply drop them from the attribute. (It would be more precise to round up or down, but assuming our users are not Olympic athletes in training, a second here or there won't matter. Besides, Nike+ seems to always record these subsecond durations as ".000" anyway.)

```
run.duration = this.model.get("metricSummary").duration.split(".")[0];
```

The **distance** property can also use some adjustment. In addition to rounding it to a reasonable number of decimal places, we can convert from kilometers to miles for our US users. A single statement takes care of both.

```
run.distance = Math.round(62. *
    this.model.get("metricSummary").distance)/100 +
    " Miles";
```

The **calories** property is fine as it is, so we'll just copy it into our temporary object.

```
run.calories = this.model.get("metricSummary").calories;
```

Finally, if you're an avid runner, you might have noticed that there's an important value missing from the Nike+ attributes: the average pace for the run in minutes per mile. We have the data to calculate it, so let's add that as well.

```
var secs = _(run.duration.split(":")).reduce(function(sum, num) {
    return sum*60+parseInt(num,10); }, 0);
var pace = moment.duration(1000*secs/parseFloat(run.distance));
run.pace = pace.minutes() + ":" + _(pace.seconds()).pad(2, "0");
```

Now we have a new object to pass to the template.

```
this.$el.html(this.template(run));
```

We'll also need to modify both templates to match the new markup. Here's the updated template for SummaryRows.

```
<td><%= date %></td>
<td><%= duration %></td>
<td><%= distance %></td>
<td><%= calories %></td>
<td><%= pace %></td>
```

And here's the Summary template with the additional column for Pace.

```
<thead>
  <tr>
    <th>Date</th>
    <th>Duration</th>
    <th>Distance</th>
    <th>Calories</th>
    <th>Pace</th>
  </tr>
</thead>
<tbody></tbody>
```

Now we have a much-improved summary table for our users, shown in Figure 9-4.

Date	Duration	Distance	Calories	Pace
04/09/2013	0:22:39	2.33 Miles	240	9:43
04/07/2013	0:44:59	5.08 Miles	569	8:51
04/06/2013	1:28:59	9.98 Miles	1,200	8:54
04/04/2013	0:58:44	5.98 Miles	736	9:49
04/02/2013	0:22:37	2.26 Miles	293	10:00
03/31/2013	0:34:04	3.98 Miles	445	8:33
03/30/2013	1:29:31	9.98 Miles	1,203	8:58
03/28/2013	1:04:09	6.94 Miles	852	9:14
03/26/2013	0:39:33	4.54 Miles	514	8:42
03/24/2013	0:33:49	3.91 Miles	455	8:38

FIGURE 9-4: *An improved summary table with cleaner-looking data*

Views for Visualizations

Now that we've seen how to use Backbone.js views to separate data from its presentation, we can consider how to use the same approach for data visualizations. When the presentation is simple HTML markup—as in the previous section's tables—it's easy to use templates to view a model. But templates aren't sophisticated enough to handle data visualizations, so we'll need to modify our approach for those.

The data from the Nike+ service offers lots of opportunity for visualizations. Each run, for example, may include a record of the user's heart rate, instantaneous pace, and cumulative distance, recorded every 10 seconds. Runs may also include the user's GPS coordinates captured every second. That type of data lends itself to both charts and maps, and in this section, we'll add both to our application.

Step 1: Define the Additional Views

As we did in the previous section, we'll rely on Yeoman to create the scaffolding for our additional views. One view, which we'll call *Details,* will act as the overall view for the details of an individual run. Within that view, we'll create three additional views, each showing a different aspect of the run. We can think of these views in a hierarchy.

Details   A detailed view of a single run

Properties   The full set of properties associated with the run

Chart   Charts showing performance during the run

Map   A map of the run's route

To start the development of these views, we return to the command line and execute four Yeoman commands.

```
$ yo backbone:view details
$ yo backbone:view properties
$ yo backbone:view charts
$ yo backbone:view map
```

Step 2: Implement the Details View

The Details view is really nothing more than a container for its three children, so its implementation is about as easy as it gets. We create a new view for each of the children, render the view, and add the resulting markup to the Details. Here is the complete code for this view:

```
Running.Views.Details = Backbone.View.extend({
    render: function () {
        this.$el.empty();
        this.$el.append(
            new Running.Views.Properties({model: this.model}).render().el
        );
        this.$el.append(
            new Running.Views.Charts({model: this.model}).render().el
        );
        this.$el.append(
            new Running.Views.Map({model: this.model}).render().el
        );
```

```
        return this;
    }
});
```

Unlike the previous views we've created, this view doesn't have an `initialize()` method. That's because the Details view doesn't have to listen for changes to the model, so there's nothing to do during initialization. In other words, the Details view itself doesn't actually depend on any of the properties of the Run model. (The child views, on the other hand, depend greatly on those properties.)

The `render()` method itself first clears out any existing content from its element. This line makes it safe to call the `render()` method multiple times. The next three statements create each of the child views. Notice that all of the child views have the same model, which is the model for the Details view as well. This capability is the power of the model/view architecture; one data object—in our case, a run—can be presented in many different ways. While the `render()` method creates each of these child views, it also calls their `render()` methods, and it appends the resulting content (their `el` properties) into its own `el`.

Step 3: Implement the Properties View

For the Properties view, we want to show all of the properties that Nike+ has associated with the run. Those properties are determined by the data returned by the Nike+ service; here's an example:

```
{
    "activityId": "2126456911",
    "activityType": "RUN",
    "startTime": "2013-04-09T10:54:33Z",
    "activityTimeZone": "GMT-04:00",
    "status": "COMPLETE",
    "deviceType": "IPOD",
    "metricSummary": {
        "calories": 240,
        "fuel": 790,
        "distance": 3.7524,
        "steps": 0,
        "duration": "0:22:39.000"
    },
    "tags": [
        { "tagType": "WEATHER", "tagValue": "SUNNY"     },
        { "tagType": "NOTE"                             },
        { "tagType": "TERRAIN", "tagValue": "TRAIL"     },
        { "tagType": "SHOES",   "tagValue": "Neo Trail" },
        { "tagType": "EMOTION", "tagValue": "GREAT"     }
    ],
    "metrics": [
        { "intervalMetric": 10, "intervalUnit": "SEC",
          "metricType": "SPEED", "values": [/* Data continues... */] },
        { "intervalMetric": 10, "intervalUnit": "SEC",
          "metricType": "HEARTRATE", "values": [/* Data continues... */] },
```

```
        { "intervalMetric": 10, "intervalUnit": "SEC",
          "metricType": "DISTANCE", "values": [/* Data continues... */] },
    ],
    "gps": {
        "elevationLoss": 114.400024,
        "elevationGain": 109.00003,
        "elevationMax": 296.2,
        "elevationMin": 257,
        "intervalMetric": 10,
        "intervalUnit": "SEC",
        "waypoints": [/* Data continues... */]
    }
}
```

That data can certainly benefit from a bit of cleanup to make it more user-friendly. To do that we'll take advantage of the Underscore.string library we added to the project before. We can make sure that library is available by "mixing it into" the main Underscore.js library. We'll do that right at the start of the JavaScript file for the Properties view.

```
/*Global Running, Backbone, JST, _*/

_.mixin(_.str.exports());

Running.Views = Running.Views || {};

// Code continues...
```

Notice that we've also added the global variable for Underscore.js (_) to the initial comment in the file.

The most straightforward way to present this information in HTML is with a description list (<dl>). Each property can be an individual item in the list, with a description term (<dt>) holding the property name and the description data (<dd>) its value. To implement this, we set the **tagName** property of the view to be "dl", and we create a generic list item template. Here's the start of our Properties view code:

```
Running.Views.Properties = Backbone.View.extend({
    template: JST["app/scripts/templates/properties.ejs"],
    tagName: "dl",
    initialize: function () {
        this.listenTo(this.model, "change", this.render);
        return this;
    },
    render: function () {
        // More code goes here
        return this;
    }
});
```

And here's the simple template that the view will use.

```
<dt><%= key %></dt>
<dd><%= value %></dd>
```

A quick glance at the Nike+ data shows that it contains nested objects. The `metricSummary` property of the main object is itself an object. We need a function that will iterate through all the properties in the input object, building the HTML markup as it does. A recursive function can be particularly effective here, since it can call itself whenever it reaches another nested object. Next, we add an `obj2Html()` method to our view. At its core, this method will use the Underscore.js `reduce()` function, which is well suited to the task at hand.

```
obj2Html: function(obj) {
    return (
        _(obj).reduce(function(html, value, key) {

            // Create the markup for the current
            // key/value pair and add it to the html variable

            return html;

        }, "", this)
    );
}
```

As we process each property, the first thing we can do is improve the key name. For example, we'd like to replace `startTime` with `Start Time`. That's where Underscore.string comes in. Its `humanize()` function turns camelCase into separate words, and its `titleize()` function ensures that each word begins with an upper-case letter. We'll use chaining to perform both operations in one statement.

```
key = _.chain(key).humanize().titleize().value();
```

Now we can consider the value. If it is an array, we'll replace it with a string that shows the array length.

```
if (_(value).isArray()) {
    value = "[" + value.length + " items]";
}
```

Next we check to see if the value is an object. If it is, then we'll call the `obj2Html()` method recursively.

```
if (_(value).isObject()) {
    html += this.obj2Html(value);
```

For other types, we convert the value to a string, format it a bit with Underscore.string, and make use of our template.

```
} else {
    value = _(value.toString().toLowerCase()).titleize();
    html += this.template({ key: key, value: value });
}
```

There are a few other minor improvements we can make to the presentation, which you can find in the book's source code. The last piece of the view is implementing the render() method. In that method, we use toJSON() to get an object corresponding to the Run model, and then we start the obj2Html() recursion with that object.

```
render: function () {
    this.$el.html(this.obj2Html(this.model.toJSON()));
    return this;
}
```

The result is a complete picture of the properties of the run, shown in Figure 9-5.

Activity	2126456911
Activity Type	Run
Start Time	2013-04-09t10:54:33z
Activity Time Z...	GMT-04:00
Status	Complete
Device Type	iPod
Calories	240
Fuel	790
Distance	3.7524
Steps	0
Duration	0:22:39.000
Weather	Sunny
Terrain	Trail
Shoes	Neo Trail
Emotion	Great
Speed Data	[136 items]
Heartrate Data	[136 items]
Distance Data	[136 items]
Elevation Loss	114.400024
Elevation Max	296.2
Elevation Min	257
Waypoints	[266 items]

FIGURE 9-5: *The completed Properties view shows all of the data associated with a run.*

Step 4: Implement the Map View

To show users maps of their runs, we rely on the Leaflet library from Chapter 6. Using the library will require some small modifications to the normal Backbone.js view implementation, but, as we'll see, those same modifications will come in handy for other views as well. Leaflet builds its maps in a containing element in the page (typically a `<div>`), and that containing element must have an `id` attribute so that Leaflet can find it. Backbone.js will take care of adding that `id` if we include an `id` property in the view. That's easy enough.

```
Running.Views.Map = Backbone.View.extend({
    id: "map",
```

With `<div id="map"></div>` available in the page's markup, we can create a Leaflet map with the following statement:

```
var map = L.map(this.id);
```

We might be tempted to do that directly in the view's `render()` method, but there's a problem with that approach. Adding (and removing) elements in a web page requires a lot of computation by the browser. When JavaScript code does that frequently, the performance of the page can suffer significantly. To reduce this problem, Backbone.js tries to minimize the number of times it adds (or removes) elements, and one way to do that is to add many elements at once rather than adding each element independently. It employs that approach when it implements a view's `render()` method. Before adding any elements to the page, it lets the view finish constructing its entire markup; only then does it add that markup to the page.

The problem here is that when `render()` is called the first time, there won't (yet) be a `<div id="map"></div>` anywhere in the page. If we call Leaflet, it won't be able to find the container for its map, and it will generate an error. What we need to do is defer the part of `render()` that draws the map until after Backbone.js has added the map container to the page.

Fortunately, Underscore.js has a utility function called `defer()` to do just that. Instead of drawing the map directly in the `render()` method, we'll create a separate method. Then, in the `render()` method, we'll defer execution of that new method. Here's what the code to do that looks like:

```
render: function () {
    _.defer(_(function(){ this.drawMap(); }).bind(this));
},
drawMap: function () {
    var map = L.map(this.id);
    // Code continues...
}
```

As you can see, we're actually using a couple of Underscore.js functions in our `render()` method. In addition to `defer()`, we also take advantage of `bind()`. The latter function ensures that the `this` value when `drawMap()` is eventually called is the same as the `this` value within the view.

There's one change we can make to further improve this implementation. Although there won't be a `<div id="map"></div>` in the page when `render()` is first called, that element will exist in subsequent calls to `render()`. In those cases, we don't need to defer the execution of `drawMap()`. That leads to the following code for our `render()` method.

```
render: function () {
    if (document.getElementById(this.id)) {
        this.drawMap();
    } else {
        _.defer(_(function(){ this.drawMap(); }).bind(this));
    }
    return this;
},
```

As long as we're making optimizations, let's also change the `initialize()` method slightly. The default method that Yeoman creates is this:

```
initialize: function () {
    this.listenTo(this.model, "change", this.render);
},
```

For the Map view, however, we don't really care if any property of the Run model changes. The only property the view needs is **gps**, so we can tell Backbone.js to bother us only if that specific property changes.

```
initialize: function () {
    this.listenTo(this.model, "change:gps", this.render);
    return this;
},
```

You might be wondering, "Why would the **gps** property of the Run model ever change?" I'll get to that when I cover the quirks of the Nike+ REST API in Chapter 10.

With the preliminaries out of the way, we can implement the `drawMap()` function, which turns out to be a very easy implementation. The steps are as follows:

1. Make sure the model has a **gps** property and there are waypoints associated with it.
2. If an old map exists, remove it.
3. Extract the GPS coordinates from the waypoints array.
4. Create a path using those coordinates.
5. Create a map that contains that path, and draw the path on the map.
6. Add the map tiles.

The resulting code is a straightforward implementation of those steps.

```
drawMap: function () {
    if (this.model.get("gps") && this.model.get("gps").waypoints) {
        if (this.map) {
            this.map.remove();
        }
        var points = _(this.model.get("gps").waypoints).map(function(pt) {
            return [pt.latitude, pt.longitude];
        });
        var path = new L.Polyline(points, {color: "#1788cc"});
        this.map = L.map(this.id).fitBounds(path.getBounds())
            .addLayer(path);
        var tiles = L.tileLayer(
            "http://server.arcgisonline.com/ArcGIS/rest/services/Canvas/"+
            "World_Light_Gray_Base/MapServer/tile/{z}/{y}/{x}",
            {
                attribution: "Tiles &copy; Esri &mdash; "+
                             "Esri, DeLorme, NAVTEQ",
                maxZoom: 16
            }
        );
        this.map.addLayer(tiles);
    }
}
```

As you can see from the code, we're storing a reference to the Leaflet map object as a property of the view. From within the view, we can access that object using this.map.

The result is a nice map of the run's route, shown in Figure 9-6.

FIGURE 9-6: A map view shows the route of a run.

Step 5: Implement the Charts View

The last remaining view that we need to implement is the Charts view, where we want to show pace, heart rate, and elevation during the run. This view is the most complex, but nearly all of the code is identical to the example in "Tracking Data Values" on page 65, so there's no need to repeat it here.

You can see the interactive result in Figure 9-7.

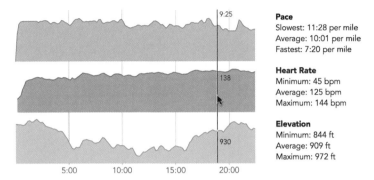

FIGURE 9-7: *An alternative view shows charts of the run.*

The source code for the book includes the complete implementation. If you're looking in detail at that implementation, there a few points to note:

- ▸ Just as with Leaflet and the map container, Flot expects a container for its chart to be present in the web page. We can use the same `defer` trick to prevent Flot errors.

- ▸ Nike+ returns at least four types of charts as metrics: distance, heart rate, speed, and GPS signal strength. We really only care about the first two. At first, it might seem easiest to calculate pace from speed, but speed isn't present in all activities. Distance, however, is present, and we can derive pace from distance and time.

- ▸ If GPS waypoint data is available, we can also graph elevation, but that data is in a separate attribute of the model (not the `metrics` attribute).

- ▸ As of this writing, there's a bit of a bug in Nike's response for GPS data. It claims that the measurements are on the same time scale as the other metrics (every 10 seconds), but in fact the GPS measurements are reported on different intervals. To work around this bug, we ignore the reported interval and calculate one ourselves. Also, we want to normalize the elevation graph to the same time scale as all the others. Doing that will give us the additional benefit of averaging the GPS elevation data; averaging is useful here because GPS elevation measurements aren't generally very accurate.

Summing Up

In this chapter, we've starting building an entire web application based on data and data visualizations. To help organize and coordinate our application, we based it on the Backbone.js library, and we relied on the Yeoman tool to create the application's scaffolding and boilerplate code and templates. Backbone.js lets us separate our application into models and views so that the code responsible for managing the data doesn't have to worry about how that data is presented (and vice versa).

In the next chapter, we'll enable our application to communicate with the Nike+ interface, and we'll add some finishing touches to improve user interaction with the page.

10

Building Data-Driven Web Applications: Part 2

In Chapter 9, we set up the framework of our web application and walked through the visualizations that will be displayed for each view. But before our web application is complete, we have several other details to attend to. First, we have to make the web application communicate with the Nike+ service and account for some quirks specific to that service. Then we'll work on making our application easier to navigate. In this chapter we'll look at the following:

▶ How to connect application models with an external REST API

▶ How to support web browser conventions in a single-page application

Connecting with the Nike+ Service

Although our example application relies on the Nike+ service for its data, we haven't looked at the details of that service's interface. As I've mentioned, Nike+ doesn't quite conform to common REST API conventions that application libraries such as Backbone.js expect. But Nike+ isn't very unusual in that regard. There really isn't a true *standard* for REST APIs, and many other services take approaches similar to Nike+'s. Fortunately Backbone.js anticipates this variation. As we'll see in the following steps, extending Backbone.js to support REST API variations isn't all that difficult.

Step 1: Authorize Users

As you might expect, Nike+ doesn't allow anyone on the Internet to retrieve details for any user's runs. Users expect at least some level of privacy for that information. Before our app can retrieve any running information, therefore, it will need the user's permission. We won't go into the details of that process here, but its result will be an `authorization_token`. This object is an arbitrary string that our app will have to include with every Nike+ request. If the token is missing or invalid, Nike+ will deny our app access to the data.

Up until now we've let Backbone.js handle all of the details of the REST API. Next, we'll have to modify how Backbone.js constructs its AJAX calls. Fortunately, this isn't as tricky as it sounds. All we need to do is add a `sync()` method to our Runs collection. When a `sync()` method is present in a collection, Backbone.js calls it whenever it makes an AJAX request. (If there is no such method for a collection, Backbone.js calls its primary `Backbone.sync()` method.) We'll define the new method directly in the collection.

```
Running.Collections.Runs = Backbone.Collection.extend({

    sync: function(method, collection, options) {
        // Handle the AJAX request
    }
```

As you can see, `sync()` is passed a `method` (`GET`, `POST`, etc.), the collection in question, and an object containing options for the request. To send the authorization token to Nike+, we can add it as a parameter using this `options` object.

```
sync: function(method, collection, options) {
    options = options || {};
    _(options).extend({
        data: { authorization_token: this.settings.authorization_token }
```

```
    });
    Backbone.sync(method, collection, options);
}
```

The first line in the method makes sure that the **options** parameter exists. If the caller doesn't provide a value, we set it to an empty object ({}). The next statement adds a **data** property to the **options** object using the **extend()** utility from Underscore.js. The **data** property is itself an object, and in it we store the authorization token. We'll look at how to do that next, but first let's finish up the **sync()** method. Once we've added the token, our request is a standard AJAX request, so we can let Backbone.js take it from there by calling **Backbone.sync()**.

Now we can turn our attention to the **settings** object from which our **sync()** method obtained the authorization token. We're using that object to hold properties related to the collection as a whole. It's the collection's equivalent of a model's attributes. Backbone.js doesn't create this object for us automatically, but it's easy enough to do it ourselves. We'll do it in the collection's **initialize()** method. That method accepts two parameters: an array of models for the collection, and any collection options.

```
Running.Collections.Runs = Backbone.Collection.extend({

    initialize: function(models, options) {
        this.settings = { authorization_token: "" };
        options = options || {};
        _(this.settings).extend(_(options)
            .pick(_(this.settings).keys()));
    },
```

The first statement in the **initialize()** method defines a **settings** object for the collection and establishes default values for that object. Since there isn't an appropriate default value for the authorization token, we'll use an empty string.

The next statement makes sure that the **options** object exists. If none is passed as a parameter, we'll at least have an empty object.

The final statement extracts all the keys in the settings, finds any values in the **options** object with the same keys, and updates the **settings** object by extending it with those new key values. Once again, we take advantage of some Underscore.js utilities: **extend()** and **pick()**.

When we first create the Runs collection, we can pass the authorization token as a parameter. We supply an empty array as the first parameter because we don't have any models for the collection. Those will come from Nike+. In the following code fragment, we're using a dummy value for the authorization token. A real application would use code that Nike provides to get the true value.

```
var runs = new Running.Collections.Runs([], {
    authorization_token: "authorize me"
});
```

With just a small bit of extra code, we've added the authorization token to our AJAX requests to Nike+.

Step 2: Accept the Nike+ Response

When our collection queries Nike+ for a list of user activities, Backbone.js is prepared for a response in a particular format. More specifically, Backbone.js expects the response to be a simple array of models.

```
[
    { "activityId": "2126456911", /* Data continues... */ },
    { "activityId": "2125290225", /* Data continues... */ },
    { "activityId": "2124784253", /* Data continues... */ },
    // Data set continues...
]
```

In fact, however, Nike+ returns its response as an object. The array of activities is one property of the object.

```
{
    "data": [
        { "activityId": "2126456911", /* Data continues... */ },
        { "activityId": "2125290225", /* Data continues... */ },
        { "activityId": "2124784253", /* Data continues... */ },
        // Data set continues...
    ],
    // Response continues...
}
```

To help Backbone.js cope with this response, we add a **parse()** method to our collection. The job of that function is to take the response that the server provides and return the response that Backbone.js expects.

```
Running.Collections.Runs = Backbone.Collection.extend({

    parse: function(response) {
        return response.data;
    },
```

In our case, we just return the **data** property of the response.

Step 3: Page the Collection

The next aspect of the Nike+ API we'll tackle is its paging. When we request the activities for a user, the service doesn't normally return *all* of them. Users may have thousands of activities stored in Nike+, and returning all of them at once might overwhelm the app. It could certainly add a noticeable delay, as the app would have to wait for the entire response before it could process it. To avoid this problem, Nike+ divides user activities into pages, and it responds with one page of activities at a time. We'll have to adjust our app for that behavior, but we'll gain the benefit of a more responsive user experience.

The first adjustment we'll make is in our request. We can add parameters to that request to indicate how many activities we're prepared to accept in the response. The two parameters are offset and count. The offset tells Nike+ which activity we want to be first in the response, while count indicates how many activities Nike+ should return. If we wanted the first 20 activities, for example, we can set offset to 1 and count to 20. Then, to get the next 20 activities, we'd set offset to 21 (and keep count at 20).

We add these parameters to our request the same way we added the authorization token—in the sync() method.

```
sync: function(method, collection, options) {
    options = options || {};
    _(options).extend({
        data: {
            authorization_token: this.settings.authorization_token,
            count: this.settings.count,
            offset: this.settings.offset
        }
    });
    Backbone.sync(method, collection, options);
}
```

We will also have to provide default values for those settings during initialization.

```
initialize: function(models, options) {
    this.settings = {
        authorization_token: "",
        count: 25,
        offset: 1
    };
```

Those values will get the first 25 activities, but that's only a start. Our users will probably want to see all of their runs, not just the first 25. To get the additional activities, we'll have to make more requests to the server. Once we get the first 25 activities, we can request the next 25. And once those arrive, we can ask for 25 more. We'll keep at this until either we reach some reasonable limit or the server runs out of activities.

First we define a reasonable limit as another settings value. In the following code, we're using 10000 as that limit.

```
initialize: function(models, options) {
    this.settings = {
        authorization_token: "",
        count: 25,
```

```
        offset: 1,
        max: 10000
    };
```

Next we need to modify the fetch() method for our collection since the standard Backbone.js fetch() can't handle paging. There are three steps in our implementation of the method:

1. Save a copy of whatever options Backbone.js is using for the request.
2. Extend those options by adding a callback function when the request succeeds.
3. Pass control to the normal Backbone.js fetch() method for collections.

Each of those steps is a line in the following implementation. The last one might seem a little tricky, but it makes sense if you take it one piece at a time. The expression Backbone.Collection.prototype.fetch refers to the normal fetch() method of a Backbone.js collection. We execute this method using .call() so that we can set the context for the method to be our collection. That's the first **this** parameter of call(). The second parameter holds the options for fetch(), which are just the extended options we created in Step 2.

```
Running.Collections.Runs = Backbone.Collection.extend({

    fetch: function(options) {
        this.fetchoptions = options = options || {};
        _(this.fetchoptions).extend({ success: this.fetchMore });
        return Backbone.Collection.prototype.fetch.call(
            this, this.fetchoptions
        );
    },
```

By adding a **success** callback to the AJAX request, we're asking to be notified when the request completes. In fact, we've said that we want the this.fetchMore() function to be called. It's time to write that function; it, too, is a method of the Runs collection. This function checks to see if there are more activities left. If so, it executes another call to Backbone.js's regular collection fetch() just as in the preceding code.

```
fetchMore: function() {
    if (this.settings.offset < this.settings.max) {
        Backbone.Collection.prototype.fetch.call(this, this.fetchoptions);
    }
}
```

Since fetchMore() is looking at the settings to decide when to stop, we'll need to update those values. Because we already have a parse() method, and because Backbone calls this method with each response, that's a convenient place for the update. Let's add a bit of code before the return statement. If the number of activities that the server returns is less than the number we asked for, then we've exhausted the list of activities. We'll set the `offset` to the `max` so `fetchMore()` knows to stop. Otherwise, we increment `offset` by the number of activities.

```
parse: function(response) {
    if (response.data.length < this.settings.count) {
        this.settings.offset = this.settings.max;
    } else {
        this.settings.offset += this.settings.count;
    }
    return response.data;
}
```

The code we've written so far is almost complete, but it has a problem. When Backbone.js fetches a collection, it assumes that it's fetching the whole collection. By default, therefore, each fetched response replaces the models already in the collection with those in the response. That behavior is fine the first time we call `fetch()`, but it's definitely not okay for `fetchMore()`, which is meant to add to the collection instead of replacing it. Fortunately, we can easily tweak this behavior by setting the `remove` option.

In our `fetch()` method, we set that option to `true` so Backbone.js will start a new collection.

```
fetch: function(options) {
    this.fetchoptions = options = options || {};
    _(this.fetchoptions).extend({
        success: this.fetchMore,
        remove: true
    });
    return Backbone.Collection.prototype.fetch.call(this,
        this.fetchoptions
    );
}
```

Now, in the `fetchMore()` method, we can reset this option to `false`, and Backbone.js will add to models instead of replacing them in the collection.

```
fetchMore: function() {
    this.fetchoptions.remove = false;
    if (this.settings.offset < this.settings.max) {
        Backbone.Collection.prototype.fetch.call(this, this.fetchoptions);
    }
}
```

There is still a small problem with the `fetchMore()` method. That code references properties of the collection (`this.fetchoptions` and `this.settings`), but the method will be called asynchronously when the AJAX request completes. When that occurs, the collection won't be in context, so `this` won't be set to the collection. To fix that, we can bind `fetchMore()` to the collection during initialization. Once again, an Underscore.js utility function comes in handy.

```
initialize: function(models, options) {
    _.bindAll(this, "fetchMore");
```

For the final part of this step, we can make our collection a little friendlier to code that uses it. To keep fetching additional pages, we've set the success callback for the fetch() options. What happens if the code that uses our collection has its own callback? Unfortunately, we've erased that callback to substitute our own. It would be better to simply set aside an existing callback function and then restore it once we've finished fetching the entire collection. We'll do that first in our fetch() method. Here's the full code for the method:

```
fetch: function(options) {
    this.fetchoptions = options = options || {};
    this.fetchsuccess = options.success;
    _(this.fetchoptions).extend({
        success: this.fetchMore,
        remove: true
        });
    return Backbone.Collection.prototype.fetch.call(this,
        this.fetchoptions
    );
}
```

And here's the code for fetchMore():

```
fetchMore: function() {
    this.fetchoptions.remove = false;
    if (this.settings.offset < this.settings.max) {
        Backbone.Collection.prototype.fetch.call(this, this.fetchoptions);
    } else if (this.fetchsuccess) {
        this.fetchsuccess();
    }
}
```

Now we can execute that callback in fetchMore() when we've exhausted the server's list.

Step 4: Dynamically Update the View

By fetching the collection of runs in pages, we've made our application much more responsive. We can start displaying summary data for the first 25 runs even while we're waiting to retrieve the rest of the user's runs from the server. To do that effectively, though, we need to make a small change to our Summary view. As it stands now, our view is listening for any changes to the collection. When a change occurs, it renders the view from scratch.

```
initialize: function () {
    this.listenTo(this.collection, "change", this.render);
    return this;
}
```

Every time we fetch a new page of runs, the collection will change and our code will re-render the entire view. That's almost certainly going to be annoying to our users, as each fetched page will cause the browser to temporarily blank out the page and then refill it. Instead, we'd like to render only views for the newly added models, leaving existing model views alone. To do that, we can listen for an **"add"** event instead of a **"change"** event. And when this event triggers, we can just render the view for that model. We've already implemented the code to create and render a view for a single Run model: the **renderRun()** method. Our Summary view, therefore, can be modified as shown here:

```
initialize: function () {
    this.listenTo(this.collection, "add", this.renderRun);
    return this;
}
```

Now as our collection fetches new Run models from the server, they'll be added to the collection, triggering an **"add"** event, which our view captures. The view then renders each run on the page.

Step 5: Filter the Collection

Although our app is interested only in running, the Nike+ service supports a variety of athletic activities. When our collection fetches from the service, the response will include those other activities as well. To avoid including them in our app, we can filter them from the response.

We could filter the response manually, checking every activity and removing those that aren't runs. That's a lot of work, however, and Backbone.js gives us an easier approach. To take advantage of Backbone.js, we'll first add a **validate()** method to our Run model. This method takes as parameters the attributes of a potential model as well as any options used when it was created or modified. In our case, we care only about the attributes. We'll check to make sure the **activityType** equals **"RUN"**.

```
Running.Models.Run = Backbone.Model.extend({
    validate: function(attributes, options) {
        if (attributes.activityType.toUpperCase() !== "RUN") {
            return "Not a run";
        }
    },
```

You can see from this code how **validate()** functions should behave. If there is an error in the model, then **validate()** returns a value. The specifics of the value don't matter as long as JavaScript considers it true. If there is no error, then **validate()** doesn't need to return anything at all.

Now that our model has a **validate()** method, we need to make sure Backbone.js calls it. Backbone.js automatically checks with **validate()** whenever a model is created or modified by the code, but it doesn't normally validate responses from the server. In our case, however, we do want to validate the server responses. That requires that we set the `validate()` property in the `fetch()` options for our Runs collection. Here's the full `fetch()` method with this change included.

```
Running.Collections.Runs = Backbone.Collection.extend({
    fetch: function(options) {
        this.fetchoptions = options = options || {};
        this.fetchsuccess = options.success;
        _(this.fetchoptions).extend({
            success: this.fetchMore,
            remove: true,
            validate: true
        });
        return Backbone.Collection.prototype.fetch.call(this,
          this.fetchoptions
        );
    },
```

Now when Backbone.js receives server responses, it passes all of the models in those responses through the model's `validate()` method. Any model that fails validation is removed from the collection, and our app never has to bother with activities that aren't runs.

Step 6: Parse the Response

As long as we're adding code to the Run model, there's another change that will make Backbone.js happy. Backbone.js requires models to have an attribute that makes each object unique; it can use this identifier to distinguish one run from any other. By default, Backbone.js expects this attribute to be `id`, as that's a common convention. Nike+, however, doesn't have an `id` attribute for its runs. Instead, the service uses the `activityId` attribute. We can tell Backbone.js about this with an extra property in the model.

```
Running.Models.Run = Backbone.Model.extend({
    idAttribute: "activityId",
```

This property lets Backbone.js know that for our runs, the `activityId` property is the unique identifier.

Step 7: Retrieve Details

So far we've relied on the collection's `fetch()` method to get running data. That method retrieves a list of runs from the server. When Nike+ returns a list of activities, however, it doesn't include the full details of each activity. It returns summary information, but it omits the detailed metrics arrays and any GPS data. Getting those details requires additional requests, so we need to make one more change to our Backbone.js app.

We'll first request the detailed metrics that are the basis for the Charts view. When the Runs collection fetches its list of runs from the server, each Run model will initially have an empty `metrics` array. To get the details for this array, we must make another request to the server with the activity identifier included in the request URL. For example, if the URL to get a list of runs is *https://api.nike.com/v1/me/sport/activities/*, then the URL to get the details for a specific run, including its metrics, is *https://api.nike.com/v1/me/sport/activities/2126456911/*. The number *2126456911* at the end of that URL is the run's `activityId`.

Thanks to the steps we've taken earlier in this section, it's easy to get these details in Backbone.js. All we have to do is `fetch()` the model.

```
run.fetch();
```

Backbone.js knows the root of the URL because we set that in the Runs collection (and our model is a member of that collection). Backbone.js also knows that the unique identifier for each run is the `activityId` because we set that property in the previous step. And, fortunately for us, Backbone.js is smart enough to combine those bits of information and make the request.

We will have to help Backbone.js in one respect, though. The Nike+ app requires an authorization token for all requests, and so far we've added code for that token only to the collection. We have to add the same code to the model. This code is almost identical to the code from Step 1 in this section:

```
Running.Models.Run = Backbone.Model.extend({
    sync: function(method, model, options) {
        options = options || {};
        _(options).extend({
            data: {
                authorization_token:
                    this.collection.settings.authorization_token
            }
        });
        Backbone.sync(method, model, options);
    },
```

❶

We first make sure that the `options` object exists, then extend it by adding the authorization token. Finally, we defer to the regular Backbone.js `sync()` method. At ❶, we get the value for the token directly from the collection. We can use `this.collection` here because Backbone.js sets the `collection` property of the model to reference the collection to which it belongs.

Now we have to decide when and where to call a model's `fetch()` method. We don't actually need the metrics details for the Summary view on the main page of our app; we should bother getting that data only when we're creating a Details view. We can conveniently do that in the view's `initialize()` method.

```
Running.Views.Details = Backbone.View.extend({
    initialize: function () {
        if (!this.model.get("metrics") ||
            this.model.get("metrics").length === 0) {
            this.model.fetch();
        }
    },
```

You might think that the asynchronous nature of the request could cause problems for our view. After all, we're trying to draw the charts when we render the newly created view. Won't it draw the charts before the server has responded (that is, before we have any data for the charts)? In fact, it's almost guaranteed that our view will be trying to draw its charts before the data is available. Nonetheless, because of the way we've structured our views, there is no problem.

The magic is in a single statement in the `initialize()` method of our Charts view.

```
Running.Views.Charts = Backbone.View.extend({
    initialize: function () {
        this.listenTo(this.model,
            "change:metrics change:gps", this.render);
        // Code continues...
```

That statement tells Backbone.js that our view wants to know whenever the `metrics` (or `gps`) property of the associated model changes. When the server responds to a `fetch()` and updates that property, Backbone.js calls the view's `render()` method and will try (again) to draw the charts.

There's quite a lot going on in this process, so it may help to look at it one step at a time.

1. The application calls the `fetch()` method of a Runs collection.
2. Backbone.js sends a request to the server for a list of activities.
3. The server's response includes summary information for each activity, which Backbone.js uses to create the initial Run models.
4. The application creates a Details view for a specific Run model.
5. The `initialize()` method of this view calls the `fetch()` method of the particular model.
6. Backbone.js sends a request to the server for that activity's details.
7. Meanwhile, the application renders the Details view it just created.
8. The Details view creates a Charts view and renders that view.
9. Because there is no data for any charts, the Charts view doesn't actually add anything to the page, but it is waiting to hear of any relevant changes to the model.
10. Eventually the server responds to the request in Step 6 with details for the activity.
11. Backbone.js updates the model with the new details and notices that, as a result, the `metrics` property has changed.
12. Backbone.js triggers the change event for which the Charts view has been listening.
13. The Charts view receives the event trigger and again renders itself.
14. Because chart data is now available, the `render()` method is able to create the charts and add them to the page.

Whew! It's a good thing that Backbone.js takes care of all that complexity.

At this point we've managed to retrieve the detailed metrics for a run, but we haven't yet added any GPS data. Nike+ requires an additional request for that data, so we'll use a similar process. In this case, though, we can't rely on Backbone .js because the URL for the GPS request is unique to Nike+. That URL is formed by taking the individual activity's URL and appending */gps*—for example, *https://api .nike.com/v1/me/sport/activities/2126456911/gps/*.

To make the additional request, we can add some code to the regular `fetch()` method. We'll request the GPS data at the same time Backbone.js asks for the metrics details. The basic approach, which the following code fragment illustrates, is simple. We'll first see if the activity even has any GPS data. We can do that by checking the `isGpsActivity` property, which the server provides on activity summaries. If it does, then we can request it. In either case, we also want to execute the normal `fetch()` process for the model. We do that by getting a reference to the standard `fetch()` method for the model (`Backbone.Model.prototype.fetch`) and then calling that method. We pass it the same `options` passed to us.

```
Running.Models.Run = Backbone.Model.extend({
    fetch: function(options) {
        if (this.get("isGpsActivity")) {
            // Request GPS details from the server
        }
        return Backbone.Model.prototype.fetch.call(this, options);
    },
```

Next, to make the request to Nike+, we can use jQuery's AJAX function. Since we're asking for JavaScript objects (JSON data), the `$.getJSON()` function is the most appropriate. First we set aside a reference to the run by assigning `this` to the local variable `model`. We'll need that variable because `this` won't reference the model when jQuery executes our callback. Then we call `$.getJSON()` with three parameters. First is the URL for the request. We get that from Backbone.js by calling the `url()` method for the model and appending the trailing */gps*. The second parameter is the data values to be included with the request. As always, we need to include an authorization token. Just as we did before, we can get that token's value from the collection. The final parameter is a callback function that JQuery executes when it receives the server's response. In our case, the function simply sets the `gps` property of the model to the response data.

```
if (this.get("isGpsActivity")) {
    var model = this;
    $.getJSON(
        this.url() + "/gps",
        { authorization_token:
          this.collection.settings.authorization_token },
        function(data) { model.set("gps", data); }
    );
}
```

Not surprisingly, the process of retrieving GPS data works the same way as retrieving the detailed metrics. Initially our Map view won't have the data it needs to create a map for the run. Because it's listening for changes to the **gps** property of the model, however, it will be notified when that data is available. At that point it can complete the **render** function and the user will be able to view a nice map of the run.

Putting It All Together

At this point in the chapter, we have all the pieces for a simple data-driven web application. Now we'll take those pieces and assemble them into the app. At the end of this section, we'll have a complete application. Users start the app by visiting a web page, and our JavaScript code takes it from there. The result is a *single-page application,* or SPA. SPAs have become popular because JavaScript code can respond to user interaction immediately in the browser, which is much quicker than traditional websites communicating with a server located halfway across the Internet. Users are often pleased with the snappy and responsive result.

Even though our app is executing in a single web page, our users still expect certain behaviors from their web browsers. They expect to be able to bookmark a page, share it with friends, or navigate using the browser's forward and back buttons. Traditional websites can rely on the browser to support all of those behaviors, but a single-page application can't. As we'll see in the steps that follow, we have to write some additional code to give our users the behavior they expect.

Step 1: Create a Backbone.js Router

So far we've looked at three Backbone.js components—models, collections, and views—all of which may be helpful in any JavaScript application. The fourth component, the *router,* is especially helpful for single-page applications. You won't be surprised to learn that we can use Yeoman to create the scaffolding for a router.

```
$ yo backbone:router app
   create app/scripts/routes/app.js
   invoke   backbone-mocha:router
   create     test/routers/app.spec.js
```

Notice that we've named our router **app.** As you might expect from this name, we're using this router as the main controller for our application. That approach has pros and cons. Some developers feel that a router should be limited strictly to routing, while others view the router as the natural place to coordinate the overall application. For a simple example such as ours, there isn't really any harm in adding a bit of extra code to the router to control the app. In complex applications, however, it might be better to separate routing from application control. One of the nice things about Backbone.js is that it's happy to support either approach.

With the scaffolding in place, we can start adding our router code to the *app.js* file. The first property we'll define is the **routes.** This property is an object whose keys are URL fragments and whose values are methods of the router. Here's our starting point.

```
Running.Routers.App = Backbone.Router.extend({
    routes: {
        "":          "summary",
        "runs/:id": "details"
    },
});
```

The first route has an empty URL fragment (""). When a user visits our page without specifying a path, the router will call its summary() method. If, for example, we were hosting our app using the *greatrunningapp.com* domain name, then users entering *http://greatrunningapp.com/* in their browsers would trigger that route. Before we look at the second route, let's see what the summary() method does.

The code is exactly what we've seen before. The summary() method creates a new Runs collection, fetches that collection, creates a Summary view of the collection, and renders that view onto the page. Users visiting the home page for our app will see a summary of their runs.

```
summary: function() {
    this.runs = new Running.Collections.Runs([],
        {authorizationToken: "authorize me"});
    this.runs.fetch();
    this.summaryView = new Running.Views.Summary({collection: this.runs});
    $("body").html(this.summaryView.render().el);
},
```

Now we can consider our second route. It has a URL fragment of *runs/:id*. The *runs/* part is a standard URL path, while *:id* is how Backbone.js identifies an arbitrary variable. With this route, we're telling Backbone.js to look for a URL that starts out as *http://greatrunningapp.com/runs/* and to consider whatever follows as the value for the id parameter. We'll use that parameter in the router's details() method. Here's how we'll start developing that method:

```
details: function(id) {
    this.run = new Running.Models.Run();
    this.run.id = id;
    this.run.fetch();
    this.detailsView = new Running.Views.Details({model: this.run});
    $("body").html(this.detailsView.render().el);
    },
```

As you can see, the code is almost the same as the summary() method, except we're showing only a single run instead of the whole collection. We create a new Run model, set its id to the value in the URL, fetch the model from the server, create a Details view, and render that view on the page.

The router lets users go straight to an individual run by using the appropriate URL. A URL of *http://greatrunningapp.com/runs/2126456911*, for example, will fetch and display the details for the run that has an activityId equal to 2126456911.

Notice that the router doesn't have to worry about what specific attribute defines the model's unique identifier. It uses the generic `id` property. Only the model itself needs to know the actual property name that the server uses.

With the router in place, our single-page application can support multiple URLs. One shows a summary of all runs, while others show the details of a specific run. Because the URLs are distinct, our users can treat them just like different web pages. They can bookmark them, email them, or share them on social networks. And whenever they or their friends return to a URL, it will show the same contents as before. That's exactly how users expect the Web to behave.

There is another behavior that users expect, though, that we haven't yet supported. Users expect to use their browser's back and forward buttons to navigate through their browsing histories. Fortunately, Backbone.js has a utility that takes care of that functionality. It's the *history* feature, and we can enable it during the app router's initialization.

```
Running.Routers.App = Backbone.Router.extend({
    initialize: function() {
        Backbone.history.start({pushState: true});
    },
```

For our simple app, that's all we have to do to handle browsing histories. Backbone.js takes care of everything else.

✳ **NOTE:** Support for multiple URLs will probably require some configuration of your web server. More specifically, you'll want the server to map all URLs to the same *index.html* file. The details of this configuration depend on the web server technology. With open source Apache servers, the *.htaccess* file can define the mapping.

Step 2: Support Run Models Outside of Any Collection

Unfortunately, if we try to use the preceding code with our existing Run model, we'll encounter some problems. First among them is the fact that our Run model relies on its parent collection. It finds the authorization token, for example, using `this.collection.settings.authorization_token`. When the browser goes directly to the URL for a specific run, however, there won't be a collection. In the following code, we make some tweaks to address this:

```
Running.Routers.App = Backbone.Router.extend({
    routes: {
        "":         "summary",
        "runs/:id": "details"
    },
    initialize: function(options) {
        this.options = options;
        Backbone.history.start({pushState: true});
    },
```

```
        summary: function() {
            this.runs = new Running.Collections.Runs([],
❶              {authorizationToken: this.options.token});
            this.runs.fetch();
            this.summaryView = new Running.Views.Summary({
                collection: this.runs});
            $("body").html(this.summaryView.render().el);
        },
        details: function(id) {
            this.run = new Running.Models.Run({},
❷              {authorizationToken: this.options.token});
            this.run.id = id;
            this.run.fetch();
            this.detailsView = new Running.Views.Details({
                model: this.run});
            $("body").html(this.detailsView.render().el);
    });
```

Now we provide the token to the Run model when we create it at ❷. We also make its value an option passed to the collection on creation at ❶.

Next we need to modify the Run model to use this new parameter. We'll handle the token the same way we do in the Runs collection.

```
Running.Models.Run = Backbone.Model.extend({
    initialize: function(attrs, options) {
        this.settings = {  authorization_token: "" };
        options = options || {};
        if (this.collection) {
            _(this.settings).extend(_(this.collection.settings)
                .pick(_(this.settings).keys()));
        }
        _(this.settings).extend(_(options)
            .pick(_(this.settings).keys()));
    },
```

We start by defining default values for all the settings. Unlike with the collection, the only setting our model needs is the authorization_token. Next we make sure that we have an options object. If none was provided, we create an empty one. For the third step, we check to see if the model is part of a collection by looking at this.collection. If that property exists, then we grab any settings from the collection and override our defaults. The final step overrides the result with any settings passed to our constructor as options. When, as in the preceding code, our router provides an authorization_token value, that's the value our model will use. When the model is part of a collection, there is no specific token associated with the model. In that case, we fall back to the collection's token.

Now that we have an authorization token, we can add it to the model's AJAX requests. The code is again pretty much the same as our code in the Runs collection. We'll need a property that specifies the URL for the REST service, and we'll need to override the regular sync() method to add the token to any requests.

```
urlRoot: "https://api.nike.com/v1/me/sport/activities",

sync: function(method, model, options) {
    options = options || {};
    _(options).extend({
        data: { authorization_token: this.settings.authorization_token }
    });
    Backbone.sync(method, model, options);
},
```

This extra code takes care of the authorization, but there's still a problem with our model. In the previous section, Run models existed only as part of a Runs collection, and the act of fetching that collection populated each of its models with summary attributes, including, for example, `isGpsActivity`. The model could safely check that property whenever we tried to fetch the model details and, if appropriate, simultaneously initiate a request for the GPS data. Now, however, we're creating a Run model on its own without the benefit of a collection. When we fetch the model, the only property we'll know is the unique identifier. We can't decide whether or not to request GPS data, therefore, until after the server responds to the fetch.

To separate the request for GPS data from the general fetch, we can move that request to its own method. The code is the same as before (except, of course, we get the authorization token from local settings).

```
fetchGps: function() {
    if (this.get("isGpsActivity") && !this.get("gps")) {
        var model = this;
        $.getJSON(
            this.url() + "/gps",
            { authorization_token: this.settings.authorization_token },
            function(data) { model.set("gps", data); }
        );
    }
}
```

To trigger this method, we'll tell Backbone.js that whenever the model changes, it should call the `fetchGps()` method.

```
initialize: function(attrs, options) {
    this.on("change", this.fetchGps, this);
```

Backbone.js will detect just such a change when the `fetch()` response arrives and populates the model, at which time our code can safely check `isGpsActivity()` and make the additional request.

Step 3: Let Users Change Views

Now that our app can correctly display two different views, it's time to let our users in on the fun. For this step, we'll give them an easy way to change back and forth between the views. Let's first consider the Summary view. It would be nice if a user could click on any run that appears in the table and be instantly taken to the detailed view for that run.

Our first decision is where to put the code that listens for clicks. At first, it might seem like the SummaryRow view is a natural place for that code. That view is responsible for rendering the row, so it seems logical to let that view handle events related to the row. If we wanted to do that, Backbone.js makes it very simple; all we need is an extra property and an extra method in the view. They might look like the following:

```
Running.Views.SummaryRow = Backbone.View.extend({
    events: {
        "click": "clicked"
    },
    clicked: function() {
        // Do something to show the Details view for this.model
    },
```

The **events** property is an object that lists the events of interest to our view. In this case there's only one: the **click** event. The value—in this case, **clicked**—identifies the method that Backbone.js should call when the event occurs. We've skipped the details of that method for now.

There is nothing technically wrong with this approach, and if we were to continue the implementation, it would probably work just fine. It is, however, very inefficient. Consider a user who has hundreds of runs stored on Nike+. The summary table would have hundreds of rows, and each row would have its own function listening for **click** events. Those event handlers can use up a lot of memory and other resources in the browser and make our app sluggish. Fortunately, there's a different approach that's far less stressful to the browser.

Instead of having potentially hundreds of event handlers, each listening for clicks on a single row, we'd be better off with one event handler listening for clicks on all of the table rows. Since the Summary view is responsible for all of those rows, it's the natural place to add that handler. We can still take advantage of Backbone.js to make its implementation easy by adding an **events** object to our view. In this case, we can do even better, though. We don't care about **click** events on the table header; only the rows in the table body matter. By adding a jQuery-style selector after the event name, we can restrict our handler to elements that match that selector.

```
Running.Views.Summary = Backbone.View.extend({
    events: {
        "click tbody": "clicked"
    },
```

The preceding code asks Backbone.js to watch for `click` events within the `<tbody>` element of our view. When an event occurs, Backbone.js will call the `clicked()` method of our view.

Before we develop any code for that `clicked()` method, we need a way for it to figure out which specific run model the user has selected. The event handler will be able to tell which row the user clicked, but how will it know which model that row represents? To make the answer easy for the handler, we can embed the necessary information directly in the markup for the row. That requires a few small adjustments to the `renderRun()` method we created earlier.

The revised method still creates a SummaryRow view for each model, renders that view, and appends the result to the table body. Now, though, we'll add one extra step just before the row is added to the page. We add a special attribute, `data-id`, to the row and set its value equal to the model's unique identifier. We use `data-id` because the HTML5 standard allows any attribute with a name that begins with `data-`. Custom attributes in this form won't violate the standard and won't cause browser errors.

```
renderRun: function (run) {
    var row = new Running.Views.SummaryRow({ model: run });
    row.render();
    row.$el.attr("data-id", run.id);
    this.$("tbody").append(row.$el);
},
```

The resulting markup for a run with an identifier of 2126456911 would look like the following example:

```
<tr data-id="2126456911">
    <td>04/09/2013</td>
    <td>0:22:39</td>
    <td>2.33 Miles</td>
    <td>240</td>
    <td>9:43</td>
</tr>
```

Once we've made sure that the markup in the page has a reference back to the Run models, we can take advantage of that markup in our `clicked` event handler. When Backbone.js calls the handler, it passes it an event object. From that object, we can find the target of the event. In the case of a `click` event, the target is the HTML element on which the user clicked.

```
clicked: function (ev) {
    var $target = $(ev.target)
```

From the preceding markup, it's clear that most of the table row is made up of table cells (`<td>` elements), so a table cell will be the likely target of the `click` event. We can use the jQuery `parents()` function to find the table row that is the parent of the click target.

```
clicked: function (ev) {
    var $target = $(ev.target)
    var id = $target.attr("data-id") ||
            $target.parents("[data-id]").attr("data-id");
```

Once we've found that parent row, we extract the `data-id` attribute value. To be on the safe side, we also handle the case in which the user somehow manages to click on the table row itself rather than an individual table cell.

After retrieving the attribute value, our view knows which run the user selected; now it has to do something with the information. It might be tempting to have the Summary view directly render the Details view for the run, but that action would not be appropriate. A Backbone.js view should take responsibility only for itself and any child views that it contains. That approach allows the view to be safely reused in a variety of contexts. Our Summary view, for example, might well be used in a context in which the Details view isn't even available. In that case, trying to switch directly to the Details view would, at best, generate an error.

Because the Summary view cannot itself respond to the user clicking on a table row, it should instead follow the hierarchy of the application and, in effect, pass the information "up the chain of command." Backbone.js provides a convenient mechanism for this type of communication: custom events. Instead of responding directly to the user click, the Summary view triggers a custom event. Other parts can listen for this event and respond appropriately. If no other code is listening for the event, then nothing happens, but at least the Summary view can say that it's done its job.

Here's how we can generate a custom event in our view:

```
clicked: function (ev) {
    var $target = $(ev.target)
    var id = $target.attr("data-id") ||
            $target.parents("[data-id]").attr("data-id");
    this.trigger("select", id);
}
```

We call the event `select` to indicate that the user has selected a specific run, and we pass the identifier of that run as a parameter associated with the event. At this point, the Summary view is complete.

The component that should respond to this custom event is the same component that created the Summary view in the first place: our app router. We'll first need to listen for the event. We can do that right after we create it in the `summary()` method.

```
Running.Routers.App = Backbone.Router.extend({
    summary: function() {
        this.runs = new Running.Collections.Runs([],
            {authorizationToken: this.options.token});
        this.runs.fetch();
        this.summaryView = new Running.Views.Summary({
            collection: this.runs});
```

```
$("body").html(this.summaryView.render().el);
    this.summaryView.on("select", this.selected, this);
},
```

When the user selects a specific run from the Summary view, Backbone.js calls our router's **selected()** method, which will receive any event data as parameters. In our case, the event data is the unique identifier, so that becomes the method's parameter.

```
Running.Routers.App = Backbone.Router.extend({
    selected: function(id) {
        this.navigate("runs/" + id, { trigger: true });
    }
```

As you can see, the event handler code is quite simple. It constructs a URL that corresponds to the Details view (**"runs/" + id**) and passes that URL to the router's own **navigate()** method. That method updates the browser's navigation history. The second parameter (**{ trigger: true }**) tells Backbone.js to also act as if the user had actually navigated to the URL. Because we've set up the **details()** method to respond to URLs of the form *runs/:id*, Backbone.js will call **details()**, and our router will show the details for the selected run.

When users are looking at a Details view, we'd also like to provide a button to let them easily navigate to the Summary view. As with the Summary view, we can add an event handler for the button and trigger a custom event when a user clicks it.

```
Running.Views.Details = Backbone.View.extend({
    events: {
        "click button": "clicked"
    },
    clicked: function () {
        this.trigger("summarize");
    }
```

And, of course, we need to listen for that custom event in our router.

```
Running.Routers.App = Backbone.Router.extend({
    details: function(id) {
        // Set up the Details view
        // Code continues...
        this.detailsView.on("summarize", this.summarize, this);
    },
    summarize: function() {
        this.navigate("", { trigger: true });
    },
```

Once again we respond to the user by constructing an appropriate URL and triggering a navigation to it.

You might be wondering why we have to explicitly trigger the navigation change. Shouldn't that be the default behavior? Although that may seem reasonable, in most cases it wouldn't be appropriate. Our application is simple enough that triggering the route works fine. More complex applications, however, probably want to take different actions depending on whether the user performs an action within the app or navigates directly to a particular URL. It's better to have different code handling each of those cases. In the first case the app would still want to update the browser's history, but it wouldn't want to trigger a full navigation action.

Step 4: Fine-Tuning the Application

At this point our app is completely functional. Our users can view their summaries, bookmark and share details of specific runs, and navigate the app using the browser's back and forward buttons. Before we can call it complete, however, there's one last bit of housekeeping for us. The app's performance isn't optimal, and, even more critically, it *leaks* memory, using small amounts of the browser's memory without ever releasing them.

The most obvious problem is in the router's **summary()** method, reproduced here:

```
Running.Routers.App = Backbone.Router.extend({
    summary: function() {
        this.runs = new Running.Collections.Runs([],
            {authorizationToken: this.options.token});
        this.runs.fetch();
        this.summaryView = new Running.Views.Summary({
            collection: this.runs});
        $("body").html(this.summaryView.render().el);
        this.summaryView.on("select", this.selected, this);
    },
```

Every time this method executes, it creates a new collection, fetches that collection, and renders a Summary view for the collection. Clearly we have to go through those steps the first time the method executes, but there is no need to repeat them later. Neither the collection nor its view will change if the user selects a specific run and then returns to the summary. Let's add a check to the method so that we take those steps only if the view doesn't already exist.

```
summary: function() {
    if (!this.summaryView) {
        this.runs = new Running.Collections.Runs([],
            {authorizationToken: this.options.token});
        this.runs.fetch();
        this.summaryView = new Running.Views.Summary({
            collection: this.runs});
        this.summaryView.render();
        this.summaryView.on("select", this.selected, this);
    }
}
```

```
    $("body").html(this.summaryView.el);
},
```

We can also add a check in the `details()` method. When that method executes and a Summary view is present, we can "set aside" the Summary view's markup using jQuery's `detach()` function. That will keep the markup and its event handlers ready for a quick reinsertion onto the page should the user return to the summary.

```
details: function(id) {
    if (this.summaryView) {
        this.summaryView.$el.detach();
    }
    this.run = new Running.Models.Run({},
        {authorizationToken: this.options.token});
    this.run.id = id;
    this.run.fetch();
    $("body").html(this.detailsView.render().el);
    this.detailsView.on("summarize", this.summarize, this);
},
```

Those changes make switching to and from the Summary view more efficient. We can also make some similar changes for the Details view. In the `details()` method we don't have to fetch the run if it's already present in the collection. We can add a check, and if the data for the run is already available, we won't bother with the fetch.

```
details: function(id) {
    if (!this.runs || !(this.run = this.runs.get(id))) {
        this.run = new Running.Models.Run({},
            {authorizationToken: this.options.token});
        this.run.id = id;
        this.run.fetch();
    }
    if (this.summaryView) {
        this.summaryView.$el.detach();
    }
    this.detailsView = new Running.Views.Details({model: this.run});
    $("body").html(this.detailsView.render().el);
    this.detailsView.on("summarize", this.summarize, this);
},
```

In the `summary()` method, we don't want to simply set aside the Details view as we did for the Summary view. That's because there may be hundreds of Details views hanging around if a user starts looking at all of the runs available. Instead, we want to cleanly delete the Details view. That lets the browser know that it can release any memory that the view is consuming.

As you can see from the following code, we'll do that in three steps.

1. Remove the event handler we added to the Details view to catch `summarize` events.
2. Call the view's `remove()` method so it releases any memory it's holding internally.
3. Set `this.detailsView` to `null` to indicate that the view no longer exists.

```
summary: function() {
    if (this.detailsView) {
        this.detailsView.off("summarize");
        this.detailsView.remove();
        this.detailsView = null;
    }
    if (!this.summaryView) {
        this.runs = new Running.Collections.Runs([],
            {authorizationToken: this.options.token});
        this.runs.fetch();
        this.summaryView = new Running.Views.Summary({
            collection: this.runs});
        this.summaryView.render();
        this.summaryView.on("select", this.selected, this);
    }
    $("body").html(this.summaryView.el);
},
```

And with that change, our application is complete! You can take a look at the final result in the book's source code (*http://jsDataV.is/source/*).

Summing Up

In this chapter, we completed a data-driven web application. First, we saw how Backbone.js gives us the flexibility to interact with REST APIs that don't quite follow the normal conventions. Then we worked with a Backbone.js router to make sure our single-page application behaves like a full website so that our users can interact with it just as they would expect.

Index

Symbols

A

B

mousedown event, 208
mouseout event, 72, 73, 104
mouseovers, 31
-moz- prefix, 166
multiple data sets, graphing on line
    charts, 17

N

navigate() method, 348
navigation plug-in, 60
network graphs, 130–138. *See also*
    force-directed network
    graphs
    adding interactivity, 137–138
    adding nodes to, 132–133
    automating layout of, 134–136
    connecting nodes with edges,
        133–134
    libraries required, 130–131
    preparing data, 131
    when to use, 130
new Date() function, 247
Node.js platform, 298
node_modules/ folder, 299
nodeName property, 144
nodes, in network graphs
    adding, 132–133
    connecting with edges, 133–134
nonbreaking space ( ), 104
normalRangeMin option, 94

O

obj2Html() method, 320, 321
object() function, 284
offset field, 216
offset parameter, 331
<ol> element, 155
omit() function, 286
.on() function, 62, 241
onAdd() method, 207–208
opacity property, 220
OpenStreetMap, 35, 200
options attribute, 214
options object, 207, 343
options parameter, 329
options variable, 63
ordered lists, 155
overflow property, 163

P

package.json file, 299
padding, 40
padding-left property, 162
pairs() function, 284
parents() function, 346
parse() function, 330, 332
<path> element, 188, 189, 192, 195, 247,
        248, 259, 262
pause() function, 213
pick() function, 285–286, 329
pickColor function, 123
pie charts, 21–25
    defining data to display, 23
    drawing, 23–24
    labeling, 24–25
    vs. line charts, 21–22
    titles for, 24–25
    when to use, 22, 46
pixel (px) units, 161
plot extension, 51
plot() function, 55, 58–59, 61–62, 63,
        68–69, 71
plothover events, 72
plotObj.draw() function, 58–59
plotObj.setupGrid() function, 58–59
plotselected event, 62
pluck() function, 291
pointOffset() function, 72
polyline() function, 204, 205, 206
position property, 72, 128
position: relative style, 142
prefix parameter, 78
ProgrammableWeb, 87
Properties view, 318–321
pure libraries, 297
px (pixel) units, 161

Q

qTip2 library, 148
querySelectorAll() function, 195

R

r attribute, 238
radar charts, 41–45
    creating, 44–45
    defining data to display, 42–44
    when to use, 41–42, 46

U

underscore character (_), 274
Underscore.js library, 270
   arrays
      combining, 278–280
      extracting elements by
         position, 275–277
      finding elements in, 281–282
      generating, 282–283
      overview, 275
      removing invalid data values,
         280–281
   collections
      finding elements in collection,
         290–291
      iteration utilities, 289–290
      overview, 288–289
      rearranging, 292–293
      testing, 292
   enhancing objects
      cleaning up object subsets,
         285–286
      keys and values, 283–285
      overview, 283
      updating attributes, 286–288
   memoizing JavaScript functions
      using, 274–275
Underscore.string library, 301, 319, 320
union() function, 278
uniq() function, 279, 282
update() function, 238
url() method, 339

V

validate() method, 335, 336
values() function, 284
.values property, 258
van Wijk, Jarke J., 120
variables
   charting many, 94–101
   local, 57
Venturini, Tommaso, 135
vertical axis
   extending range of, in line
      charts, 18
   fixing in bar charts, 9–10
verticalLines property, 18, 23
*Visual Display of Quantitative
      Information, The* (Tufte), 90

visualization. *See* D3.js library;
      map-based visualization
VMM.Timeline constructor, 173
volume property, 106

W

web applications, data-driven
   adding unique dependencies,
      301–302
   authorizing users, 328–330
   collections
      defining, 306–307
      filtering, 335–336
      paging, 330–334
      supporting run models outside
         of, 342–344
   creating Backbone.js router,
      340–342
   defining new project, 298–300
   fine-tuning the app, 349–351
   installing development tools, 298
   model
      defining application's, 303–304
      implementing, 304–306
   overview, 295–296
   responses
      accepting, 330
      parsing, 336
   retrieving details, 336–340
   selecting application library, 297
   views
      additional, defining, 317
      allowing users to change,
         345–349
      Charts view, 322–324
      Details view, 317–318
      dynamically updating, 334–335
      main view, 307–314
      Map view, 322–324
      Properties view, 318–321
-webkit- prefix, 166
.when() function, 84
where() function, 291
width variable, 226–227
Wied, Patrick, 125
Wikimedia Commons, 188
wind property, 38
window.onload event, 8
wins2 array, 13
without method, 281